The Notation of Western Music

To Jane

The Notation
of Western Music

An Introduction

Richard Rastall

St. Martin's Press
New York

Library of Congress Cataloging in Publication Number: 82-62938
ISBN 0–312–57963–2

First published in Great Britain by J. M. Dent & Sons Ltd.

First U.S. Edition

Contents

v

Contents

PART II
Didactic Notations

PART III
Tablatures

PART IV
Staff Notation Since 1600

Contents

Preface

In 1974, after several years of decoding work, a Hurrian love-song dating from *c*. 1800 B.C. was at last transcribed and performed.[1] This song caused a major revision of our ideas about the antiquity of musical notation, for it ante-dated the previously known oldest notation by more than a millennium. The existence of such an early example of written music may remind us of the vast field covered by the words 'musical notation', a term that we normally think of as having a limited application in both date and scope. So large is the subject of notation in general that a whole series, not a book, would be needed to cover it. In choosing to deal only with western notation I have severely limited the subject chronologically as well as geographically; and even the geographical limitation is somewhat exclusively applied, for I have not discussed the notation of certain peripheral areas such as ancient Greece and Byzantium. This book does not aim at comprehensive descriptions of notations, but rather at a limited exploration of their underlying principles: and so, although its basic organization is chronological, it is not particularly concerned to chart the earliest or latest example of this or that notational device.

My general aim explains also the absence of photographs and reproductions of early sources. This is not a transcription-book, in which the reader is guided through the notation of specific pieces. My illustrations of early sources are transliterations (a system used by Johannes Wolf, among others), for I believe that notation can and should be studied as a discipline separate from those of musical and textual paleography, codicology, and other related subjects. My experience as a teacher is that a student finds it confusing to cope with two or more of these simultaneously from the start, even if the different disciplines must later be fused (with others) into the larger discipline that we call Musicology. Nevertheless, I should be the last to discourage anyone to study the sources themselves: indeed, the serious student must do so as soon as this book has served its immediate purpose, for I have been able to give only very brief examples. The notes to each chapter therefore include references to the main facsimiles of music discussed.

Bibliography on musical notation falls into three categories: the sources themselves, to which we may add facsimile publications; works specifically on notation, including theoretical writings; and other works (such as interpretative works or music histories) in which notation is discussed in passing. My debt to certain writers will be very obvious—Willi Apel in the second category and Robert Donington in the third, for instance. I owe much to Carl Parrish, too, not merely for his clear exposition of medieval notation but also for the illustrative plates in his book, which—since they are easily-accessible and extremely well chosen—I have thought it proper to cite. Most of all, the debt is to Johannes Wolf, who provided the starting-point for all subsequent historical work on notation. It is a pity that his fine portfolio of examples, the *Musikalische Schrifttafeln* (Bückeburg, 1930), is too rare to be cited usefully. I have thought it helpful to list the principal relevant works in the notes to each chapter, and there are abbreviated references in the text and notes. All cited works are included in full in the Select Bibliography, where abbreviations are explained.

Many friends have helped in the preparation of this book. Hilda Kenner and Benedict Sarnaker drew my attention to matter that I might otherwise have missed; Donald Ireland and Jack Pilgrim enlightened me on aspects of plainsong and tonic sol-fa, respectively; Raffaella Ferrari, Ronald Martin and Brian Richardson helped with the translation of terms and quotations; Keith Dennis, Margaret Ireland and Susan Wanless provided several stimulating discussions, including one that produced the definition of notation given on p. 2; David Fallows kindly allowed me to read his *New Grove* article 'Tempo and Expression Marks'; to Michael Talbot I owe some of the ideas expressed in Chapter 13 (see the notes), and he kindly sent me that part of the draft Editorial Guidelines for the *New Vivaldi Edition* which deals with the editorial treatment of accidentals; and Ian Bent, whose friendship and scholarship have put me incalculably in his debt over the years, read the typescript and made valuable suggestions. To all of these I am extremely grateful. They are not responsible for any inadequacies remaining in this book, of course, nor for the use that I have made of their expertise.

I am grateful also to my typist, Isabel Tupper: the burden of reading my script was not lightened by my use of the common medieval scribal abbreviations, which she learned for the purpose. Most of all my debt is to my wife, Jane, who read, commented and encouraged at all stages. That the book has been completed is largely due to her and the dedication to her is proper, although inadequate as an expression of gratitude.

Lastly I should like to record my gratitude to Malcolm Gerratt and Julia Kellerman, of Dent, for their patience and understanding.

Leeds, September 1980   Richard Rastall

Acknowledgments

The author is grateful for permission to reproduce copyright material in the figures, as follows:

Fig. 58	by permission of the Staatsbibliothek Preussischer Kulturbesitz, Berlin
Figs 63(a), 67(a)	by permission of the Syndics of the Fitzwilliam Museum, Cambridge
Figs 67(b), 90(a)	by kind permission of the Provost and Fellows of King's College, Cambridge
Fig. 55	by permission of the Master and Fellows of Trinity College, Cambridge
Figs 57(d), 60(b) and (c), 77	by permission of the Syndics of Cambridge University Library
Fig. 51	Musée Condé, Chantilly
Fig. 89(d)	by permission of the Governers and Guardians of Archbishop Marsh's Library, Dublin
Fig. 64(b)	Edinburgh University Library
Fig. 46(d)	The British Library, London
Figs 50 and 57(c)	Real Monasterio de San Lorenzo del' Escorial, Madrid
Fig. 96(a)	Music Division, The New York Public Library: Astor, Lenox and Tildem Foundations
Figs 55, 64(a)	The Bodleian Library, Oxford
Fig. 81(b)	by permission of the present owner
Fig. 6(a)	Stiftsbibliothek, St Gall
Fig. 6(c)	Abbaye Saint-Pierre, Solesmes
Fig. 120(b)	Archiv der Gesellschaft der Musikfreunde in Wien
Fig. 73(f)	Bild-Archiv der Österreichischen Nationalbibliothek, Vienna
Fig. 34(c)	Bibliothèque de la Faculté de Médecine de Montpellier
Fig. 73(b)	Bärenreiter-Verlag, Cassell

Fig. 131(c)	reprinted by permission of Belwin-Mills Music Ltd, 250 Purley Way, Croydon, Surrey, England, and Belwin-Mills Publishing Corporation, New York
Fig. 107(a)	by kind permission of Chappell Music Ltd
Fig. 63(b)	Broude Brothers Ltd, New York
Fig. 133(a)	Dover Publications, Inc., New York
Figs 130(b), (c), (d) and (f)	Faber and Faber Ltd, London
Fig. 92(c)	by kind permission of Chappell Music Ltd
Figs 108(b), 109(d), 111(c) and 114(a)	by kind permission of Heugel et Cie., Paris
Fig. 129(a)	Klavar Music Foundation of Great Britain, Lincoln
Fig. 73(c)	by permission of Georg Olms Verlag, Hildesheim, and Breitkopf and Härtel, Wiesbaden
Fig. 132	C. F. Peters Corporation, New York
Fig. 61(a)	Stainer and Bell, Ltd, London, and Galaxy Music Corporation, New York
Figs 121(a) and (b), 122(b), (c) and (d), 129(a) and (b)	Universal Edition (Alfred A. Kalmus Ltd)
Figs 131(d), 133(b)	Universal Edition (London) Ltd

In this book pitches are referred to in the Helmholtz system, in which c'–b' denotes the octave from middle C upwards. A fuller explanation is shown in Figure 72 (I), p. 122.

We commonly use note-names to denote both a note-shape and a duration: for instance, 'crotchet' can mean either the shape ♩ or the duration of one beat in $\frac{4}{4}$ time, etc., according to context. In this book names are thus used from Chapter 4 onwards, normally abbreviated as follows:

Max = maxima
D   = duplex long
L   = long
B   = breve
S   = semibreve
M   = minim
Sm   = semiminim
F   = fusa
Sf   = semifusa
C   = crotchet
Q   = quaver
Sq   = semiquaver
Dsq = demi-semiquaver

Introduction:
The Nature of Musical Notation

Notation can be divided into two classes:
1. 'Phonetic' notation, in which sounds are represented by letters, numbers or other signs, or in which verbal instructions are given. Chinese and ancient Greek notations are phonetic, as are the tablatures discussed in Part III of this book.
2. 'Diastematic' or intervallic notation, in which sounds are represented graphically.

Staff notation is diastematic in its representation of pitch and duration, which depends upon the conventions of 'high' and 'low' in the vertical plane and duration moving from left to right horizontally. The representations of other parameters in staff notation are normally phonetic, such as the indications p[iano], pizz[icato], etc.

Clearly, since the various parameters are notated in different ways, staff notation cannot be called either phonetic or diastematic as a whole. However, it is the notation of pitch that has most exercised the ingenuity of western musicians in the last thousand years, so that pitch-notation is the most sensible choice for a criterion by which western notations can be classified. When we say, therefore, that a notation is phonetic or diastematic, we refer specifically to its method of notating pitch.

Musical characteristics and notational precision

Most of us, if asked for a definition of musical notation, would probably say something like the following: 'The system of written symbols by means of which a composer records the music that exists in his imagination, and which thus acts as a set of instructions to a performer or performers who will create the sound of the music.' Such a definition is certainly acceptable for most written music, but it cannot stand without modification. Anyone brought up on Tonic

1

Sol-fa rather than staff notation will immediately query 'system' in the singular, and the most cursory study of Wolf's *Handbuch der Notationskunde* shows that in the West alone many quite different (and not easily-classifiable) systems have been in operation. Those familiar with medieval notations will ask if the notation itself, far from being a mere tool for the transmission of music, did not sometimes influence the kind of music that was composed. Present-day composers who use 'inspirational' notations do not specify at all closely the sounds that they expect to be produced: they only set certain limits to the methods of the performance or to particular musical parameters. To what extent does such notation represent sounds imagined by the composer?

To take account of these objections several changes are needed in our definition. 'System' is misleading in a definition, although it may be accurate enough as the description of a notational arrangement; written symbols may (and in the West usually do) include verbal instructions; a composer may record musical ideas without controlling individual parameters as precisely as 'music that exists in his imagination' suggests; and his purpose may not be performance. (A notation used for other purposes is, of course, a notational parasite: study-scores, Schenker's analytical notation, and so on, could not exist unless performance-notation existed first. But that would be no reason to exclude them from this book, even were it always possible to do so.) Finally, we cannot always assume a composer (in the writing down of folk songs, for instance).

With all this in mind, I offer the following as a definition of musical notation: 'The written symbols (which may include verbal instructions) by which musical ideas are represented and preserved for future performance or study.' Any notation that conforms to this definition will give at least some of the following information about the musical characteristics of any single musical sound:

1. Its pitch.
2. Its duration.
3. Its loudness.
4. The type of attack.

When two or more sounds are put together, notation may also show

5. Pitch-relationships: chords (simultaneous sounding) and melody (consecutive sounding).
6. Duration-relationships: rhythm, tempo (the frequency of stresses) and metre (the shape of stress-patterns).

Finally, the notation may show

7. 'Expression': the deliberate variation of any of the above elements for expressive purposes. (I do not forget that this definition is circular: but we can study a composer's action and the means that he uses without discussing the validity of his motives.)

These characteristics are not all equally important, and only in the relatively recent past have composers normally tried to show all of them with any precision. The earliest written music in the West showed little more than the relative pitch of consecutive notes, and that very imprecisely; duration (and therefore rhythm) was not shown until the late twelfth century, while indications of tempo (and therefore more precise duration) occur only in the seventeenth; loudness was normally indicated only from the seventeenth century onwards; and the same is true for the notation of attack and other 'expressive' characteristics.

Historically, then, notation has tended to show an increasing number of musical parameters more and more precisely, though we must not assume a consistent increase in the composer's requirements from notation. The purposes to which notation has been put are, roughly:

(i) An *aide-mémoire*: a reminder of music which has been learned aurally and is really sung from memory.

(ii) A 'skeleton' notation showing the composer the main outlines of the work's structure, from which he can construct a performance. This often involves certain conventions, and both memory and improvisation play a large part: the composer is usually directing a performance in which others are involved.

(iii) A 'skeleton' notation, detailed enough to allow others to construct a performance in the composer's absence. This could be a solo performance, or not; it may involve known conventions (of instrumentation, for example), or special verbal instructions from the composer, or even written non-musical principles.

(iv) A notation detailed enough to give the performer very little latitude in following the composer's intentions: memory and improvisation do not play much part, if any.

(v) A notation giving such precise information that the performer has virtually no latitude, and follows the composer's intentions as closely as possible in all respects.

(vi) Inspirational notation, in which visual symbols or ideas expressed graphically and/or in words inspire the performer to certain actions.

3

(vii) A visual analogue for the listener, from which no performance could be reconstructed.

(viii) Notation intended, not for performance, but to give instruction in musical procedures.

It would be surprising if such a variety of purposes did not give rise to a similar variety of notations. Nos (i) to (vii) are roughly in chronological order, although they do not quite constitute a straight-line progression. Situation (iii), for example, is both medieval and twentieth century; (vi) and (vii) obviously do not belong to the same scheme of things as (i) to (v), although they are very recent; and (viii), which is a situation encountered from the tenth century to the twentieth, gave rise to completely different notational systems in the early examples, whereas the notation of later examples is virtually no different from that of other types of music.

Situations (i) to (v) require a notation of increasing precision. This partly reflects the composer's increasing wish to make the performer present the music exactly as it was originally envisaged: in other words, the composer's more precise wishes have to be transmitted through more precise notation. Most composers, however, would probably favour some latitude in performance as necessary for the spontaneity and tiny unpredictabilities that make a performance 'come alive'. For, quite apart from any individual 'interpretations', one essential of musical performance is the human element—the subtle variation of all the musical elements discussed above—that makes each performance an individual recreation of the music, slightly different from all other performances, even by the same person. That is why most composers happily accept that conventional staff notation has certain in-built limitations of precision. The precision of the composer's intention must be matched by the precision of the notation that transmits that intention; and latitude in performance requires a comparable element of notational imprecision.

It is therefore in the realms of precise performance that composers have rejected conventional staff notation. Those composers who have preferred to commit their music to an electronic tape, thus exercising complete control over all the musical parameters involved, have also required a notation of comparable precision. Notation for such music is often a set of precise instructions which will enable an electronic engineer to make up a tape in which the performance of the music will in no way differ from that on the composer's original tape.

I have discussed the matter of composers' varying needs for precision because it is our only weapon against the 'progressive' view.

However we may fight against it intellectually, most of us have grown up to accept the Darwinian theory of evolution and its application to musical history, notation and many other subjects. The very word 'progress' implies a transition from barbarism to civilization, from ignorance to knowledge or wisdom; and in consequence it is hard not to sit in judgement when we study the history of a subject over a period of a thousand years. It is still occasionally argued, for instance, that thirteenth-century secular song must have been sung in free rhythm, because the songs are notated non-rhythmically although the means to notate rhythms were at hand (cf. the polyphony of that century). The argument goes that if the songs were to be sung in set rhythms, they could and would have been notated in those rhythms. The truth is, I believe, that rhythmic notation was unnecessary to monophony (as opposed to polyphony, for which it was vital) and not a part of the secular singer's equipment (as opposed to that of the church singer of polyphony, who used notation considerably more to aid his aural memory).

The composer's or scribe's choice of musical parameters to be notated is not, then, merely a matter of availability. A purely oral tradition requires nothing to be written down, which is why nothing survives that can be identified as medieval minstrels' music; a *mainly* oral tradition requires certain parameters to be notated (perhaps only pitch), and the scribe chooses what these shall be; a tradition which is only partly oral requires more parameters (rhythm and metre, for instance, and perhaps some expression). The reasons behind the scribe's choice are a matter of musical history rather than of notation. But the story of notation can be seen as the continuous exercise of this choice, and not a progression from darkness to light. From the beginning of our study we shall find that notation is concerned with the transmission of relevant information: that is, it is well suited to the music that it serves.

This has its corollary. Systems of notation have been invented as they were found necessary, and modified or abandoned as they were found inadequate: so the story of musical notation in western Europe is one of innovations, changes and disappearances. Even staff notation, which we tend to regard as the only and unchanging system, has altered greatly in the course of its development. Originally it was exclusively a vocal notation, but by the end of the thirteenth century it was in use for purely instrumental music: from then on it was, as it is always assumed to be, an all-purpose notation, capable of transmitting music for voice or any instrument. Of the other early vocal

5

notations, the system of syllable-heighting relied on a text, was therefore not suitable for instrumental music, and was quickly abandoned as clumsy in operation; methods of using letters for notes were found unsatisfactory for vocal music (where the letters could no doubt be confused with the text) but had four centuries' good use in instrumental tablatures; and Tonic Sol-fa, specially devised for singers in the nineteenth century (although descended from the medieval solmization system), might well have been used for instrumental music but apparently never was. Roughly speaking (and concerning ourselves only with pitch-notation), an all-purpose notation has generally been thought desirable, and a notation which is especially suitable for the voice will not be acceptable to instrumentalists, and *vice versa*.

It may be instructive to speculate on the reasons for this. In vocal music, the performer has only the tension of his vocal chords to guide him in pitching a note, and his ear to criticize the note once it is sung. Unless he possesses true 'perfect' or 'absolute' pitch (and such people are rare) he has no absolute pitch-reference which will allow him to sing a note at any time absolutely in tune. Hence a singer concerns himself with relative, rather than with absolute, pitch. He performs by calculating intervals between notes, not by singing each note individually. The successful vocal notations have been those which recognize this: Guido's use of clefs and coloured stave-lines to show where the semitones are; the solmization-syllables to identify the intervals in a hexachord; and the later use of sol-fa syllables for the same purpose, in a modified system to suit the possibilities of modulation from one key to another.

The instrumentalist's need, on the other hand, is generally for precise instructions to play each individual note. Given these, he can discharge the physical requirements of playing two notes, and the notes will sound correctly without him knowing in advance the precise intervallic relationship between them. The most successful instrumental notations have been those that provide the performer with precise instructions on the placing of his fingers on the strings, holes or keys of the instrument.

Why, then, has staff notation successfully held its place for almost 1000 years as an all-purpose notation? Probably because it has just enough of the necessary characteristics for singers and instrumentalists alike to read it in the way that they wish to. For singers, staff notation shows the movement up or down, and also the type of each interval (3rd, 5th, etc.). The precise interval has to be worked out according to the clef and any accidentals, but an experienced singer can do this in most keys quite successfully at sight. For instrumentalists, the placing of any note on the staff (again, with accidentals taken into account) relates precisely to a note-name of which the fingering on the instrument is known. This involves a 'middle process'—the relating of the note-name to the written symbol on one side and the fingering on the other—which is absent from the most successful instrumental notations. On the other hand, staff notation is flexible enough to imply alternative meanings to an instrumentalist:

1. it can show the true pitch of the note required, so that retuning a lute-string, for instance, would necessitate a change in the relationship between note-name and fingering;

or

2. it can show the fingering required, and a change of tuning will result in a different sound.

The first of these is the meaning normally assumed: the second comes into play in cases such as the *scordatura* tunings of the seventeenth century or the transpositions used for certain orchestral instruments.

Staff notation and tablature

A second reason for the success of staff notation is that vocal and instrumental music have often been interchangeable, and transcription from one notation to another therefore highly inconvenient (and so commercially lucrative: witness the sixteenth-century printed lute intabulations of polyphony). This interchangeability of medium that staff notation allows has been used to particularly good purpose in keyboard music. In the sixteenth century, when the keyboard repertory was still separating itself from the rest of the vocal and instrumental repertory, it was useful—and probably necessary—for an organist to be able to read from open score. It was therefore possible for any work in score to be played by a good keyboard performer, or for any keyboard music in score to be played by other instruments. In some cases, such as Bermudo's *Declaración de Instrumentos* (1555), score was used deliberately to give a choice; sometimes it is not certain that keyboard performance was intended (it is assumed for Frescobaldi's *Recercari et Canzoni Franzese* (1615), for instance, only because the composer was an organist); and occasionally the use of score is at least partly didactic and designed to show the part-writing, as it is in Bach's *Die Kunst der Fuge*.

Willi Apel called a score 'keyboard partitura' (NPM, xxiii f), but I do not think that a special name is necessary. 'Keyboard music in open score' is less elegant, but unequivocal. Besides, this layout must not be confused with that most commonly used for keyboard music, namely, a condensed score of two or three staves on which the various voices are written two or more to a staff. Unfortunately, this is always called 'keyboard score', although in fact it is not a score but a tablature. A score presents each voice-part on its own staff (see below), while a tablature presents two or more voices on each staff or comparable area of the page—that is, the music is 'intabulated'. This nomenclature is neither consistent nor wholly logical: a Bach two-part invention is both keyboard score and open score, and an orchestral score does not cease to be such because two flutes are written on a single staff. But I have tried to use these terms realistically, and in this book 'score' implies basically one part per staff, 'keyboard score' is a two- or three-staff system specifically for keyboard, and 'tablature' refers to all intabulations other than keyboard score.

In this last class, the exclusion of keyboard score removes the only type of intabulation consisting wholly of staff notation. 'Tablature' will therefore apply only to notations in which letters or numbers are used exclusively or in part:

1. letter notations, in which pitch is indicated by the letter-names of the notes; and

2. *Griffschrift*, sensibly translated as 'finger-notation' by Apel (NPM, 54), which directs the performer to make certain mechanical actions which, on a specified instrument, will produce the required sound.

Most examples of the first are in fact vocal notations, discussed in Part II, although German organ tablature is another. In this, the relationship of music and medium is so close that I have thought it reasonable to place German organ tablature in Part III among other notations referred to as 'tablatures'. The Spanish keyboard tablatures, which in concept lie half way between *Griffschrift* and *Tonschrift* (pitch notation), can then properly be placed between the German tablature and the real finger-notation tablatures.

The format of the musical source

Following the discussion of tablature and scores, it will be useful here to describe the main ways in which polyphonic music has in the past been ordered on the page, and to explain briefly the implications of the

8

layout for the manner of performance. In all but the last of the formats described here, the layout was originally intended to accommodate all the performers at one copy of the music.

1. A score shows each voice-part on its own staff, with groups of staves making up 'systems'. If simultaneous musical events are aligned vertically, then a vertical reading of the system shows what is happening in the music at any given moment. From the late twelfth century to the beginning of the sixteenth, score-layout implied that the different voices had approximately the same rhythms and movement: for this reason it was usually considered necessary to write the text once only, below the lowest voice. In the later sixteenth century score-layout was used for didactic purposes, and in the seventeenth also for keyboard music (see above). At the latter time, the close liaison between singer and accompanist caused scores to be used for Italian 'monody', although this may also have been influenced by the large master-scores in which the complete musical and verbal texts of operas were set down. This last use of score continues to the present day, and it presupposes individual parts for the performers.

2. *Cantus lateralis* (music in which the parts are 'side by side') lays out the various voice-parts separately, so that each singer reads from a particular area of the open page. In the earliest form, the motet-layout of the thirteenth century, the Tenor is written right across the bottom of the open spread, with the two upper parts above it, one on each page. (The Tenor, 'holding-part', is the lowest voice in this texture, with Motetus and Triplex above. The Tenor moves more slowly, often in ligatures, and is thus shorter in written length than the upper parts.) For shorter pieces of music, this layout was contracted to take up only a single page.

The normal layout for soloist vocal polyphony in the fourteenth and fifteenth centuries also used a single page, with the parts written separately in order (usually Cantus, Tenor, Contratenor). With four parts, such as was used in sacred music of the fifteenth and early sixteenth centuries, this layout used both pages of the open spread, with the Cantus on the upper half of the left-hand page, the Tenor below it and the Altus and Bassus facing them on the recto. This is by no means invariable, however, and the disposition of voices varies considerably when there are five or more. The large choir-books of the fifteenth century, from which a whole choir could read at a lectern, of necessity take up both pages of the open book.

Just before the middle of the sixteenth century Jacques Moderne used a modified choir-book layout for some of his chanson publications (Reese MR, 290): here, the upper voice on each page is printed upside-down so that, when the book is laid on a table, two persons on one side of the table and two on the other can all read from the same book. This idea was later used in England, mainly for the two-part amateur repertory of the seventeenth century. However, the late English use of it probably derives from table-format proper, not from Moderne's modified choir-book format.

'Table-format' is another type of *cantus lateralis*. It came into being in the late sixteenth century, when choir-book layout was no longer normally used. In instrumental (or mixed vocal and instrumental) consorts it became usual for the performers to sit around a table with a single copy placed flat between them. In this case, the music can face in all four directions (not in only two, as with Moderne's prints), so that the performers really sit *round* the table and not merely on opposite sides of it. Table-format is a peculiarly English layout, and had a short life-span. Its chief asset seems to have been its ability to work equally well for different types of consort: the Cantus and lute-part often appear together on the left-hand page in two-part score, apparently so that the singer can accompany himself, while the other parts, which are really optional voices, can be performed vocally and/or instrumentally as desired.

3. Part-books came into being in the late fifteenth century. As choirs became larger there came a point at which choir-books could not be increased in size to accommodate the greater number of singers. In the Eton, Lambeth and Caius choir-books (*c.* 1500–20) the page-size has reached its reasonable maximum: for a larger page the cost of parchment would be prohibitive and paper would tear, while the notation would take too long to write. (For reasons of legibility these late choir-books are in black notation.) The solution for a large choir was to write the individual voice-parts in separate books, from which two or three singers could read. This format was retained for sacred vocal music until the nineteenth century, when church musicians finally took up the vocal score which had been normal in secular vocal music since the seventeenth century; and parts (although of rather larger format now) have continued in use for instrumentalists.

Primary and secondary interpretations

Finally, I must discuss briefly a subject that I passed by earlier in writing on the role of notation in the composer-performer relationship. When we look at a piece of music and ask 'What does this notation mean?' we expect there to be only one correct answer, such as 'That note is a minim, and should be held for two beats' or 'This passage is to be played with the volume increasing from piano to forte'. We assume, in other words, that the composer and performer have a basic common understanding of what is implied by the notation. The assumption is generally correct, though notation constantly changes, giving rise to heated academic arguments (as in medieval theoretical writings) or a set of explanations by the composer himself (as has often been the case in the present century). This common understanding results in what we may call the primary interpretation of the written music.

There may nevertheless be quite marked differences in performance according to (usually) regional conventions or preferences. An Italian singer performing from Franconian notation would not have sung the same rhythms as a French singer reading from the same copy; and a late eighteenth-century Parisian performance of *Messiah* would have been noticeably different from a German one in both rhythms and articulation. In each case the performers brought their own conventions to the performance, thus adding a *secondary interpretation* to their common understanding of the notation. Moreover, this secondary interpretation may be applied to music which is in some way notationally non-committal, an even more difficult situation to assess. What rhythms were applied to medieval secular songs notated non-rhythmically, and were the same rhythmic principles applied by everybody?

The questions to be asked are many and complex. Shall we ever find the answers to such problems as the rhythm of medieval monody, or the questions concerning over-dotting and the assimilation of triplets in the eighteenth century? Perhaps not. Certainly these matters have been, and still are, live issues, constantly debated. It is not possible to ignore them for the purposes of this book, for they usually affect, and are affected by, the notation to which they refer. But they are problems of performance-practice rather than of notation, and I shall discuss them only when notational considerations demand it.

Part I
The Development of Staff Notation

1. The Notation of the St Gall Manuscripts

The notation of pitch

Diastematic notation is closely related to marks used for speech-accentuation. The signs for long and short duration in ancient Greek music, – and ᴗ , survive as signs of syllable-length in poetry, and the basic accentuation-signs of Greek declamation, ⁄ and ⸜ , are now used in the French language (as is the form combining them, ᴧ), although with regard to pronunciation rather than declamation. This is not to argue any causal relationships: I wish only to demonstrate that such signs are equally applicable to pronunciation, declamation and music. That such signs were used for these various purposes is the main reason why it has been difficult to prove which of the pre-Christian notations is the real precursor of the notation of the western Church. Although the issue is still not finally settled, there is general agreement that the earliest surviving western notation was probably derived from the accentuation-signs of classical literature. These signs, which were in use between *c.* 200 B.C. and *c.* A.D. 200, are usually ascribed to Aristophanes of Byzantium (b. ?257 B.C.).

In the musical notation of the Christian Church these signs became *neumes* (the Greek *neuma* means 'a sign'). The earliest surviving manuscripts of neumatic notation, dating from the ninth and tenth centuries, originated in the monastery of St Gall in Switzerland. They show a highly-developed notational style, in marked contrast to the more primitive Paleofrankish notation, of which ninth-century examples are also known. Hence, although the earliest musical repertory is written in Sangallian neumes, that notation is unlikely to be the earliest western notation, and much work has to be done on other schools of neumatic notation before any line of development can be clearly seen. The discussion that follows is not, therefore, intended to imply that Sangallian neumes are the ancestor of all western staff notation.

Dom Eugène Cardine ('Sémiologie grégorienne', 2) has distinguished four groups of declamation-signs which became neumes:
(a) the *accentus acutus* ╱ and the *accentus gravis* ╲;
(b) the abbreviation-signs **,** and ∴;
(c) the contraction-signs ∼ and ↳; and
(d) the interrogation-marks ⱱ and ⱱ.
The signs of the first group showed respectively the raising and lowering of the voice: in their use as neumes the acutus became the *virga* ('rod'), while the gravis was modified to a *punctum* ('dot' or 'point') or a *tractulus* ('little stroke'). This modification of the gravis is natural for a right-handed scribe: for while the acutus requires a movement easily accomplished by the wrist, the gravis needs a more difficult movement of fingers only, or else a use of the whole arm that is not easily controlled.[1] A punctum is the simplest and most natural solution, although in the earliest manuscripts (up to the tenth century) it is often written at speed and takes the form of the tractulus.

Between the ninth century and the end of the twelfth neumatic notation developed, at least in some places, to the point at which it has remained ever since when used for plainsong. (In polyphony, as we shall see, the notation developed further.) During these three centuries or more the virga and punctum were used for single notes, usually for upward and downward movement respectively. For groups of two or three notes to be sung to a single syllable they were combined to form more complex shapes called 'ligatures' (that is, a group of notes 'bound' or 'tied' to one another). Figure 1 shows the probable development of 'simple' Sangallian neumes. It will be seen that the neumatic notation is closely related to the column before it: many of the shapes are the same but the neumes tend to be cursive, made with fewer lifts of the pen.

More complex neumes, containing four or more notes, were made by combining these ligatures with either a single note or with another ligature. These are known as 'compound neumes'. The name of a compound neume indicates both the ligature with which it begins and the manner of its modification: for example, the *podatus subbipunctis* is a podatus followed by two descending puncta; the *climacus resupinus* is a climacus 'bent backwards', with an ascending note following it. Figure 2 shows some of the most common forms. As the last example indicates, a ligature can be modified more than once, and in theory could go on being modified no matter how long the melisma was. In practice, a much-modified ligature usually took the shapes of shorter ligatures in the course of its modification, and the

16

Figure 1. Simple Neumes

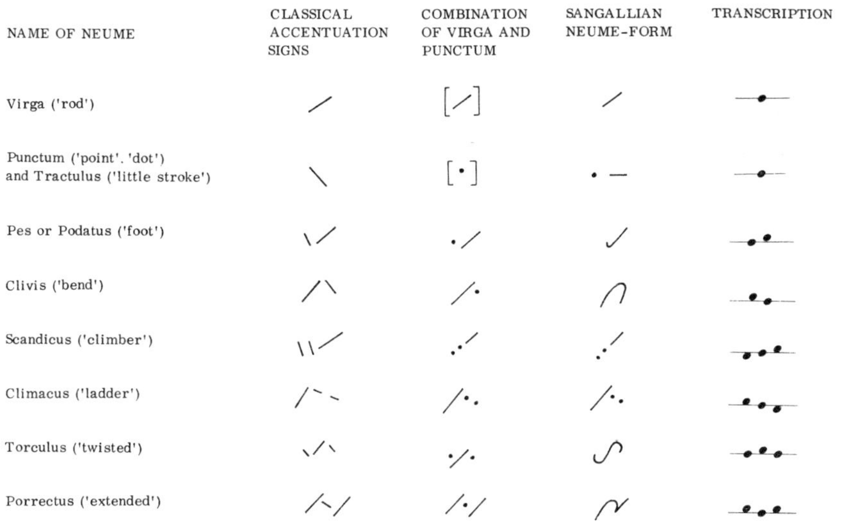

NAME OF NEUME	CLASSICAL ACCENTUATION SIGNS	COMBINATION OF VIRGA AND PUNCTUM	SANGALLIAN NEUME-FORM	TRANSCRIPTION
Virga ('rod')	/	[/]	/	—•—
Punctum ('point', 'dot') and Tractulus ('little stroke')	\	[•]	• —	—•—
Pes or Podatus ('foot')	\/	•/	/	—••
Clivis ('bend')	/\	/•	∩	—••—
Scandicus ('climber')	\\/	.:/	.:/	—•••—
Climacus ('ladder')	/˜˲	/••	/••	—•••—
Torculus ('twisted')	\/\	•/•	∿	—•••—
Porrectus ('extended')	/˜/	/•/	∩/	—•••—

(In transcribing neumes I have chosen to use plain note-heads: these indicate regular, but not precisely-measured, durations in the Solesmes method of performance.)

Figure 2. Compound Neumes

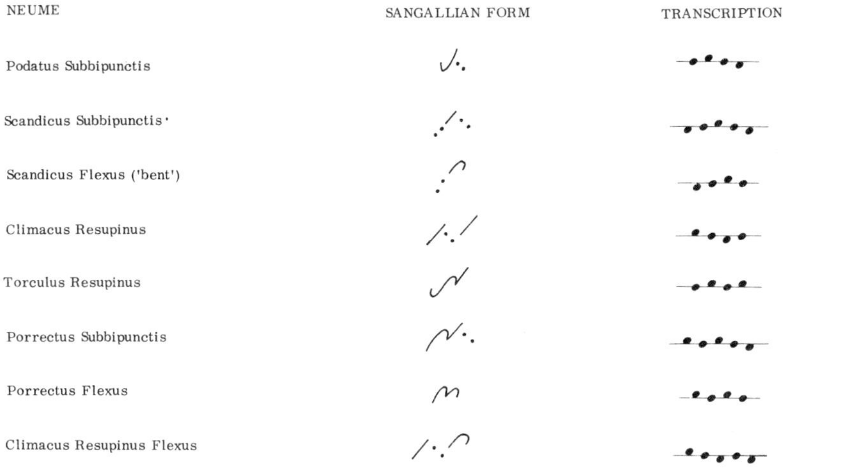

NEUME	SANGALLIAN FORM	TRANSCRIPTION
Podatus Subbipunctis	∕••	—••••—
Scandicus Subbipunctis·	.:/••	—•••••—
Scandicus Flexus ('bent')	.:∩	—••••
Climacus Resupinus	/•./	—••••—
Torculus Resupinus	∿/	—••••—
Porrectus Subbipunctis	∩/••	—•••••—
Porrectus Flexus	∽	—••••—
Climacus Resupinus Flexus	/•.∩	—•••••—

climacus resupinus flexus shown could equally well be regarded as a climacus closely followed by a heighted clivis. Scribes probably found it more convenient to add simple neumes together in a very long melisma, rather than writing rarely-used modifications.

17

The neumes so far discussed, whether simple or compound, are concerned solely with the pitch of each note in relation to the notes on either side: that is, the direction of melodic movement is shown, but not the precise intervals. No accentuation or durational changes are shown, either, although the accentuation is assumed to belong to the first note of each group. The St Gall manuscripts do in fact notate a great number of rhythmic and other subtleties, shown by means of special neumes, by Romanian letters and signs, and by certain modifications of the normal neume-shapes. These will be discussed in turn.

Special neumes

Cardine's second group of neumes derived from declamation-signs comprises those which 'involve a unison'. The first (see Figure 3) originally signified the elision of a vowel: in notation it is variously called *stropha, apostropha* or *strophicus*. However, it is most commonly found in a group of two or three at the same pitch—such a group being called *bistropha* or *tristropha*—or in even larger groups. In the old Solesmes tradition these are performed with two and three times the duration of a single note—that is, as a single longer note, fairly precisely measured. Cardine's assertion that the constituent notes should be sung separately is supported by instances of chants containing such a neume used as a tenor in motet style: the polyphony usually separates the neume into constituent notes separately sung. The special forms of these neumes must nevertheless indicate a way of performance for which a bivirga or trivirga (see below) would not be appropriate. Cardine believes that the use of the elision-sign in apostrophic neumes shows that those notes were to be sung lightly.

The *trigon* was originally an abbreviation-sign. According to Cardine it was used, like the stropha, to indicate a lighter manner of singing. The trigon exemplifies Cardine's description (SG, 2) of a neume as a 'written gesture': for, despite its shape, its first two notes are at the same pitch, again sung separately.

Cardine points out (ibid., 71) that Sangallian notation does not use puncta together at the unison. The neumes of which the bistropha and tristropha are lightly-sung versions are the bivirga and trivirga: these are groups of two or three virgae at the unison, sung separately in a normal manner.

18

Figure 3. Apostrophic Neumes

NEUME	SANGALLIAN FORM	TRANSCRIPTION
Stropha	,	•
Bistropha	,,	• •
Tristropha	,,,	• • •
Trigon	∴	• • •
Bivirga	//	• •
Trivirga	///	• • •

The neumes of Cardine's third group use the contraction-sign ⁓ or a similar, but upright, form ♮ or 5. The *oriscus* ('limit'), which uses the upright forms, is normally a single note at the same pitch as the preceding note and followed by one of lower pitch. It is found also, even when the following note is *not* lower in pitch, as the second of two unison notes which carry the same vowel without a consonant between (Cardine SG, 99, gives '*te ex*spectant' as an example, the oriscus being on the second syllable). In each case the oriscus is sung as a separate note (the old Solesmes tradition makes the unison notes a single note of double length).

The *pressus* ('closed') takes several forms: the melodic configurations are those in which the oriscus is used, but with a different disposition of syllables. The *pressus major* (Figure 4) consists of a virga, oriscus and punctum: the first two notes are at the same pitch, sung separately, and take a single syllable. This syllable may be shared by the punctum, or the punctum may have a syllable of its own. The *pressus minor* consists of an oriscus and a punctum, the first being in unison with the preceding note. After a clivis or torculus, the pressus minor may be joined to the ligature before, as in Figure 4(b).

Several other neume-forms use the oriscus and are closely related to those just discussed (see Cardine's list in SG, 4, nos 18–24). Of these, the *salicus* ('leaper') must be discussed, partly because it is a common neume and partly because Cardine's interpretation of it (which contradicts the traditional Solesmes interpretation) raises an important general principle for all neumes in this group. The salicus (c) is a modified scandicus in which the second note is an oriscus. According to the monks of Solesmes (LU, ix) the accent is on the second note of the three, not on the first (as would be the case with a scandicus). Apel (GC, 110) shares the view of several scholars that this is not the correct interpretation, and prefers the suggestion that the middle note is either chromatically inflected or is a micro-tone. This would require the middle note to be sung rather lightly, not with an accent and slight lengthening. Cardine's suggestion is closer to the Solesmes tradition (and he produces interesting evidence to support it: SG, 102), namely, that it is the note after the oriscus that takes the accent. Clearly, this interpretation has important consequences for all the neumes just discussed, giving as it does to the oriscus the function of throwing the accentuation on to a later note than expected.

Figure 4. Neumes of the Oriscus Group

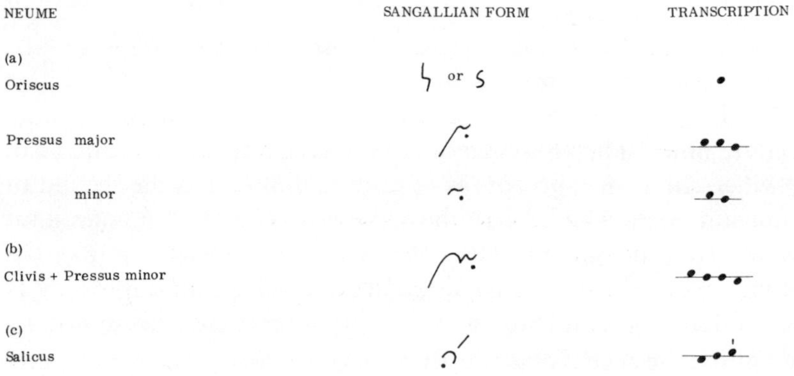

NEUME	SANGALLIAN FORM	TRANSCRIPTION
(a) Oriscus		
Pressus major		
minor		
(b) Clivis + Pressus minor		
(c) Salicus		

Cardine's last group consists of neumes using the question-mark, a sign that 'lends itself to representing a vocal phenomenon related to the ascending inflexion of an interrogative phrase' (SG, 2). To be more accurate, we are concerned here with a single note, the *quilisma* ('roll'): but since this note is invariably found in ligature it is convenient to discuss it in its simplest context, that of the *quilisma-pes*. The Sangallian shape of the quilisma-pes is shown in Figure 5(a): a note written as two or three small loops is bound to a following virga. One Sangallian source uses the form of question-mark found in the region of Troyes (b): but this form came to be used exclusively in Messine notation. The note before a quilisma is normally lower in pitch: usually this preceding note (and perhaps a whole ligature) shares a syllable with the quilisma-pes (c), although the quilisma can begin a new syllable. The virga with which the quilisma-pes ends can be modified (see below) or extended (d) in the obvious ways.

Cardine remarks that the oldest of the Sangallian manuscripts, MS

359 of the monastery's collection, uses the two- and three-loop forms quite deliberately, the former indicating the ascent of a whole tone and the latter all other intervals (in practice, almost always a semitone). This does not apply in the other manuscripts, where the two forms are used indiscriminately.

Figure 5. Quilisma Neumes

The manner of performance of the quilisma has been the subject of much discussion in the past. Most scholars have regarded it as an ornamental note, and at one time there was general (if agnostic) agreement that it should be sung as a short trill, or mordent (LU, vii: Apel GC, 114). Cardine, who is much concerned with duration and accentuation, rejects this theory. He believes that the note should be sung lightly, the accent being thrown on to a later note (SG, 126), and his argument is certainly persuasive.

Liquescence

Liquescent neumes are a result of the close relationship between words and music in Gregorian chant. Certain letter-combinations are difficult to sing smoothly, clearly and without undue emphasis: liquescence is a notational modification indicating a style of performance which helps the singer's pronunciation at those points.

A liquescent neume is a modified ligature. There are many contexts in which liquescence can be used (see PM II, 38: Cardine SG, 133 f), the most common being consonant-groups which include a liquid (l, m, n, r) or plosive (d, t). The liquescent note is sung lightly as an indeterminate vowel which, placed between the two syllables concerned, serves to articulate the change from one to the other. Liquescence is also commonly used when two vowels come together, in which case no extra vowel is sung.

In the Gradual 'Liberasti nos' (shown in Parrish NMM, plate II, and discussed ibid., 17) the word 'affligentibus' is given two liquescent neumes (Figure 6(a): for the sign over the three neumes on '-bus', see below). The performance of this word is shown in (b). (In my transcriptions of chant liquescent notes are written small and the slurs indicate the extent of individual neumes where necessary.)

Figure 6. Liquescence

(a)

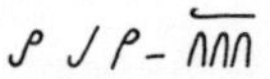

af fli genti bus

(St Gall, Stiftsbibliothek, MS 359, f.125r)

(b)

a – f^e – fli – gen^e – ti – bus

(c)

af – fli – gen – ti – bus

(Graduale Romanum, p. 366)

Figure 6(c) shows the notation of this word in the Solesmes editions. It illustrates the two classes into which liquescence can be divided (Stanbrook GM, 33 ff):
1. that which modifies a particular neume as seen in other versions of the chant, the existing last note being made semivocal, as in the first syllable of Figure 6 (a torculus); and
2. that in which the semivocal note is additional to the neume found in other versions, as in the third syllable of Figure 6 (a punctum).
In all cases it is the last note of the ligature that becomes semivocal. Figure 7 shows the commonest liquescent neumes. The precise form of the modification depends on whether the last note is a bound virga or a punctum: in the former case the stroke is shortened, and in the latter a more curved shape is used. The liquescent scandicus and climacus resupinus are modifications of forms that are themselves modified by the substitution of a pes for the punctum-plus-virga formation. Liquescence of the second class more often concerns neumes ending in a bound virga.

Figure 7. Liquescent Neumes

NEUME	NORMAL FORM	LIQUESCENT FORM AND NAME
First Class		
Pes	✓	 ✓　　Epiphonus ('semivocal')

Figure 7. *Continued*

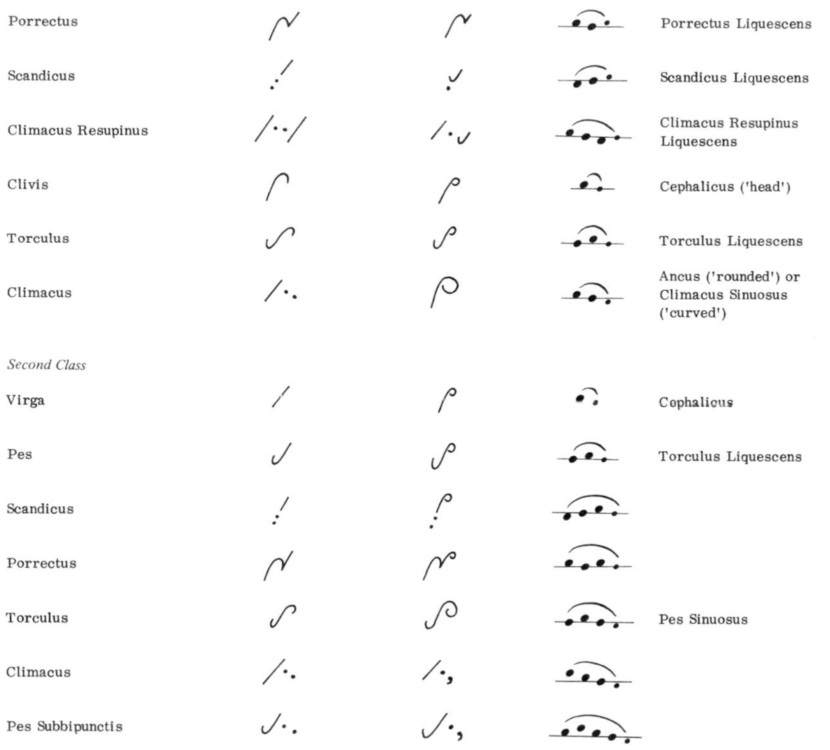

Porrectus			Porrectus Liquescens
Scandicus			Scandicus Liquescens
Climacus Resupinus			Climacus Resupinus Liquescens
Clivis			Cephalicus ('head')
Torculus			Torculus Liquescens
Climacus			Ancus ('rounded') or Climacus Sinuosus ('curved')
Second Class			
Virga			Cephalicus
Pes			Torculus Liquescens
Scandicus			
Porrectus			
Torculus			Pes Sinuosus
Climacus			
Pes Subbipunctis			

Rhythmic modifications and Romanian letters

Sangallian notation is not concerned only with pitch-relationships. The earliest manuscripts show considerable modification of the basic notation, especially with respect to duration. Most neumes lend themselves to modification in one of the following ways:

1. the addition of a short stroke, called an *episema* ('added to the sign'), above the neume;
2. the addition of the episema to a part of the neume;
3. the lengthening or enlarging of part of the neume.

In each case the note concerned is lengthened in performance. Some scribes used the tractulus (also known as *virga jacens*, 'thrown rod') as a modified punctum, especially in those ligatures where the punctum appears as a separate note. Figure 8 shows some common modifications of these three types.

23

Figure 8. Rhythmic Modifications

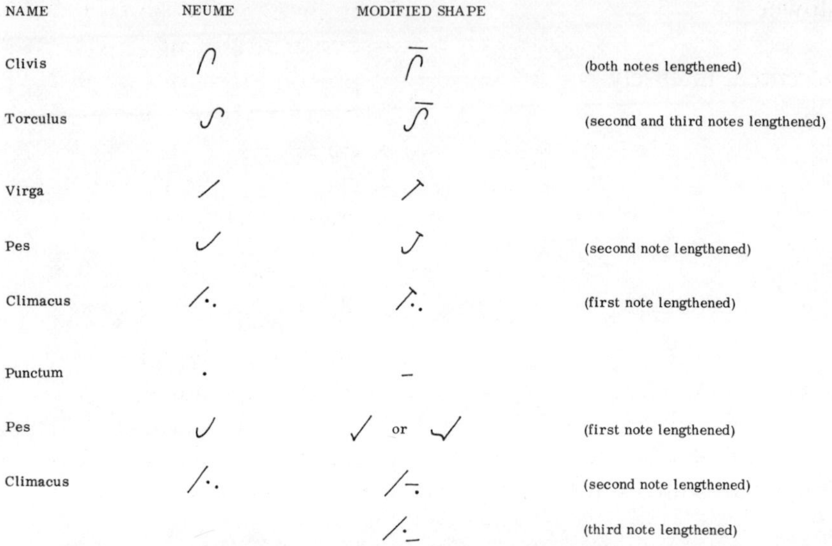

NAME	NEUME	MODIFIED SHAPE	
Clivis			(both notes lengthened)
Torculus			(second and third notes lengthened)
Virga			
Pes			(second note lengthened)
Climacus			(first note lengthened)
Punctum			
Pes		or	(first note lengthened)
Climacus			(second note lengthened)
			(third note lengthened)

The invention of these modifications and the use of the episema is sometimes attributed to Romanus, a papal emissary to St Gall *c.* 789. We have it on the authority of Notker Balbulus that Romanus was responsible for adding letters above the chant, with equally subtle rhythmic effect. The Romanian letters explained by Notker (GS I, 95 f) fall into two main classes (Stanbrook GM, 39 ff):
1. the first shows the singer the direction of the tune, or warns him that the interval is larger than expected;
2. the second deals with duration and accent.
A third and much smaller class modifies the letters of the two main classes. The table which follows shows the letters most commonly found.

ROMANIAN LETTERS

Class 1

rising in pitch

- a = altius (higher)
- l = levare (rise)
- s = sursum (lift up)

falling in pitch

- d = deprimatur (lowered)
- i = iusum, inferius (lower)

the same pitch

- e = equaliter (equally)

Class 2

faster

c = cito, celeriter (quickly)

slower	t = trahere, tenere (drag, hold)
	x = exspectare (wait)
accented, intensely	p = pressio (accent)
	f = cum fragore (with much noise)
	k = clange, clamitat (with noise, cries aloud)

Class 3

	b = bene (well)
	m = mediocriter (moderately)
	v = valde (very much)

Messine notation, too, sometimes used letters, some not found in Sangallian sources and others with different meanings (Murray GC, 59):

MESSINE LETTERS

Class 1

| falling in pitch | h = humiliter (lower) |
| the same pitch | nl = ne leves (do not rise) |

Class 2

slower	a = auge (lengthen)
at normal speed	nt = ne teneas (do not lengthen)
	st = statim, strictim (no delay, straight on)

Class 3

| | n = naturaliter (of normal value) |

The Messine letters, although obviously derived from Romanian letters in idea, seem to be more corrective. They are not used as much as the Romanian letters, and their use is much less consistent.

In general, Romanian letters affect only one note in a neume, although some manuscripts use so many modifications that letters appear almost constantly through the chant, c and t being very frequent. It is also possible for the scribe to make a letter valid for several notes by extending a line from the letter above all the notes to be modified (see above, Figure 6(a), for an example).

However strange we may find a notation that acts principally as an *aide-mémoire,* that used at St Gall was certainly very sophisticated. At least, the singing—the actual performance of the music—was very sophisticated, and the notation reflected this. The Romanian letters (and perhaps also the episema and other rhythmic modifications) seem to have been the means by which Romanus, a Roman cantor trained in the performance-traditions of the papal chapel, notated some of the subtleties of performance for German monks who had no such tradition. Recent research indicates that the performance of plainsong became less sophisticated in the ensuing centuries.[2] The notation followed the same trend. From the tenth century until the fifteenth we can see the various schools of neumatic notation gradually losing the subtlety of the Sangallian neumes.

2. Later Neumatic Notations and the Development of the Staff

Accent-neumes and point-neumes

The Sangallian is only one type of neumatic notation. Many others were in use during the Middle Ages, and some of them may be older than that of St Gall, even if their surviving sources are later. At no time was medieval musical notation standardized: it was always subject to mutual influence between one place and another. Although the notations of the main centres of plainsong are easily recognizable, even in a particular monastery a piece might be notated slightly differently by different scribes. Deviations are more marked in sources originating in other places, such as a related monastery, even in the same geographical area; and when a notation travelled widely (as Norman notation did) it is often possible to say only that a notation is basically of one type but with strong characteristics of another. Moreover, as we shall see, a notation could change gradually to take on very different characteristics.

There is no short cut to the understanding of the various schools of neumatic notation: each must be studied, compared and transcribed. One must note its use of virgae and puncta; the disposition of neume-elements in ligature, and the method of joining them; the incidence of liquescence and other special neumes; and the consistency of the thickness of pen-strokes in different directions.

In this work it is useful to follow Carl Parrish (NMM, 10) in classifying neumatic notations as accent-neumes, point-neumes or mixed point and accent-neumes. Sangallian, French, Norman and Beneventan notations are accent-neumes: that is, they use mainly strokes (virgae) in a cursive hand that makes ligatures really 'bound' together, as a comparison of the torculus in these four notations will show (Figure 9(a)). Aquitanian notation, on the other hand, is classified as point-neumes. It uses the virga relatively rarely in ligature, so that the ligatures are not 'tied' at all in most cases. When they are, they still take the form of dots joined together by very thin pen-strokes: and the virga is itself only a tailed punctum (b). The French call this 'notation à points superposés' (Pothier MG, 51 ff), which is perhaps a better description than the English 'point-neumes'. Note that the order of vertically-disposed puncta is downwards, as it is also in the Beneventan climacus (c).

Paleofrankish and Messine notations are regarded by Parrish as mixed point and accent-neumes. In the case of Messine notation this is probably correct. Paleofrankish notation, however, should be classified as point-neumes, although at first sight it seems to use more strokes than Aquitanian notation and many fewer than the accent-neumes (d). The inclined strokes are not single notes (virga or punctum) but lines connecting non-existent points at either end. Thus an apparent virga is in fact a pes (there is no virga). Moreover, climacus and scandicus forms consist of unbound puncta or tractuli (see Parrish NMM, 14 f and plate I). Parrish points out that several neumes have two forms. In the case of podatus and clivis, the simpler form represents step-wise movement and the bent form a larger interval. If Paleofrankish notation is indeed a point-neume notation, this must cast considerable doubt on the possibility of it being an ancestor of Sangallian neumes.

Figure 9. Accent-Neumes and Point-Neumes

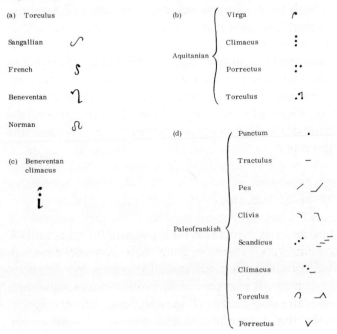

It is neither possible nor necessary in this book to discuss in detail the different characteristics of the various neume-schools. But it will be useful to tabulate the forms taken by the scandicus at various places and times, which will tell us much about the disposition of neume-elements, etc. (Figure 10).

Figure 10. Scandicus Forms

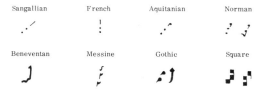

These are given in approximate chronological order from Sangallian to Square (the most recent). Two things can be seen: first, that certain types of neume are apparently derived from earlier types (Gothic from Messine, Square from Norman); and second, that much of the difference between the earlier and later types is due to a gradual change from a relatively thin pen to the thick-cut quill of the 'Gothic' era, with its characteristic thick and thin strokes at right angles to each other. This is, no doubt, one reason why later notations lost the Romanian letters and other notational subtleties of St Gall: the change to a thicker pen, both for script and for music, gradually forced the notation to be simpler. This was by no means the only period at which scribes, preferring to use the same type of pen for both words and music, allowed notation to be modified by their choice (see Chapter 6, last section). In the case of neumatic notations the result was the two late medieval notations which appeared in the late twelfth or thirteenth century, Gothic or Hufnagel ('hoof-nail', i.e. horse-shoe nail, from the shape of its virga) and Square. From the latter, all later staff notation developed.

The development of the staff

Neumatic notation sets out principally to show melodic rise and fall, but only approximately. This can be done more precisely by using exactly the same notation but with the addition of one or more horizontal lines as points of reference. The earliest manuscripts, and indeed many of the later ones, have the music written *in campo aperto* ('in the open field': that is, without guidelines): if the neumes are written in a horizontal row there is no way of telling how large are the intervals suggested by the notation. In this case the neumes are called Oratorical or Chironomic. 'Chironomy' comes from the Greek for 'gesticulation', and chironomic notation may refer to a method of conducting still to be found in monasteries, whereby the choir-leader indicates the intervals of the chant by raising his hand to a greater or smaller distance above his desk.

Even among the earliest manuscripts, however, there are some that place the neumes more or less carefully above or below an imaginary line. This 'heighted' notation is known as Diastematic (i.e. intervallic), the word here having a much more restricted meaning than that for which we used it in the Introduction. Diastematic writing of the ninth and tenth centuries is not usually accurate enough to be transcribed without the help of later, staff-notated concordances, but a few eleventh-century examples are precise enough for a transcription to be made with some confidence.

Two notational aids were soon added: a clef to show the pitch of the imaginary line, and a *custos* at the end of a line to show the pitch of the first note on the new line. These two show some preoccupation with problems of pitch on the part of singers. The use of a note letter-name at the beginning of the line could be for any or all of three reasons: to fix the chant at a particular (more or less standard) pitch, in a comfortable part of the vocal range; to indicate a convenient reciting-pitch; or to act as a warning of a semitone which must be sung correctly if the chant is to be sung in its proper mode. The most commonly-used letter, f (i.e. f below middle c), would fulfil all of these functions, while that next most frequently found, c (for middle c), would certainly have fulfilled the first and last, if only occasionally the second. As for the custos or direct (known in the sixteenth century as 'index' or 'director'), that was evidently designed to cope with an extension of the same problem, namely, how to move the eye from the end of one line of music to the beginning of the next without losing the pitch or making any sort of break in the music. The direct is basically some sort of note, modified by the addition of an easily-distinguishable tail so that it shall not be sung. Placed at the end of a line, it marks the pitch of the following note: the singer is then able to pitch that note in advance, and so can find his bearings at the beginning of the next line even if the clef changes. Indeed, a direct makes a change of clef no problem at all, during a line or between lines. Directs were used throughout the period of frequent clef-changes (up to the seventeenth century) and, by the inertia of tradition, far beyond. The tail of a direct is very often a diagonal one, with or without a hook at the end. In Aquitanian neumes, the direct is a punctum with a line through; in square notation the note-head may be shortened; and in Ars Nova notation the direct may also serve the very useful function of showing that the following note is colored or otherwise. Figure 11 will give some idea of the variety of shapes used. although it is only a very small selection.

Figure 11. Directs

In setting out a page of text a scribe would first cut guide-lines in the parchment with a knife, both for the script itself and to mark off the margins at the top, bottom and sides of the page. It is therefore hardly surprising that in the late tenth century the imaginary line used for heighting the neumes became an actual line, dry-drawn with the other guide-lines. This was sometimes regarded as legible enough, and manuscripts exist with a fully-developed dry-drawn staff of four lines. But in general ink lines were found to be more legible: some manuscripts have a single line inked over, while others added a second, third and fourth line in ink. In many cases, however, the 'problem' notes c' and f are the only ones inked in a four-line dry-drawn staff. Even on a fully inked staff, the lines for these notes are often distinguished by being coloured yellow (sometimes green) and red, respectively. In all cases the notes are placed both on and between the lines. The lines thus represent d, f, a and c', or f, a, c' and e', according to the tessitura of the chant: low-lying chants occasionally dispense with the c' line, so that the lines represent B, d, f and a. Chant has never used more than four stave-lines.

With the extension of the staff came a less restricted use of letters as clefs. Although F and C continued to be used most often, D, A and E (for d, a and e') were also used, all on lines. Only the rather special forms ♭ and ♮ were used in the spaces between stave-lines. These forms of the letter b, necessary because of the use of both flat and natural inflexions of the note, were known as B *durum* or *quadratum* ('hard', 'square') and B *mollum* or *rotundum* ('soft', 'round'), respectively. The round form has remained as a letter b, and its use to flatten a note was extended later to all other notes of the scale: the square form turned itself into ♯, and thence into ♯, ♮, and h. Hence the present German terminology of B = B♭ and H = B♮.[1]

The credit for making these improvements standard, if not for their invention, is given to Guido of Arezzo (*c.* 995–*c.*1050), a monk who had found great difficulty in teaching chant to boys.[2] In particular, Guido found that notational means were needed to give warning of the semitones in the scale, and hence his advocacy of coloured stave-lines (red for F, yellow for C) and the use of such clefs as were necessary. The colouring of the stave-lines was probably his own idea. In addition, Guido devised the system of solmization (see Chapter 9) which was to be a standard aid to singers and players for almost 600 years. These three aids to a large extent overlapped in their aims, and one or more were bound to be redundant if all three were used. The coloured stave-lines fairly quickly fell out of use (due to the inconvenience to scribes, probably, rather than to any notational inferiority to clefs), the C and F clefs being most often used and thus taking their place. Red staves became normal, giving way to black ones only in the fifteenth century for polyphony and the late nineteenth century for plainsong. Solmization remained a necessity, although not strictly a notational device, as music made increasing use of chromatic inflexion.

Guido used Aquitanian neumes, a type of notation especially suited to placing on a staff because of its use of separated puncta. Messine notation and its derivative, Gothic or Hufnagel notation, were also suited to use with a staff, for similar reasons. Other types of neume were used, of course, even on the fully-developed staff: and, as we shall see, the appearance of square notation was probably due to the use of less suitable neumes on a staff.

Square notation

I have already suggested that Sangallian neumes cannot be regarded as the direct ancestor of all later staff notation. The reason for this is that square notation is derived from French neumes (that is, the notational style used in the Isle de France), and these are not a direct descendant of the Sangallian style, although the two are closely related. Parrish

(NMM, 18) lists the differences, which can be seen by comparing my Figures 1, 2 and 12:

French neumes have vertical strokes rather than oblique.

French neumes have variations in thickness, due to a different type of pen.

The French clivis and other neumes have a more pointed shape than in the notation of St Gall.

There are no Romanian letters or other rhythmic modifications in the French neumes.

French notation, like that of St Gall, is basically an oratorical notation. It is of course possible to 'height' both, but the accuracy of pitch-representation is limited by the accent-neume nature of both notations, even if a staff were used. The problem is the virga, whose long straight shape gives no precise pitch-centre for the note that it represents, either as a single note or in ligature. In order to make it possible to height French notation accurately, therefore, one needs to add a 'head' to the virga and, similarly, to thicken the stroke at the relevant place in the middle of a ligature. A pen giving thicker down-strokes and thin cross-strokes produces the right effect: and it is more comfortable to use if the neumes lean a little to the right. ('Down' and 'cross' strokes are relative to the line of the arm, hand and pen. The 'lean' of the notation varies a little, and depends on the thickness and angle of the cut of the pen, as well as on the angle of the scribe's hand.) Given these three modifications, Norman notation is the result (Figure 12). Norman notation is also an accent-neume notation, of course (so it is misleading to call it, as the French do, a 'notation à points liés'—i.e. of dots bound together), but it is almost as susceptible of precise heighting as Aquitanian neumes. Those places which used Norman notation were, apparently, particularly anxious to establish some means of notating precise pitch-reference, and it is almost exclusively with Norman notation that we find letters used to give the pitch in manuscripts of the tenth and eleventh centuries (Chapter 8).

The notation of precise pitch with Norman neumes followed the course that we might expect. Written *in campo aperto* during the eleventh century, the notation became very accurately heighted and was then used with stave-lines, perhaps because the provision of letters was too cumbersome. In the twelfth century Norman neumes were placed on a fully-developed staff, and soon afterwards we find that the pen used is rather thicker. Here, as was often the case later, polyphony encouraged innovations that were not taken up in the more

Figure 12. The Development of Square Notation

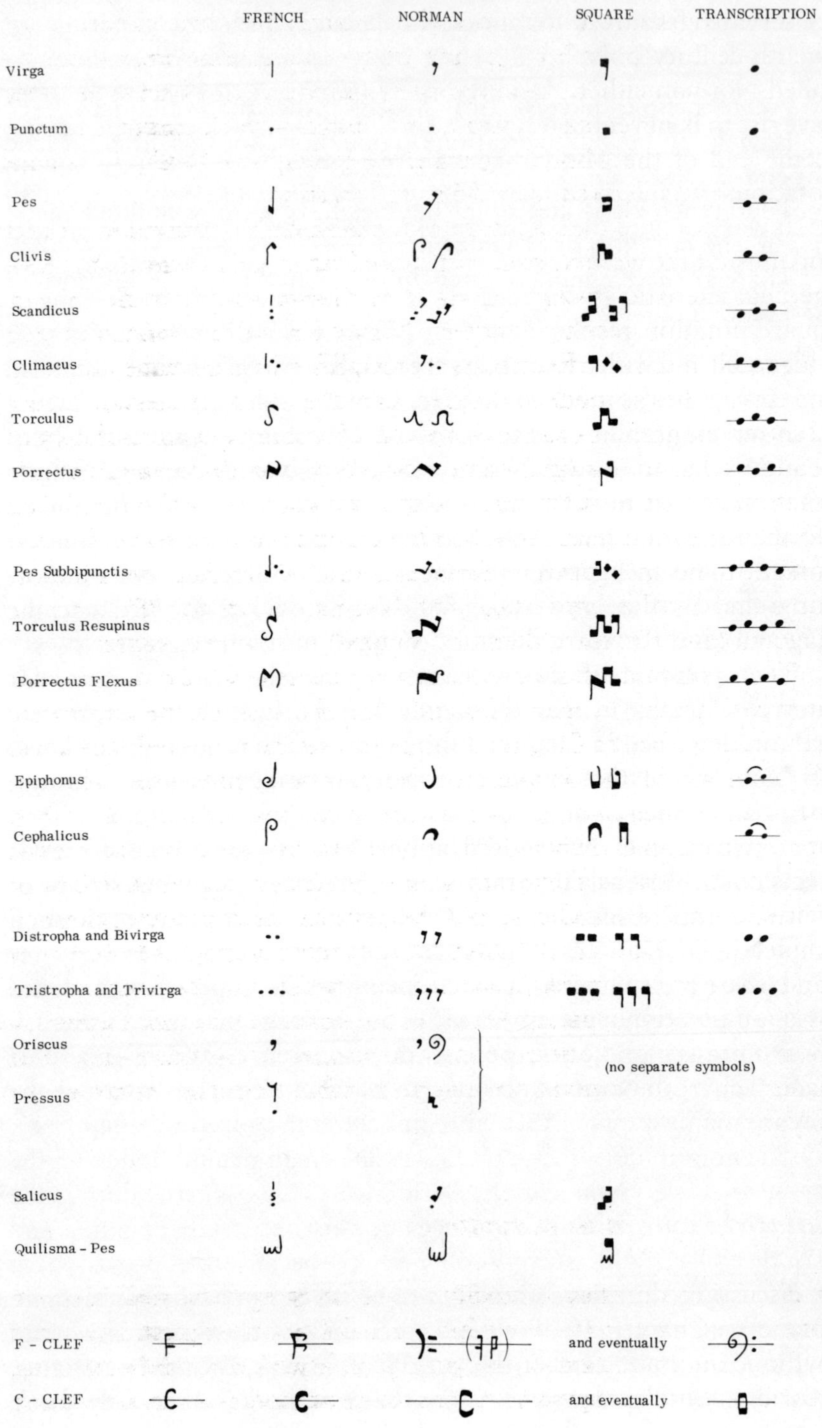

	FRENCH	NORMAN	SQUARE	TRANSCRIPTION
Virga				
Punctum				
Pes				
Clivis				
Scandicus				
Climacus				
Torculus				
Porrectus				
Pes Subbipunctis				
Torculus Resupinus				
Porrectus Flexus				
Epiphonus				
Cephalicus				
Distropha and Bivirga				
Tristropha and Trivirga				
Oriscus				
Pressus			(no separate symbols)	
Salicus				
Quilisma – Pes				
F – CLEF			and eventually	
C – CLEF			and eventually	

conservative sources of monodic music, and the notation of twelfth-century polyphony, if not quite square notation, cannot be called Norman either. A similar metamorphosis of Norman neumes gave rise to Beneventan notation; and Gothic—which continued in use to the end of the Middle Ages before giving way finally to square notation—was derived from Messine notation.

It was not until the beginning of the thirteenth century that the text and music alike were written with a quill cut in such a way that it gave the characteristic thicks and thins of Gothic script. In the music, square notation resulted: indeed, Norman notation written with a wider quill and with a few necessary simplifications *is* square notation, and this applies as much to the clefs as to the notes themselves. Figure 12 shows the graphic changes involved. (The latest examples shown of F- and C-clefs in this figure date from the sixteenth century.) Square notation at first took the same slight deviation from the vertical as Norman notation had, though it later tended to be vertical: but the puncta found in ligatures (climacus, etc.), which had been almost horizontal in the later stages of Norman notation (■), became diagonal (and therefore diamond-shaped) in square notation.

The evolution of square notation was not wholly a gain, for intervallic precision was won only for the loss of the expressive features described in Chapter 1. Square notation is not only the latest but also one of the simplest of the plainsong notations. The old distinction—such as it was—between punctum and virga was lost, those two neumes being used largely interchangeably; the salicus seems not to exist as a separate neume, its place being taken by one of the two forms of scandicus; and the notation of liquescence is much simpler and more limited than in some earlier notations. On the other hand, there are compensations of clarity, which may be felt to off-set losses of subtlety. In particular, all of the ligatures are much clearer, as are the pressus and oriscus forms. It was no doubt this clarity that made square notation obviously suitable for the notation of polyphony.

Notated rhythm in plainsong

In discussing durational modifications in Sangallian and Messine notations (Chapter 1) I have been careful not to suggest any strict rhythmic interpretation. In the past there have been widely-differing theories about the rhythmic performance of medieval monody (both sacred and secular) notated in neumes. As far as chant is concerned, there is now probably a consensus of opinion favouring an approximation to speech-rhythm, although it seems clear that some hymns were performed rhythmically (More, 'The performance of Plainsong', 125). From the mid-fourteenth century, and more especially from the second half of the fifteenth, polyphonic settings of chant tunes sometimes notated the chant in such a way that smaller note-values were used for the less important syllables, suggesting that in *alternatim* performance the plainsong sections might be performed rather similarly. By the middle of the sixteenth century service-books sometimes used a quasi-mensural notation in which the virga and punctum had long and short values (not strictly measured, but approximating to their relative mensural values, Long and Breve), with the rhombic punctum (Semibreve) for the least important syllables. From the early seventeenth century onwards quasi-mensural notation using virga, punctum and rhombic punctum was normal in service-books, and it remained so until the Solesmes editions of the late nineteenth century. Figure 13, taken from a *Canon Missae ad usum Episcoporum ac Prelatorum* (Rome 1852) in my possession, is typical of such notation. The notation represents 'an attempt to stylize in note-values *a free speech-rhythm*' (More, op. cit., 127, discussing the intonation of a fourteenth-century polyphonic setting of *Magnificat*: the italics are hers).

Figure 13. Quasi-Mensural Chant

Per om-ni-a sae-cu-la sae-cu - lo - rum

(■ is a note of normal length; ▮ a long note; ♦ a short note)

This example is sung by the celebrant alone, so that speech-rhythm is possible, as it would be with trained singers. But should a large congregation attempt to sing in this way the result would surely be a mensural performance. The difference between stylized speech-rhythm and strictly mensural performance is ultimately one of degree, therefore. Thus the question of rhythm in chants notated 'mensurally' is a matter of performance-practice, and need not concern us here in any detail. However, the use of mensural note-shapes for both chant and polyphony raises the difficult problem of the relationship between the notations of these two types of music, and in particular the notational devices known as 'stroke' notation and 'strene' notation: these are discussed in Chapter 7.

3. Modal Notation

The notations so far discussed could be used for polyphony as well as for monody. Two rows of unheighted or only roughly-heighted neumes are the same sort of *aide-mémoire* for two-part polyphony that a single row provides for monody, and likewise cannot be transcribed unless diastematic concordances exist. Early polyphony that can be transcribed melodically survives in several types of notation, both with and without the staff. As long as the two parts go along note-by-note together it is possible to produce some sort of performance by imposing the same rhythmic values on each part. But in more developed polyphony, where one part may have a melisma against a single note in the other, the rhythmic problem makes performance more difficult. The Compostella pieces, for instance, *c.* 1136 (see Parrish NMM, plate xxiii), present no difficulty as to pitch, for the music is written in notation which is nearer to square than to Norman neumes, on four-line staves and with clear clefs: but we cannot know how a contemporary performance was organized rhythmically. The non-notation of rhythm may or may not have been a serious impediment to performance for contemporary singers, but it is very unfortunate for us.

The modal patterns

The problem of rhythmic notation in polyphony was faced in the second half of the twelfth century. It is in the various copies of Leonin's *Magnus Liber Organi* (compiled *c.* 1170, although surviving manuscripts are later) that the notes and ligatures of square notation are first found incorporated into a system that we now call 'modal' because it is concerned with the modes (ways) of organizing music rhythmically (see Waite RTCP for the authoritative study). Modal notation uses ligatures to indicate certain repeated rhythmic patterns which allow a rigorous rhythmic organization to be imposed on the music. Medieval theorists recognized anything between five and nine

37

rhythmic modes, but six was the number commonly accepted.[1] The modes are based on poetic metres:[2] Figure 14 shows both the metres and the equivalent rhythmic patterns.

Figure 14. The Rhythmic Modes

MODE	RHYTHMIC PATTERN and NOTE - VALUES	MODERN NOTATION
	(– long ᴜ short)	
I	– ᴜ – ᴜ	𝄴 ♩♫ ♪♩♫ ... ♩ 𝄽
II	ᴜ – ᴜ –	𝄴 ♪♩ ♪♩ ... ♪♩ ♪𝄽
III	– ᴜ ᴜ	𝄴 ♩. ♪♩ ♩. ♪♩ ... ♩. 𝄽.
IV	ᴜ ᴜ –	𝄴 ♪♩ ♩. ♪♩ ♩. ... ♩. 𝄽.
V	– – –	𝄴 ♩. ♩. ♩. 𝄽.
VI	ᴜ ᴜ ᴜ	𝄴 ♫♫♫♫ ♩ ... ♫♩ ♪𝄽

(or ... ♫♩ ♩ 𝄽)

In this figure I have followed tradition in transcribing into crotchets and quavers. However, the theorists state that a long note (*nota longa*) lasts for two *tempora* and a short note (*nota brevis*) for one *tempus*.[3] *Tempus*, a section or unit of time, denoted the time taken to speak a syllable. By the time these theorists were writing, in the latter part of the thirteenth century, tempus meant 'beat': so it is possible that this music should be performed slowly enough for the quaver of my transcription to be a medium-fast beat.

It will be seen that the values of a *longa recta* (i.e. 'correct' longa, of two tempora) and a *brevis recta* (of one tempus) apply exclusively only to modes I, II and VI. (Mode II is not simply Mode I with an up-beat: the accent falls on the brevis.) The other three modes are *in ultra mensuram*: that is, they are 'beyond [the poetic] measure' because they include values other than the two-beat longa recta and the one-beat brevis recta:
1. the three-beat longa:
2. the two-beat brevis (not Mode V).
Of the first, little need be said, since its necessity is obvious. The second requires a rather important digression.

The alternation of longa and brevis found in the oldest of the rhythmic modes, Mode I, set the pattern in all the modes for a musical metre that we should define as 'compound duple': that is, a metre in which groups of three are further grouped into twos. The triple element is not immediately compatible with the apparently duple nature of Modes III and IV, in which a pair of breves come between longae. Strict adherence to values of one and two tempora would destroy the metrical pattern, which can be retained only if the foot remains six tempora long. For this, it is necessary for the longa to take three tempora and the two breves the other three. Of these, the second brevis fills the required duration by lasting for two tempora. It is then known as *brevis altera* (the 'second brevis' [of two]) as opposed to its one-beat partner the *brevis recta* ('correct' or 'proper breve'). From this it will be seen that the actual duration of a *brevis altera*, or 'altered breve' is that of a *longa recta*—two tempora, transcribed as an undotted crotchet. In view of this, the student of notation is warned of one absolutely essential rule of working: when calculating the rhythms of medieval music, *never try to make a direct substitution of modern for original note-values,* for there is rarely an exact equivalence. Also, modal notation can only be made to work logically if one keeps the metrical structure in mind. Always know, therefore, which are long notes and which are short, no matter what their duration in absolute terms.

The rhythmic patterns shown in Figure 14 were notated by means of the ligatures and single notes of square notation (see Figure 12), plus a short vertical stroke for a rest. The square brackets over the notes in that figure indicate the ligatures. It will be seen that the various modes have distinct ligature-patterns, each defining its mode and setting the basic rhythm. The ligature-patterns are shown below: 1 stands for a single note, 2 for a two-note ligature (binaria), 3 for a three-note ligature (ternaria) and 4 for a four-note ligature (quaternaria).

Mode I   : 3 – 2 – 2 – . . . – 2
Mode II : 2 – 2 – 2 – . . . – 3

Mode III : 1 – 3 – 3 – . . . – 3
Mode IV : 3 – 3 – 3 – . . . – 1

Mode V : 1 – 1 – 1 – . . . – 1 or 3|3|3| . . .
Mode VI : 4 – 3 – 3 – . . . – 3

39

As is shown here, there is an alternative notation (irregular but common) for Mode V, a series of ternariae with rests between. This is also the notation for a short phrase in Mode I (Figure 15).

Figure 15. Uses of the Ternaria

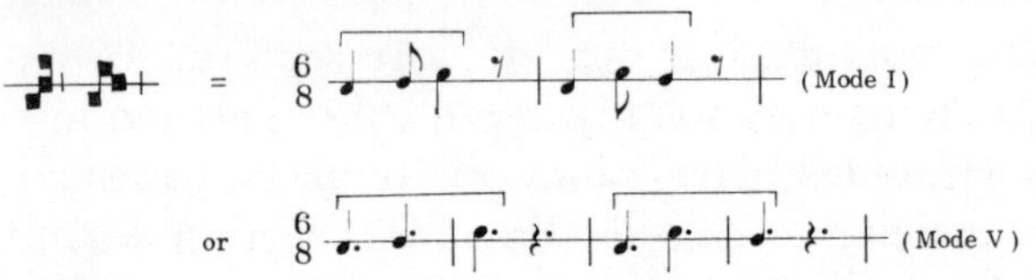

However, the Mode I pattern is usually in an upper voice and the Mode V pattern nearly always in the Tenor, so there is rarely any confusion.

It should be emphasized here that the duration of a note depends on its context. This applies also to rests, which must be evaluated according to the prevailing mode.[4] In the example of Mode II in Figure 14, the last note and rest must therefore be brevis recta and longa recta (1 + 2 tempora), not longa and brevis. As a matter of fact, there is another reason why this should be so: the general rule (not invariably adhered to) that a longa which is followed by another longa must be valued at three tempora.[5] The final note could not be a longa, therefore, because the note before it is a longa recta.

Some short examples will help to show the principles of modal notation (Figure 16).

Figure 16. Examples of the Modes

Note that the binaria notates short-long in each case: in fact, the binaria is very useful for identifying the mode, for this reason. The ternaria, on the other hand, has several interpretations, according to context: it can be long-short-long (Mode I, the most common), short-long-short (II), short-short-long (III, IV), long-long-long (V) or short-short-short (VI).

The system must be modified if a note is to be repeated in the course of a ligature (this being notationally impossible). The solution is to break down the ligature in question into smaller parts, usually a shorter ligature plus a single note. Thus the first-mode rhythm shown as Figure 17(a), normally notated as at (b), must sometimes appear in a guise such as (c) or (d).[6]

Figure 17. Notational Modifications

Two matters can be mentioned here briefly. Although modal notation used the four-line staff of plainsong, a fifth line was often added if the range required it. Also, we may note that at this time the double-bulbed flat sign ♭ was often used for the upper B♭ (bb′) to distinguish it from the lower one: this form is presumably a version of Guido's ♮ (see Figure 72).

Modifications of the basic patterns

Modal notation was used for all the musical styles of the early thirteenth century. Conductus-style, in which the parts move together rhythmically, is often notated quite strictly, as are long passages of melismatic organum. The organa, however, tend to have long-held tenor notes (usually single notes with rests) whose durations cannot be notated. These tenor notes are usually aligned vertically in score with

41

the upper parts, so that there is no doubt of the duration of each note: but in some ambiguous cases (as when both parts begin with a long single note followed by a rest) the longer-held tenor note is written with an elongated body ⌐, a shape later used for the *duplex longa* or *maxima.*

The modal system was used also in the early motets, in which the voices move at different speeds which clearly characterize them. Modes I and III—and to a lesser extent II—were much used for the faster-moving upper parts; later, the parlando triplex part was sometimes notated in Mode VI, also a fairly rare mode; tenor parts were commonly written in Mode V. Only Mode IV was very little used, and it seems to have been hardly more than a theoretical mode, recognized because it completed a logical pattern of rhythms.

In practice, the modes could be modified in various ways:

1. A longa recta could be replaced by two breves: this is known as *fractio modi* ('the breaking of the mode'), and causes a VIth-mode rhythm to be introduced temporarily. Fractio modi is accomplished in one of two ways:

(i) By means of an irregular ligature. In Figure 18(a) the first note of the third ligature (an irregular ternaria in Mode I) takes half the value from the end of the second ligature.

(ii) By means of a *plica*, the equivalent of a liquescent neume in chant. Plica ('fold') refers to the common forms in which a single note has a tail to either side (Figure 19(a)), forms clearly derived from the epiphonus and cephalicus. The tails ascend for an ascending second note and descend for a descending one. As in chant, the second note should be sung more lightly.[7] (In transcription we write a short bar through the stem.)

Figure 18 shows fractio modi notated (a) with an irregular ternaria and (b) with a plica.

Figure 18. Fractio Modi

For an ascending plica a single tail is often used, and ligatures are commonly plicated in a similar way (Figure 19(b)). As it is awkward to add a tail to such forms as the pes, scandicus and porrectus, which have a left-turned final note, this note is turned to the right so that a tail can be added (c).

Figure 19. Plicae

In polyphony a plica may indicate a changing-note (often between notes of the same pitch) or the middle note for the interval of a third: between notes a second apart it may supply an anticipation of the second note, or it may jump a third and return—the harmonic context does not always make the correct solution plain (Figure 20).

Figure 20. Plicae in Transcription

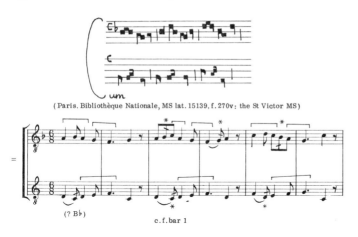

(Paris. Bibliothèque Nationale, MS lat. 15139, f. 270v: the St Victor MS)

c.f. bar 1

A note in the middle of a ligature cannot be plicated. Moreover, when a plica is used in the middle of a wider interval such as a fourth or fifth, there appear to be no rules or notational indications as to the pitch of the extra note. For both of these reasons, plicae gave way to irregular ligatures and *conjuncturae* (see below) as methods of notating fractio modi.

The secular monody of the later thirteenth century (which will not be treated separately in this book) shows a more flexible use of plicae. Sometimes the pitch of the added note is accurately shown by the length of the tail, and often a secondary head appears (Figure 21(a)), forming a small note like that now used for liquescents in the Solesmes editions. Another feature is the use of a plicated note in apposition to a single note or to the end of a ligature (b): in this latter case, it is unnecessary to turn the head of a rising ligature.

Figure 21. Plicae in Secular Notation

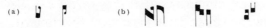

At first modal notation did not show the durations of plicated notes, but the rules are simple. If the main note is a longa of three tempora, the plica takes a third of its value (Figure 22(a)); if a longa recta, then a half (b); should the plicated note be a brevis recta, *semibreves* result, dividing the brevis into two equal parts (c).[8] In all cases, plication indicates an extra note, taking its value from that to which it is attached.

Figure 22. Duration of the Plica

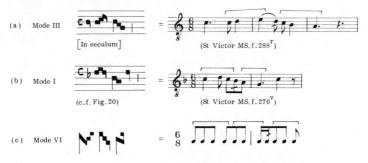

2. A longa recta can be replaced by a longa of three tempora: that is, a Vth-mode rhythm is introduced temporarily. This is the reverse of fractio modi, and is called by Apel (NPM, 234 f) *extensio modi* ('lengthening of the mode'). Single longae must be notated separately:

Figure 23. Extensio Modi

44

Comparison with an apparently similar context, Figure 17(c), will show that ambiguity could occur. But in the earlier example the change in ligature-pattern is clearly due to a repeated note, so there is no reason to think that the modal pattern has been broken.

3. Another way of producing *semibreves* was by means of a series of rhombic puncta. These, which may be as many as nine together and always appear in descending scalic formation, are called *conjunctura* or *currentes* ('joined together' or 'running'). When they follow a single note they may be used as a normal ligature: in particular, the climacus form ▌♦♦ should always be tried first simply as a ternaria. But currentes proper, whether following a single note or a ligature, share the value of the previous note, longer values coming last (Figure 24(a)). When there are so many notes in the conjunctura that their combined values on this basis would be more than the note preceding, the theorists give no help. Most such conjuncturae are substitutes for normal ligatures, for (as Waite, p. 87, points out) it is easier to write the conjunctura form than a descending stepwise ligature in square notes (b).

Figure 24. Currentes

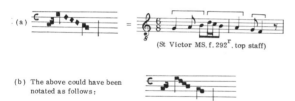

(a)

(St Victor MS. f. 292ʳ, top staff)

(b) The above could have been notated as follows:

In practice only the *clausulae* and to some extent the *caudae* of the earlier thirteenth century, and also some of the dance-tunes, are notated in more or less regular ligature-patterns. The *conductus* is syllabic in style, and therefore uses single notes rather than ligatures; and the organa are so melismatic that they are notated in a much freer way, using a wide variety of ligatures, whose rhythmic interpretation continues to cause some difficulty.

4. The Later Thirteenth Century

Mid-century innovations

Modal rhythm remained the vehicle of theoretical writing on music for the rest of the thirteenth century and its terminology was useful even to the theorists of the Ars Nova. Musically, however, the needs of the mid-thirteenth century were greater than the system could satisfy. Free melismatic music needed a more precise notation, while the syllabic style and the more rhythmically regular melismatic style needed something both more precise and more flexible than modal notation. The result of these changing needs was eventually a new notational style, in which a less limiting system of ligature-values joined with precisely-measured single notes and precisely-measured rests.

The earliest indications of these changes closely follow the first use of motet-layout, *c.* 1225, and the progressive development of the new notation can be traced in the theoretical writings of *c.* 1240 to *c.* 1280 (Waite RTCP, 10). This period, defined as 'Pre-Franconian' by Apel (NPM, Chapter IV), was notationally transitional, and is best studied—as Apel does—source by source. The earliest of the treatises, the *Discantus positio vulgaris* transmitted *c.* 1240 by Jerome of Moravia (CS I, 94–7), already includes specific note-shapes, the square virga and punctum, for the longa and brevis (hereafter, L and B, respectively). The later treatises show more and more of the features eventually codified by Franco of Cologne, and their innovations need not be catalogued here. There are, however, two differences between Franco and his immediate predecessors that must be described briefly: 1. Dietricus, writing *c.* 1275, considered the semibrevis (S) to be half of a B (Apel NPM, 296 and n.1), thus following the binary division of the B that we have already assumed in modal notation. But Master Lambert (Magister Lambertus, or Pseudo-Aristotle), writing at about the same time, deals with both the *semibrevis major* (two-thirds of a tempus) and the *semibrevis minor* (one-third), showing a ternary division of the B. In this, Lambert was followed by Franco. We may therefore regard *c*. 1275 as the turning-point at which binary division of the B gave way to ternary division: this is roughly confirmed by the sources.

2. Two different sets of rest-values emerged (set out below in Figure 35). That of Master Lambert, very close to the rests used in the Bamberg MS (Apel NPM, 302, and CS I, 278), is less logical than Franco's (itself perhaps based on John of Garland's, though much improved: see CS I, 104). Incidentally, Lambert's rests require a five-line staff, by this time normal in polyphony.

Franco of Cologne

With the *Ars Cantus Mensurabilis* of Franco of Cologne (*c*. 1280) the situation becomes clearer (CS I, 117–36, translated in Strunk SR, 139–59). Franco's work in codifying and rationalizing the workings of several slightly different systems was a real achievement. Franco states that since some musicians evidently do not understand measured music properly, he intends to explain what is good in present practice, to refute what is bad, and to make any necessary innovations to improve the system. His preliminary discussion of measurement in music was evidently intended only to clear the ground for his study of the notation, and he deals with the rhythmic modes very briefly, clearly not wanting to be involved in the current disputes except as an arbiter.

From there he goes straight to the duration of the notes (Figure 25).

Figure 25. Single Notes

◼ is a Long (either perfect or imperfect).

◼ is a Duplex Long (two longs in duration).

▪ is a Breve (proper or altered), and

◆ is a Semibreve (major or minor).

Franco explains that the tails of the L and Duplex L (D) represent length. The B, L and D are recognizable as the single notes used in modal notation. The S is the rhombic punctum of the conjunctura, and in Franco's time the S was still used only in groups of two or more, as if in ligature: it is not found as a single note until the fourteenth century.

Franco's description of the L as perfect or imperfect introduces us

47

to a very important concept, that of *perfection*. A perfect L was that of three tempora, now regarded as normal (and perfect because three was the perfect number). A perfect L could be imperfected by a B, in which case the L became an imperfect L of two tempora, the B being the third tempus in the grouping. By an extension of this concept and its terminology, we speak of a 'perfection'—that is, a ternary durational grouping. This is, of course, a useful unit of measurement in music that has no bar-lines.

The principle of alteration was retained from the modal system, and from Franco's time onwards alteration and perfection were the twin pillars of medieval mensuration, binary metres being recognized very late. The rules which arose from these principles can be summarized as follows:

1. a L followed by a single B is imperfected by it (Figure 26(a));
2. a group of two or three Bs makes a perfection, the second B of a pair being altered (b);
3. with four or more Bs together, the first imperfects the L (if any) preceding it, then they are counted in groups of three (perfections) until *either* the next L is reached, *or* only two remain (which form a perfection as before), *or* only one remains, which must imperfect the L following (c).

(In this chapter the note-values are divided by eight, the B beat being transcribed as a C.)

Figure 26. Imperfection and Alteration

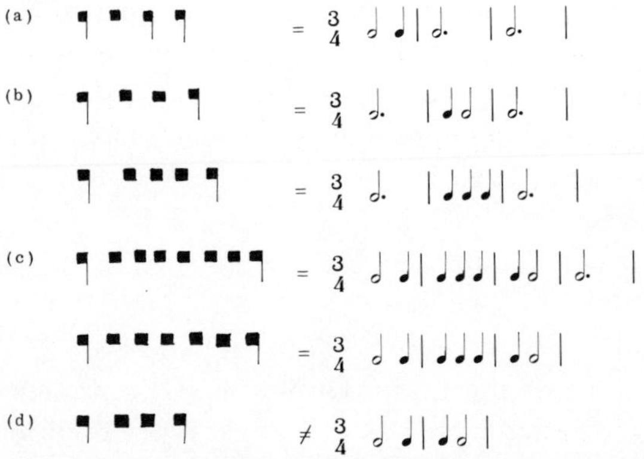

Here we see that imperfection by the note preceding takes place. The same happens if the musical phrase starts with a B followed by a L (as in Modes II and IV), since the phrase always begins at the start of a

48

perfection: that is, there is no anacrusis. Where a L could be imperfected either by a B preceding or by one following, imperfection by the note following takes place, as shown in Figure 27.

Figure 27. Imperfection

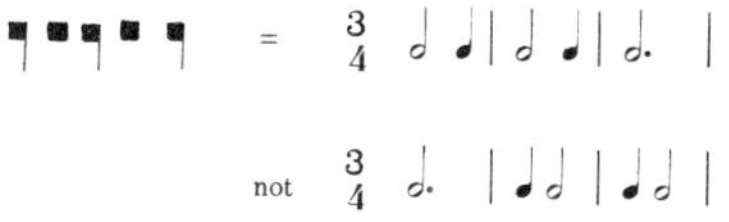

$$\blacksquare\,\bullet\,\blacksquare\,\blacksquare\,\blacksquare \quad = \quad \tfrac{3}{4}\ \; \downharpoonright\ \vert\ \downharpoonright\ \vert\ \downharpoonright\ \vert$$

$$\text{not}\quad \tfrac{3}{4}\ \;\vert\ \vert\ \vert\ \vert\ \vert$$

Similarly in Figure 26(a): but imperfection of the first note is in any case required there because the third note cannot be imperfected without contravening a rule of modal notation still in force, namely, that a L which is followed by another L is perfect (of three tempora).

Obviously, there are rhythms which could not be notated according to what has just been said. For example, the grouping L B B L would always be sung as in Figure 26(b), not as at (d). This latter rhythm, however, is made possible by Franco's use of the 'division of the mode' (*divisio modi*) or 'sign of perfection' (*signum perfectionis*), a short vertical stroke across a stave-line. For Franco this is no longer a rest (although it continued so to be used by many scribes).[1] In its new guise the sign is used to fix the end of a perfection in a place where it would not otherwise fall. Thus the group L B B L would be changed rhythmically by the insertion of a sign of perfection between the Bs, so that the first perfection must end after the first B. The two Bs can therefore no longer form a perfection by themselves: the first must imperfect the preceding L, and the second is then forced to imperfect the L following (Figure 28(a)). Similarly, the sign can alter the rhythm of any larger number of Bs by changing the way in which the notes group themselves into perfections (b).

Figure 28. The Sign of Perfection

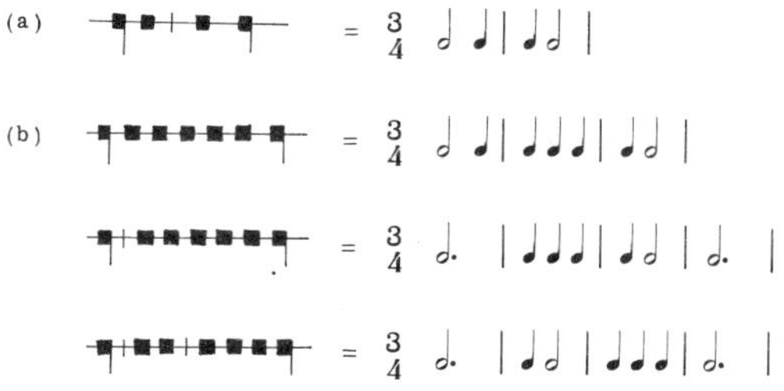

(a) ────── = $\tfrac{3}{4}$ ♩ ♩ | ♩♩ |

(b) ────── = $\tfrac{3}{4}$ ♩ ♩ | ♩♩♩ | ♩♩ |

────── = $\tfrac{3}{4}$ ♩. | ♩♩♩ | ♩♩ | ♩. |

────── = $\tfrac{3}{4}$ ♩. | ♩♩ | ♩♩♩ | ♩. |

As we noted above, ternary division of the B was then new: possibly Franco's support was decisive in suppressing binary division of the B. For Franco, a proper B is divided into either two or three Ss: in the former case the major ('larger') S comes second (Figure 29(a)). In other words, the rule of alteration applies to the S. An altered B can be divided into four, five or six Ss, a sign of perfection being used to split the five into 2 + 3 or 3 + 2 ((b)—(c)).

Figure 29. Division of the Breve

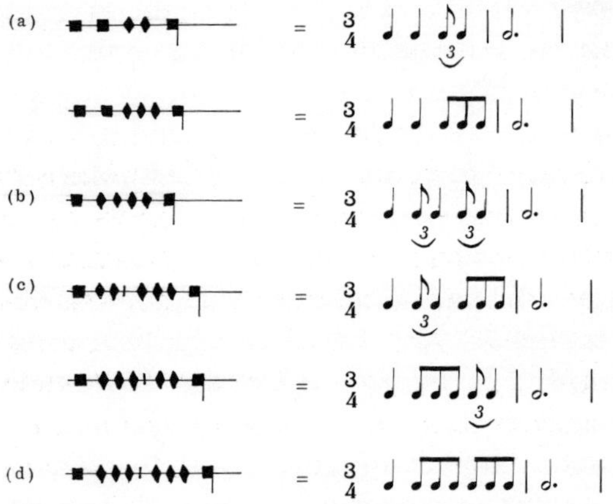

Although it is not possible for a S to imperfect a B, Franco does use a sign of perfection to divide six Ss in the time of a proper B (Figure 29(d)), perhaps merely to guide the eye.

Franco's use of ligatures is a much-improved system that allows great flexibility without ambiguity. Its limitation is, perhaps, that it is a little too complicated (a short-coming that was put right in the following century). Its fault stems from the fact that it is based on an already-existing use of ligatures that is—from a purely notational point of view—more complex than it need be. The extension of the system from this basis, however logical it may be, implies an extension of the complexity.

For a consideration of Franco's ligature-system we must take as our starting-point the forms of pes and clivis in use in plainsong notation (Figure 30(a)). These are Franco's basic ligatures, and he gives to them the values assigned to them in modal notation, B–L. This valuation gives to the ligature two basic qualities (CS I, 124):

1. Because the first note is as it would be in a plainsong ligature, the ligature is said to be 'with propriety' (*cum proprietate*).
2. When the second note is an imperfect L, the ligature is said to be

'with perfection' (*cum perfectione*), because its completion is as in a plainsong ligature.

By changing the shapes of these ligatures, the ligature-values are made to be 'without propriety' (L–L), 'without perfection' (B–B), or both (L–B). A ligature is made 'without propriety' (*sine proprietate*) by removing the tail from a descending ligature, and by adding a tail to the right of the first note of an ascending one (Figure 30(b) and (d)). Franco mentions that the tail is sometimes written on the left (b), but says that this is not really correct. A ligature is made 'without perfection' (*sine perfectione*) by turning the upper note of the ascending ligature to the right, or by using the oblique form of ligature (which is 'out of use', as Franco says, in the ascending ligature) ((c) and (d)).

Figure 30. Two-note Franconian Ligatures

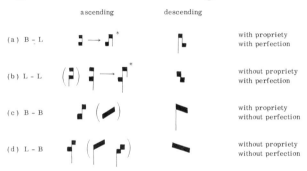

The vertically-aligned forms (ascending B–L and L–L) are not easy to write accurately if the interval is small: indeed, in modal notation the pes, scandicus and porrectus forms account for most mistranscriptions of pitch. Some scribes after Franco's time took the opportunity of modifying them by analogy with other forms, turning the head to the right and adding a compensating tail (Figure 30*). Although the older forms remained in use for plainsong and for secular monody, they quickly disappeared from polyphonic sources, and are rarely found in the fourteenth and later centuries. Similarly, the ascending oblique forms are awkward for a right-handed scribe, and were little used, although they did not disappear entirely and are occasionally found in the fourteenth and fifteenth centuries.

To the above two-note ligature forms we can add the ligature 'with shared propriety' (*cum opposita proprietate*),[2] which will be men-

51

tioned again below. Although Franco refers to this form only as part of a larger ligature, it does appear by itself.

In dealing with three-note ligatures, Franco gives only two rules:
1. An upward tail shows a ligature 'with shared propriety', in which the two notes following the tail are both Ss. Although Franco does not say so, the upward tail presumably signifies shortness: he has already said that a downward tail signifies length. At this point he does say that the S cannot stand as a single note.
2. A middle note, if it is not governed by shared propriety (in which case it is a S, as above), is a B. Franco remarks, however, that some say that this note should be a L (he probably means John of Garland: see CS I, 179).

Franco uses the word 'ligature' in two different ways, and so must we:

(a) To mean the complete symbol consisting of either two, three or more notes. This is the sense in which we normally use it, though Franco more often uses the word *figura* for this:

(b) More specifically, to mean the binding of two particular notes within the symbol. Hence he talks about ascending and descending ligatures when he is discussing the first two notes, or the last two notes of a multi-note *figura*.

It must therefore be understood that when one evaluates the first or last note of a three-note ligature that note must be treated as if it formed a two-note ligature with the note next to it. For example, in Figure 31(a) the first note forms part of a two-note ascending ligature (in the second sense above) 'without propriety', while the last forms part of a two-note descending ligature 'without perfection'. The complete symbol is therefore evaluated as L–B–B (that is, L–(B) + (L)–B, with the middle note a B), as at (b).

Figure 31. Evaluation of a Ligature

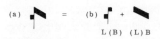

In a ligature of more than three notes the first and last are evaluated as before, and all the middle notes are Bs unless governed by shared propriety. Franco says that not more than two Ss may be bound together, a rule which is generally kept at this time: but he also says that these Ss must come at the beginning of a ligature (or as a two-note ligature), a rule that is contravened in both Franco's own examples and in Master Lambert's.

52

The plica was still in use in the late thirteenth century, and is described by Franco. As before, its purpose is to split a note into two. It should be noted that, as in modal notation, a plicated ternary L is divided as 2 + 1 tempora:[3] similarly, the ternary B is divided with the longer duration first, not in the rhythm of a pair of Ss, in which the semibrevis major comes second. (Franco does not explain the rhythm of a B plica, but harmonic considerations in the musical sources themselves confirm that this is the correct interpretation.)

The shapes that Franco gives are familiar to us (Figure 32). The direction of the tails shows whether the plica ascends or descends, and the longer tail indicates a L if it is to the right of the note and a B if it is to the left.[4] The asterisked form at (a) was still in use, but Franco explains that it is not strictly correct, because it is the wrong shape for a 'fold' (plica). The S cannot yet be plicated except in ligature.

Figure 32. Franconian Plicae

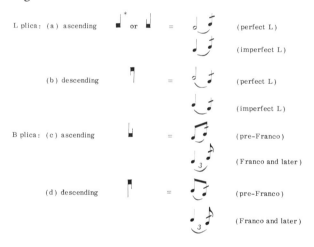

Franco's examples show a variety of ligatures with plicae attached (CS I, 125 f). The plica is always a single tail, added to the end of the ligature and referring to the final note. Both ascending and descending ligatures can be plicated, he says, whether the ligature is perfect or imperfect (ending with a L or a B). However, for the perfect ligatures he gives only the various B–L forms: and while a plica can be added to the descending L–L forms, the ascending forms present either a vertical alignment or else a form which already has a descending tail (cf. Figure 30(a) and (b)). Master Lambert seems to use a double-tailed plica on the vertical ascending B–L ligature, as well as on the descending L-L form (CS I, 277), while John of Garland puts an upward plica (but not a downward one) on the rectangular ascending B-L ligature (CS I, 100). In Figure 33(a), which shows the main two-note ligatures with plicae, the forms peculiar to Lambert and Garland are marked as such. Ligatures of three notes or more are plicated according to the same principles (b).

Figure 33. Plicated Ligatures

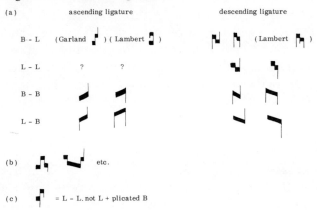

With regard to the imperfect ligatures Franco remarks that the oblique forms should always be used when a plica is added. Actually, he is talking only about the ascending form, for the descending ligature would be notated as an oblique form in any case. His reason is that if the rectangular ascending form were used, the descending plica would look like a normal tail making the final note into a L (c) (cf. Figures 30 and 33(a)). This is clearly an unsatisfactory area in the notation of the time. One solution was to use plica-forms 'in apposition' (see Figure 21(b)), and this is indeed found in sources such as the late chansonniers which use a wider variety of plica shapes than the main sources of sacred music (there are several examples, for instance, in the Chansonnier d'Arras). In general, however, the problem seems to have been avoided at this time rather than solved.

Franco does not explain the plicated ligature 'with shared propriety', although he shows one in his examples. The sources of the period show the plica attached to S-ligatures both oblique and rectangular, ascending and descending (Figure 34(a)). In most cases the ligature stands (as the name implies) for a complete B recta, so that the plica is a full minor S in duration (b). This is not quite the same as a group of three separate Ss, because the plica-note is sung more lightly.

Very rarely, the ligature is followed by Ss, the first of which makes up the B. In this case the plica divides a minor S (c):[5] we should probably assume duple division for the divided minor S, the situation being as for the divided B in modal notation (see Chapter 3, especially n. 9).

Figure 34. Ligatures 'With Shared Propriety'

Apart from the confusion in notating plicated ligatures, Franco's system is unambiguous in its working. However, his reasons for writing the treatise show that the notation of his time was not standardized, and even after his time we find pieces whose notation is not unambiguous to us, whatever it may have meant to the scribes. In this situation it is often the rests which give the clue to solving an ambiguity, for they do not follow the same principles as other symbols. The shapes of notes and ligatures show the *name* of each individual note: they do not tell us the actual durations (whether a L is perfect or imperfect, a B proper or altered, a S major or minor), this being dependent upon the context. The size of a rest, on the other hand, is directly related to its absolute duration.

Franco's notation for rests is perhaps most obviously based on that of John of Garland (itself rather unsatisfactory) in its precise values, though it may also owe much to the rather more rational system described by Master Lambert. In all cases a rest takes the form of a vertical stroke on the staff, the number of spaces covered showing the duration. In Lambert's system (Figure 35(a)) a S (half a tempus) takes one space, a proper B (one tempus) two spaces, an imperfect L three and a perfect L four. Probably Franco rejected this system on the grounds that the numerical ratios of the duration of B, imperfect L and perfect L (1, 2 and 3 tempora) are not matched by the rests (2, 3 and 4 spaces), while the minor S and major S are similarly in the wrong ratios to the B. His own rests (b) satisfy this point exactly: moreover, they allow him to use a stroke covering the complete staff (i.e. four spaces) for the 'ending-sign' (finis punctorum) used to end a piece or section.

Figure 35. Rests

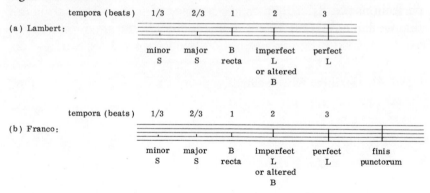

There is no separate symbol for a D-rest: two L-rests together are used. For obvious reasons, rests are neither imperfected nor altered.

The rests should not be confused with the sign of perfection: the former all sit on a staff-line, while the latter crosses a line.[6] Immediately after Franco's time the sign of perfection took the form of a dot (*punctum*).

Petrus de Cruce and the transition to Ars Nova

At about the end of the century Petrus de Cruce modified Franco's notation in order to accommodate certain musical innovations. These changes can be seen in the compositions of Petrus himself, but their precise significance is still a matter of debate. The adjective 'Petronian' has been given to this notation because Petrus was apparently responsible for two innovations which had far-reaching consequences:

1. Robert de Handlo attributes to him a new use of the sign of perfection, or dot of division (*punctum divisionis*), as it now became (CS I, 387, translated in Apel NPM, 318).

2. James of Liège [Jacobus, Jacob] says that Petrus was the first to place four Ss in the time of a perfect tempus (CS II, 401, translated in Apel NPM, 318).

The first of these innovations is a fairly logical extension of Franconian principles. Franco had used the sign of perfection either to prevent the imperfection of a L or to make plain the rhythm of a group of Bs or Ss: in other words, he used it sparingly to modify the rhythm of a small group of notes. Petrus's departure from Franco's system is in his recognition that the dot of division could be used to mark off the perfections (i.e. Bs) in a much larger group of Ss (Figure 36(a)). (Note that we can now regard the B recta as a 'perfect' B, dividing into three Ss.)

Figure 36. Rhythmic Organization of Petronian Semibreves

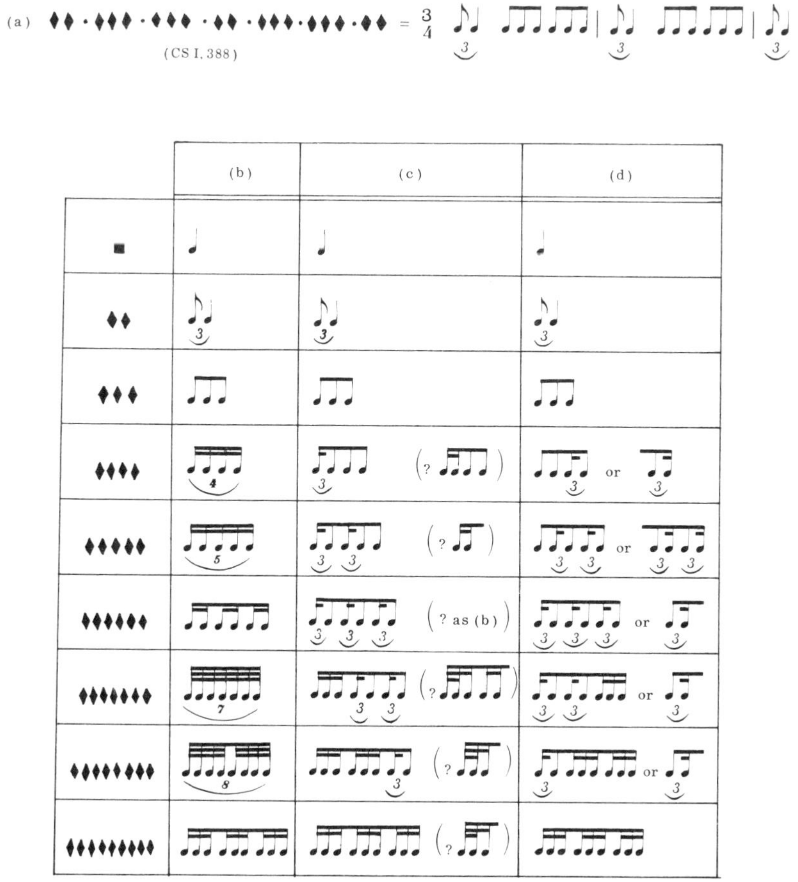

(a) [musical notation] (CS I, 388) = ¾ [musical notation]

	(b)	(c)	(d)
■	♩	♩	♩
♦♦	[2 notes, 3]	[2 notes, 3]	[2 notes, 3]
♦♦♦	[3 notes]	[3 notes]	[3 notes]
♦♦♦♦	[4 notes, 4]	[4 notes, 3] (? [notes])	[notes, 3] or [notes, 3]
♦♦♦♦♦	[5 notes, 5]	[notes, 3 3] (? [notes])	[notes, 3 3] or [notes, 3 3]
♦♦♦♦♦♦	[6 notes]	[notes, 3 3 3] (? as (b))	[notes, 3 3 3] or [notes, 3]
♦♦♦♦♦♦♦	[7 notes, 7]	[notes, 3 3] (? [notes])	[notes, 3 3] or [notes, 3]
♦♦♦♦♦♦♦♦	[8 notes, 8]	[notes, 3] (? [notes])	[notes, 3] or [notes, 3]
♦♦♦♦♦♦♦♦♦	[9 notes]	[9 notes] (? [notes])	[9 notes]

Thus far, Petrus only extended Franco's principles: his real innovation lies in the use to which he put this new-found flexibility of rhythms among the smaller note-values. His own compositions show not only groups of two or three Ss between dots, but larger groups as well. In each case the group as a whole takes up a perfect tempus. A binaria 'with shared propriety' also takes up the time of a B, and does not combine with other Ss. James of Liège, in a well-known passage (CS II, 429), says that there can be anything from two to nine Ss in a tempus: when there are two they are unequal; when three, equal; and there are also four, five, six, seven, eight and nine. These Ss, which are not distinguished notationally, are called *semibreves secundae, tertiae, quartae, quintae, sextae, septimae, octavae* and *nonae*, respectively.

The question arises as to how we should sub-divide a B beat in which there may be as many as nine Ss. Apel (NPM, 322 ff) uses the remarks of James of Liège to show that the groups of three and more should be treated as groups of equal notes: this gives groupings of sextuplets, septuplets, etc., as shown in Figure 36(b). However, this depends on a translation that is by no means certain. The original,

nunc duas semibreves ponerunt inequales; nunc tres equales,
nunc quatuor, quinque, sex, septem, octo vel novem . . .

surely does not necessarily mean

they used now two unequal semibreves, now three, now four,
five, six, seven, eight or nine equal ones . . .

but rather as I have given it in the paragraph above: that is, the equality or otherwise of groups of four and more is not stated.[7] Granted that the passage is at least ambiguous (the punctuation is Coussemaker's), we must ask ourselves whether a more organized rhythmic system is not as likely a solution. Personally, I think it a more likely one, though the matter is certainly still open to argument. Thus I prefer the rhythms shown in Figure 36(c), although that column raises questions that cannot yet be answered.

My reasons are as follows. Until the time of Franco, the Ars Antiqua had been much concerned with rhythmic organization, and in most respects Petrus de Cruce's music and its notation clearly belong to the Ars Antiqua. After the time of Petrus there are clear notational links between the late Ars Antiqua (through the *Roman de Fauvel* music) and the Ars Nova. In particular, Italian Ars Nova notation displays highly-organized rhythmic interpretations of varied groups of Ss. I do not wish to argue from effect to cause: but we should ask ourselves if it is reasonable in these circumstances to assume a free rhythmic organization, such as Apel proposed, for some music between about 1290 and 1315. I would suggest that it is much more reasonable to assume some form of rhythmic organization such as we know of both before and after the time of Petrus de Cruce. If that is accepted, then the detailed organization depends on two rules:

1. Shorter values come first.
2. Sub-division of the one-third tempus is likely to be ternary, this being the division discussed by Robert de Handlo (1326: CS I, 425).

The principle of strict rhythmic organization is supported by

Walter Odington, writing *c.* 1300, his interpretation being slightly different from those of continental writers. After discussing groups of two and three Ss, Odington moves on to the division of the B into four, five or more parts, giving an illustration of one group each of four, five and six Ss, the groups being separated by *signa rotunda*. He discusses only the group of four (CS I, 236):

> Suntque due de quatuor prioribus semibreves minores; due vero posteriores minute sunt, quasi minime seu velocissime, et sic de alliis.

This may be translated as

> And two of the first four notes are minor semibreves, the next two are actually *minute* (meaning 'smallest' or 'fastest') semibreves, and so on with the others.

Two points must be made about Coussemaker's text: first, the punctuation is unsatisfactory, since 'semibreves' is qualified by both 'minores' and 'minute' (my translation repeats 'semibreves' for clarity); second, Coussemaker uses *puncta divisionis* instead of *signa rotunda* in the musical example, despite Odington's clear statement.

I do not find all this either confusing or inadequate. Odington says three things very clearly:

1. The group of four Ss is to be strictly interpreted, using minor Ss and *semibreves minute*;
2. The longer values come first (an English preference); and
3. Groups of five or six Ss should be interpreted according to the same principles.

Odington has already explained his ternary division of the minor S into *minute*. Although he does not say whether the division gives $\frac{1}{3} + \frac{2}{3}$ or $\frac{2}{3} + \frac{1}{3}$, he treats the division of the L into Bs, the B into Ss and the S into *minute* as corresponding to each other: this may, however, be in respect only of their ternary division, without implying the method employed for interpreting two *minute* in the S.

As Odington has already said that the S can be divided into as many as seven parts (he seems to exclude divisions into eight or nine, though there is no logical reason why he should), his interpretation of S-groups is that shown in Figure 36(d). The interpretations for eight and nine Ss are conjectural.

Undoubtedly the first two decades or so of the fourteenth century present a rather confused picture of the theorists' attempts to organize rhythms using the smaller note-values. With such writers as Handlo and the younger John of Garland (cited by Handlo) we see experiments with *semibreves signatae* or *caudatae*—that is, tailed

Ss—to show the major S, a smaller value called the S minima (Odington's *minuta*), and so on. The younger Garland, like Odington, used the *signum rotundum*, or small circular punctum, to separate groups of three minima (that is, the value of a minor S: CS I, 425). Such innovations, short-lived as they were in practice if not in their basic principles, are of importance for the few sources of the period, and notably for the music in the *Roman de Fauvel*. At about the turn of the century a notation for a plicated S is also found, though only on the last of a group of three minor Ss sung to one syllable (CS I, 384 and 423).

Finally, one non-rhythmic innovation appeared at about the time of Petrus de Cruce. Throughout the century the sharp/natural sign commonly used had taken the forms # and ♮, which are very close to our modern forms. At the end of the century a third form, the *croix* ('cross'), took the shape of the first form written diagonally, ✳. This form remained in use until the early seventeenth century.

5. Ars Nova

The innovations of Ars Nova

Much of our knowledge about thirteenth-century music comes from fourteenth-century theorists, whose writings result from a conservative reaction to the notational and musical revolution of the Ars Nova (the 'New Art'). Indeed, it was the proponents of the New Art that called it so, and the apologists from the 'Old Art' of the thirteenth century that gave it the name of Ars Antiqua (or Ars Vetus). (Strictly, 'Ars Nova' refers only to French music, but it is commonly used for all fourteenth-century music from the *Roman de Fauvel* onwards, and is so used here.)

The innovations of Ars Nova notation are:
1. A process of slowing down (already implied by the sub-divisions of the B in Petronian notation) led to the adoption of the S as the beat: in this chapter and the next, therefore, the S, not the B, will be represented by the crotchet or dotted crotchet beat in transcription.
2. This first change necessitated the use of smaller note-values—the minim (*semibrevis minima*, or smallest S: hereafter M) and, before long, the semiminim (Sm).
3. Duple mensuration was given theoretical recognition on an equal footing with triple mensuration.
4. This recognition of both binary and ternary division of note-values allowed a more varied system of metres. Time-signatures were devised to indicate the metre of the music.
5. The practice arose of imperfecting a note not only by the note-value below, but also by the two values below that: the result was a new series of rhythmic possibilities.
6. Further rhythmic and metrical variety was obtained by the use of red notes, whose colour showed certain durational changes.
7. Durational changes were also effected by the use of stems and flags.
8. In addition to the dot of division (*punctum divisionis*), the dot of addition (*punctum additionis*) and the dot of syncopation (*. . . demonstrationis*) came into use.

As we have seen, some of these innovations had appeared by about the turn of the century: but it is with the *Roman de Fauvel* (Paris BN, fonds fr. 146), the music of which was added soon after 1314, that we reach the last of the transitional works. The Ars Nova really dates from the writings of Marchettus de Padua (1318) and Jean de Muris (1319). These books, however, describe two different systems, for after the *Roman de Fauvel* Italy and France went separate notational ways. Of the innovations listed above, France made no extensive use of no. 7, while in Italy nos 5 and 8 were not used. The Italian system was short-lived, however, and towards the end of the fourteenth century was infiltrated by French elements (see Chapter 6). Early in the fifteenth century the specifically Italian elements disappeared, and from then on the history of staff-notation concerns the evolution of our present system from the French.

Another development, though not a controversial one, was that the bar-line (as we shall now call it) became used systematically to mark off the end of a musical section. In this, the Ars Nova followed Franconian practice: but in addition to the Franconian *finis punctorum* the Ars Nova used a double or even triple bar-line to mark the end of an individual voice-part, a function necessitated by the general use of *cantus lateralis*. (Score-layout was little used, except in England, for the next three centuries.)

The finis punctorum was itself used for new purposes:

1. To mark off the first-and second-time endings in those dance-forms (estampie and ductia) and song-forms (mainly the ballata) which needed them. These different endings are often marked as 'open' or 'closed' according to whether the phrase does or does not cadence on the key-note of the piece ('ouvert' and 'clos' in French sources, 'aperto' and 'chiuso' in Italian).

2. In an extended form drawn across two staves, in keyboard score. This seems to fulfil the purely practical function of guiding the eye of a solo player, and it is one of the main differences between keyboard score and vocal music in score layout. Because much Ars Nova keyboard music is based on a pre-existent tune, the bar-lines are usually spaced regularly, often at a B's distance. This is for practical reasons rather than for the specific purpose of marking off metrical units comparable to the modern bar.

Italian notation

Italian notation was first described in the *Pomerium* (1318) of Marchettus of Padua, but was no longer in use when it was described in the *Tractatus* (1412) of Prosdocimus de Beldemandis. The system is an extension of the Petronian groups of Ss, each group the length of a (perfect) B and set off by a dot of division on each side. This notation is seen in a developed form in the *Roman de Fauvel* pieces, although there is argument as to the precise stage between Petronian and truly Italian notation that those pieces represent. The Italian Ars Nova extended the Petronian S-groups to include as many as twelve notes: thus any number of smaller notes up to twelve must be organized rhythmically within the length of a B. In any group in which there are fewer than the maximum possible number of smaller values, the method of organizing the rhythm is to leave the larger note-values to the end of a unit. In many cases this can be seen as an extension of the principle of alteration.

Marchettus used Ss throughout in his examples, following Petronian practice: however, it quickly became normal to use Ms for the smallest available value in each metre. In the explanation of *via naturae* ('the usual way') that follows, the notation of Marchettus can be found by replacing Ms with Ss: in practice, this makes no difference to the evaluation of notes *via naturae*.

Marchettus discusses the metres and their rhythmic organization under the separate headings of perfect and imperfect time. We shall do the same here, but we shall deal with imperfect time first.

There are four divisions of imperfect time.

Quaternaria. The simplest metre, in which the B is divided into two Ss, each of which can be subdivided into two. Hence, a maximum of four notes is found in the B. Remembering that the longer notes come at the end of a unit, the rhythmic interpretations of one, two, three or four notes in *quaternaria* are those of Figure 37(a). Where a time-signature is used, quaternaria is shown by the letter .q. . Since the S (i.e. half of a B) is now the beat, quaternaria can be transcribed straight into $\frac{2}{4}$ time: however, we normally merge pairs of units, so that $\frac{4}{4}$ results.

Octonaria. Where smaller note-values are needed, the notes can be subdivided into two again, giving eight in all: the time-signature for octonaria is .o. . The rhythmic organization of octonaria is shown in Figure 37(b). As before, we usually merge pairs of $\frac{4}{4}$ bars.

Senaria Imperfecta. If the B is divided into six in imperfect time, each beat will have three subdivisions: that is, the equivalent of ⅜ time will result. The time-signature for senaria imperfecta is .i. . The rule regarding the longer note coming at the end of the unit may have to be applied to the two halves of the unit separately. (Since ⅜ time is two beats in a modern bar, the B now takes up a whole bar in transcription.) The rhythmic organization of senaria imperfecta is as in Figure 37(c).

Figure 37. Imperfect Metres

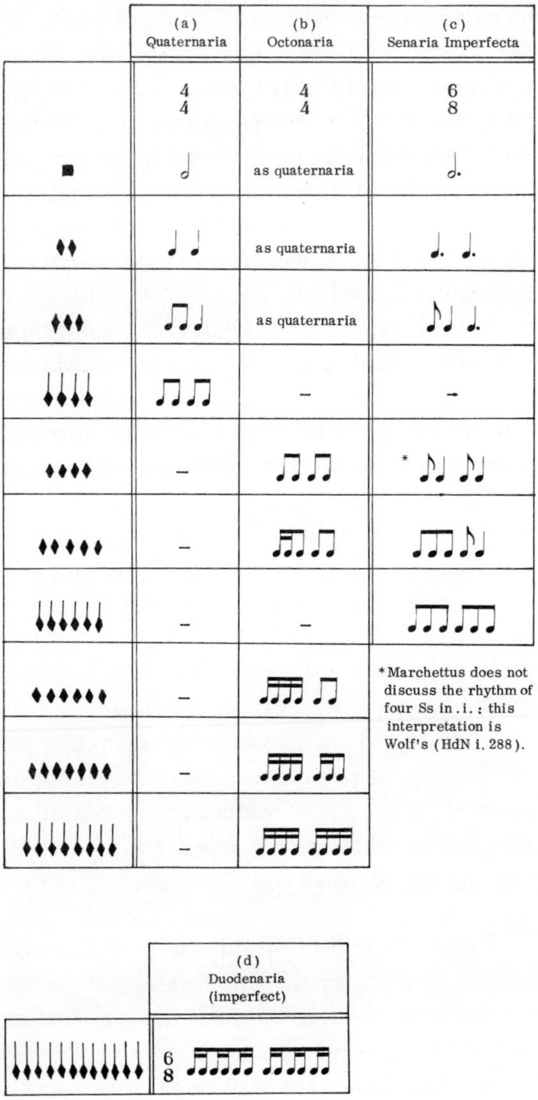

	(a) Quaternaria	(b) Octonaria	(c) Senaria Imperfecta
	4/4	4/4	6/8
■	𝅗𝅥	as quaternaria	𝅗𝅥.
♦♦	𝅗𝅥 𝅗𝅥	as quaternaria	𝅗𝅥. 𝅗𝅥.
♦♦♦	♫ 𝅗𝅥	as quaternaria	♪𝅗𝅥 𝅗𝅥.
♦♦♦♦	♫ ♫	–	–
♦♦♦♦	–	♫ ♫	* ♪♪ ♪♪
♦♦♦♦♦♦	–	♬ ♫	♬ ♪♪
♦♦♦♦♦♦	–	–	♬ ♬
♦♦♦♦♦♦	–	♬ ♫	*Marchettus does not discuss the rhythm of four Ss in .i. ; this interpretation is Wolf's (HdN i. 288).
♦♦♦♦♦♦♦	–	♬ ♬	
♦♦♦♦♦♦♦♦	–	♬ ♬	

	(d) Duodenaria (imperfect)
♦♦♦♦♦♦♦♦♦♦♦♦	6/8 ♬♬ ♬♬

Duodenaria. There are two species of duodenaria, of which that in imperfect time is rare. But if the basic metre of senaria imperfecta is required with smaller note-values, the theoretical maximum of senaria imperfecta subdivides to give twelve notes in all. The time-signature for duodenaria of either type is ·d· . It would be very difficult to formulate the rhythmic organization for this metre as we have done for the others so far; but as it happens the metre is invariably used *via artis* (discussed below), so that its rhythms are clearly shown by specific notational means. For the moment it can suffice to say that the theoretical maximum number of twelve notes in the B would give the metrical structure shown in Figure 37(d).

The divisions of perfect time are only three in number.

Senaria Perfecta. The B is divided into three beats, each of those being subdivided into two. The time-signature for senaria perfecta is ·p· , or sometimes ·Ᵽ·, i.e. per[fecta]. The rhythmic organization is as in Figure 38(a).

Duodenaria. If smaller note-values are needed, the perfect (and more common) type of duodenaria is used, twelve notes being the theoretical maximum. This metre, too, is used only *via artis*: but the theoretical maximum of notes would give the metrical structure shown in Figure 38(b).

Novenaria. The last metre to be discussed subdivides each of its three beats into three, making a theoretical maximum of nine. The modern

Figure 38. Perfect Metres

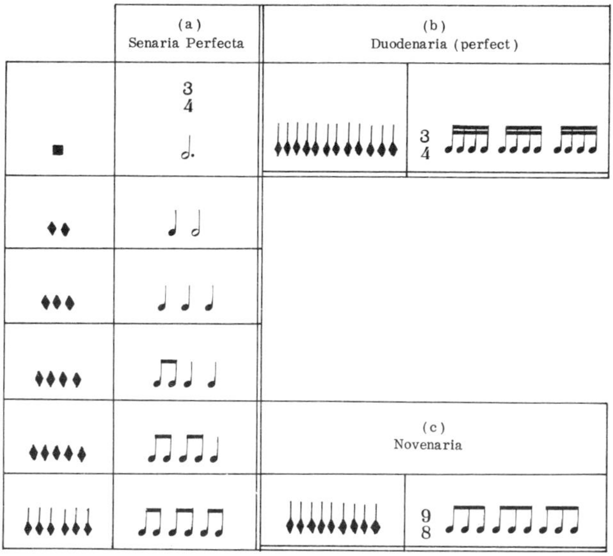

equivalent of this metre is therefore $\frac{9}{8}$. The time-signature for novenaria is ·n· . Like duodenaria, novenaria is used only *via artis*, but its theoretical maximum of notes would give the metrical structure shown in Figure 38(c).

An eighteen-fold subdivision of novenaria was theoretically recognized but never used. As it happens, the separate note-shape for the Semiminim (Sm) makes this unnecessary and also accounts for the rarity of duodenaria of both types. Twelve notes are really the most that a singer would ever need to evaluate at a time, and in practice he was rarely asked to read in groups of more than eight.

A glance at almost any example of Italian notation will show that the dot of division is not, in fact, used to separate every single B-value group from its neighbours. The reason for this is that any note-value of a B or more, including ligatures, can be assumed to constitute a whole number of Bs, independent of adjacent notes, with which they do not combine (see Figure 39, for instance, where no dots are necessary).

Although the metrical divisions of this notation are measured in terms of the B, the B is not the unit of equivalence between metres: that distinction falls on the S, according to Marchettus (GS III, 172). This means that the S in its largest value (i.e. one half or one third of a B) is an unchangeable beat, as shown in Figure 39 (where the B in senaria perfecta is half as long again as that in quaternaria).

Figure 39. Change of Time-Signature

So far, our rhythmic interpretations of the different metres have been based on the assumption that longer note-values come last—the 'usual way' (*via naturae*). These rhythms can be changed by making use of the 'artificial way' (*via artis*), by which a note which would otherwise be long is made short and *vice versa*. For this the system uses two notationally-distinguished forms of the S, the 'greater S' (*semibrevis major*) and the 'smallest S' (*semibrevis minima*): these are the two surviving forms of the *semibreves signatae*. In the former, length is indicated by means of a downward tail, and in the latter—which is, of course, the M—shortness is shown by an upward tail (Figure 40(a)). The major semibreve, like other Ss, can vary in length according to its context: but the M retains an invariable value in any one metre—one quarter of a B in quarternaria, one sixth of a B in senaria, one eighth of a B in octonaria, and so on. Figure 40(b) shows how these note-values were used.

Figure 40. Via Artis

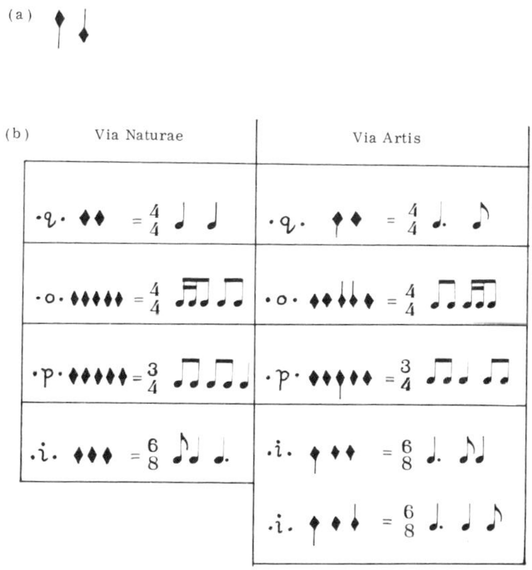

(a)

(b)

The semibrevis major is not always so easily interpreted, however, especially where syncopation is concerned in senaria imperfecta. If Wolf's interpretation shown in Figure 41(a) is correct, then (b) follows, which is logical enough but not at all obvious: and the notation of (c), though unambiguous, is perhaps a little clumsy. An irregular alternative for the latter is shown at (d), in which a *signum rotundum* ('round sign') shows the B to be shorter than its normal value. (This notation is found in the Chantilly MS: it may be a 'mixed' notation form derived from the French grouping shown in Figure 45(f).)

Figure 41. Syncopation

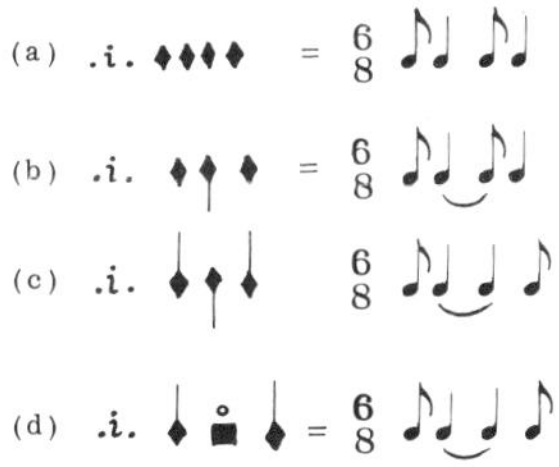

An even greater rhythmic variety was made possible by the use of *via artis* with smaller note-values. The Semiminima, or half-minim (Sm), has a flagged stem (Figure 42(a)), while a similar shape is used for triplets in the time of two Ms (b). (Sometimes the shapes of these two forms are reversed.) There are many other types of stemmed note, some of which are extremely rare and probably the quirks of individual scribes: their purpose is invariably to show particular rhythmic subtleties. Some of the more standard forms have a certain logic about them (c). These note-shapes are often useful for notating 'dotted rhythms' (otherwise very limited in this notation), for, according to the metre in use, any note can be replaced by a suitable group of smaller values. Thus in the group shown in Figure 42(d), the substitution of smaller values for the largest might result in (e).

Figure 42. Italian Note-shapes

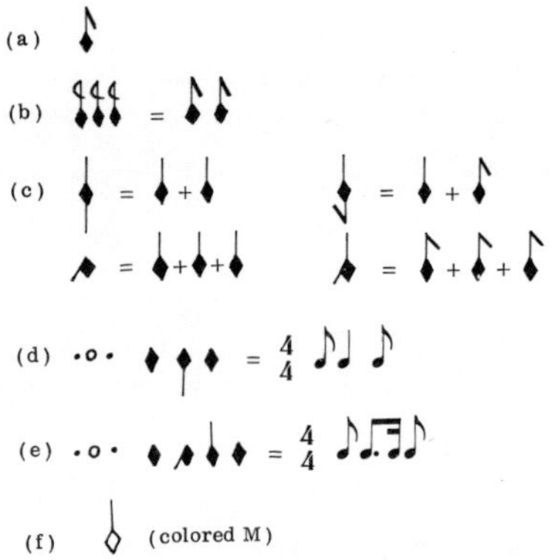

(a)

(b)

(c)

(d)

(e)

(f) (colored M)

We have seen that there existed certain tailed notes by means of which a scribe could notate the rhythm of three notes in the time of two: similar means were used to provide four in the time of three, and other such fractional values. Late in the fourteenth century a second method of doing the same thing, and of providing syncopation and hemiola rhythms, began to be used in Italian notation, namely, coloration (see below). Never very common in Italian sources (it is one of the earliest French devices used by the Italians), coloration is found in both the red and void (outline) forms. Of these forms, the red comes from France, while the void (Figure 42(f)) seems to be of Italian origin. Late in the fourteenth century the Italians also discarded the consistent use of the dot of division, taking instead the French time-signatures. This notation, characterized by the use of both Italian and French elements (the latter eventually including dots of addition and syncopation, as well), is usually known as 'Mixed Notation' (see Chapter 6).

One more feature of Italian notation must be discussed. The simpler metres do not always have a time-signature at the beginning of a piece, although changes of metre in the middle are invariably shown by one. This means that the singer must sometimes decide the metre for himself by examining the music. In octonaria, for instance, any M will invariably be one eighth of a B: a group of eight Ms between dots of division must therefore indicate octonaria. Similarly, a group of six Ms indicates senaria, a group of nine shows novenaria, and so on. In practice, the metre can be guessed at even if other values are in the group. A S, for instance, is often equal to two Ms in a mixed group of Ss and Ms.

The rests of Italian notation are those of the French (Figure 47): however, they enter fully into the Italian system, and what has been said above about note-values applies also to the corresponding rest-values. Finally, it should be noted that Italian scribes preferred a six-line staff, as opposed to the five-line staff of the French.

French notation

French Ars Nova notation was first described in the *Ars Novae Musicae* (1319) of Jean de Muris. This work was a defence of the ideas of the composer and theorist Philippe de Vitry, who can be regarded as the architect of the Ars Nova. Vitry's own treatise *Ars Nova* (*c.* 1325) gave the movement its name.

The basic principle of French notation is the application of the rules of imperfection and alteration to three different levels of mensuration, together with the possibility of duple mensuration at any level. The three levels are

1. Modus ('mode'): the division of the L into Bs;
2. Tempus ('time'): the division of the B into Ss; and
3. Prolatio ('prolation'): the division of the S into Ms.

Prolatio ('measurement') was a new term, probably referring to the measured division of the S into Ms and Sms. (The Sm, with the shape shown in Figure 42(a), was always half of a M.)

A fourth level, of theoretical rather than practical significance, also existed:

4. Maximodus: the grouping of Ls.

This has virtually no metrical significance, and there was never a time-signature for it. In modally-notated music maximodus was almost invariably imperfect, the Ls being grouped in pairs: a triplex L, recognized in Ars Nova theory (Strunk SR, 177), was so rare in practice that we can regard maximode as a grouping of Ds, Ls and L-rests, not as a division of the Maxima (triplex L).

To begin with there were time-signatures for modus. Like all French Ars Nova time-signatures they referred to the concept of perfection and imperfection, and consisted of a small rectangle containing two strokes for imperfect mode (i.e. two Bs in a L) and three for perfect mode (i.e. three Bs in a L).

Modus imperfectus: ⊡   Modus perfectus: ⊡

These signs were not really necessary, and did not last long: the type of L-rest used would immediately show whether the L were binary or ternary (Figure 47). But in any case major mode became increasingly rare, and for most of the 180 years or so of French notation modus was normally imperfect.

The time-signatures for tempus and prolatio were as in Figure 43. Perfect time (*tempus perfectum*, ternary division of the B) was indicated by the sign of perfection (i.e. completeness), the circle: similarly, the sign of imperfection, the broken circle, indicated imperfect time (*tempus imperfectum*, binary division of the B). The indications for prolation were placed inside these: at first, three dots showed perfect (major) prolation, and two dots (the imperfect number, being one less than perfection) showed imperfect (minor) prolation. The time-signatures are sometimes found thus in the Italian sources of 'mixed' notation, but in France they very early lost two dots each, so that perfect prolation showed only one dot and imperfect prolation none.

The binary and ternary divisions of tempus and prolatio combined to give four metres, each with its time-signature. These are the 'four measurements' (*quatre prolacions*) of Philippe de Vitry (Figure 43).

Figure 43. The Quatre Prolacions

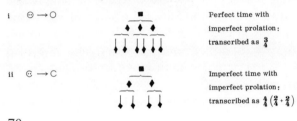

i   ⊙ → O

Perfect time with imperfect prolation: transcribed as $\frac{3}{4}$

ii   ⊖ → C

Imperfect time with imperfect prolation: transcribed as $\frac{4}{4}\left(\frac{2}{4}+\frac{2}{4}\right)$

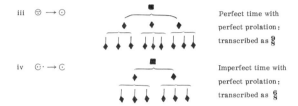

iii ⊙ → ⊙

Perfect time with perfect prolation: transcribed as $\frac{9}{8}$

iv ℂ· → ℂ

Imperfect time with perfect prolation: transcribed as $\frac{6}{8}$

The S, which is generally the beat, is normally the invariable duration: that is, it is the unit of equivalence between metres. Hence a perfect B is half as long again as an imperfect one.

We have seen that in Franconian notation the principle of alteration was applied both in perfect mode and in perfect time. Ars Nova theory allowed alteration at any level for which the mensuration was ternary. Thus in perfect time the S could be altered, as before (Figure 44(a)), and so could the M in major prolation (b). If both time and prolation were perfect, alteration might take place at both levels (c). The old rule 'L before L is perfect' had therefore now given way to the more general 'like before like is perfect' (*similis ante similem perfecta*), acting in perfect time (for the B), in major prolation (for the S) and, though very rarely, in perfect mode (for the L).

Figure 44. Alteration

(a) ○ ■ ♦♦■ $= \frac{3}{4}$ 𝅗𝅥. | 𝅘𝅥 𝅗𝅥 | 𝅗𝅥. |

(b) ℂ ♦ 𝅘𝅥𝅘𝅥 ♦ $= \frac{6}{8}$ 𝅘𝅥. 𝅘𝅥𝅮𝅘𝅥𝅮 | 𝅘𝅥.

(c) ⊙ ■ 𝅘𝅥𝅘𝅥♦■ $= \frac{9}{8}$ 𝅗𝅥. 𝅘𝅥. | 𝅘𝅥𝅮𝅘𝅥𝅮 𝅗𝅥. | 𝅗𝅥. 𝅘𝅥. |

The rules of imperfection similarly became applicable at different levels. In Franco's time a L could be imperfected by a B, but a B could not be imperfected by a S. Now, however, a B in perfect time could be imperfected by a S, and a (perfect) S in major prolation could be imperfected by a M. As before, imperfection by the note following had precedence over imperfection by that preceding (Figure 45(a)).

This was not the only way in which the principles of imperfection were extended, however, and other innovations greatly angered the opponents of Ars Nova.[1] The original type of imperfection just described, called by James of Liège 'proximate' or 'direct' imperfection (*imperfectio proxima* or *immediata*), is sometimes known as *imperfectio ad totum*—that is, imperfection of the whole note. Ars Nova theory also recognized *imperfectio ad partem* (imperfection of part of a note), in which imperfection was caused by a note two or

three values below the note affected. Thus a L might be imperfected by
a S, which would be considered to have taken its value from the last of
the (perfect) Bs of which the L was composed (Figure 45(b)): or the L
might even be affected by a M taking its value from a constituent S in
major prolation (c).

Imperfectio ad partem was logical enough if, as in these examples,
the imperfecting note was itself a part of a ternary group. Machaut
and some later composers, however, used a form of *imperfectio ad
partem* in which the ternary measurement was at the level above, but
not at the level of the imperfecting note itself (d). This may be related
to the use of two notes substituted for a single imperfecting note in
imperfectio ad totum (e), which gave rise to a grouping in which the
two notes concerned were separated, the imperfected note coming
between them (f).

Figure 45. Imperfection

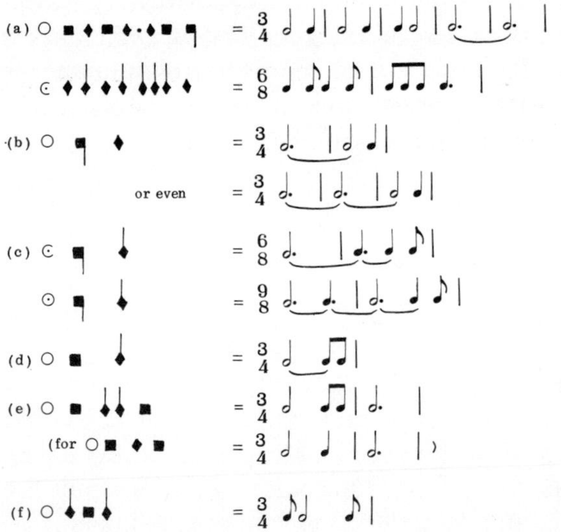

Another means used to introduce rhythmic subtleties was
coloration. Red notes were first used in the *Roman de Fauvel* pieces,
imperfect mode being shown by means of colored Ls. Here, then, a red
L is always imperfect, even in a context where it would normally be
perfect. Coloration often involves a complete group of notes which
together form a hemiola. The simplest form is shown in Figure 46(a).
The hemiola group is usually transcribed as shown here because the
coloration also implies a change of stress: that is, the group is a real $\frac{3}{2}$

bar and not simply syncopation in $\frac{3}{4}$ time. The same would of course apply to colored Ss in major prolation (a bar of $\frac{3}{4}$, not $\frac{6}{8}$).

This system applies not only to Ls in perfect mode, Bs in perfect time and Ss in major prolation, but to groups of smaller values which have the same duration when added together. Thus if a coloured B is replaced by two coloured Ss in perfect time, the hemiola still results (b). Although the value of the Ss individually is apparently not changed by the coloration here, the effect in practice is to prevent alteration of the second S (cf. (c)). That is, the two Ss together make up a B which is imperfected. In fact, there are perhaps two other reasons why a hemiola group is usually notated entirely in red:

1. It makes it possible for the singer's eye to take in a single group of notes and to see that the sum total is a whole number of perfections—i.e. that it *is* a hemiola group.

2. The scribe would have to use a different pen for red: writing whole groups in red allows him to change pens less frequently.

It is important to recognize that coloured groups can involve a wide range of note-values, not all of which will individually be affected by the coloration. Occasionally, however, a hemiola is effected through coloration of an incomplete group: this is possible if the values of surrounding notes make the rhythm unambiguous (d).

Figure 46. Coloration

Veni electa mea   (London, The British Library, Add. MS 35290 (15th cent.), f. 238r)

(Here and in later examples the broken square brackets, used to indicate coloration in transcriptions, show it also in my transliterations of the original note-values.)

The rests of fourteenth-century French notation are basically Franconian (Figure 47(a)). The B-rest is taken to be either perfect or imperfect, according to the prevailing metre of the music: but there is an invariable rule that the (perfect) B-rest cannot be imperfected, and an imperfect B-rest in *tempus perfectum* is written as two S-rests.

Similarly, it is unnecessary to have separate rests for the altered S or altered M, and the Franconian distinction between the major and minor S-rests is dispensed with.

The rests and their grouping therefore usually depend on the metre of the music. For example, in *maximodus imperfectus* the L-rests are grouped in pairs whether the L is perfect or imperfect, so that each pair has the value of a D (Figure 47(b)). In *maximodus perfectus* the rests are grouped in threes (c). In a long series of rests these pairs or threes are staggered on the staff so that the eye can take them in and count them more easily.[2]

Figure 47. Rests

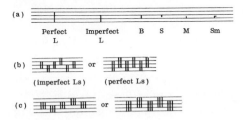

(a)　　Perfect　　Imperfect　　B　　S　　M　　Sm
　　　　L　　　　　L

(b)　　(imperfect Ls)　　(perfect Ls)

(c)

The ligatures of French notation are also derived from those of Franco of Cologne. To understand them, it is easiest to start with those forms of Franconian ligature that have no tails (Figure 48(a)). These are the basic two-note shapes. The addition of a downward tail to the left of the first will make it into the Franconian B-L ligature: so

* a downward tail to the Left shoRtens the first note.[3]

The addition of a tail to the right of the second ligature will also provide a B-L ligature: so

* a downward tail to the Right Lengthens the second note.

We therefore have two B-L forms (b).

The oblique form is also used. As in Franconian notation, the descending form is normal, the ascending one rare. There is no longer any notational significance in this, and both forms have the value L-B:

*oBLiquing makes L-B.

The rules concerning downward tails also apply to the oblique forms (c). To these we can add the two-note ligatures 'with shared propriety' (d).

Ligatures of three or more notes are evaluated as in Franconian notation, the first and last notes being evaluated separately. Any middle note (including an obliqued one) is a B unless

1. it has the long horizontal body of a D, in which case it *is* a D;

74

2. it has a downward tail to its right, in which case it is a L (a downward tail makes a L to its Left); or

3. it forms part of a ligature 'with shared propriety', in which case it is a S.

The ligature 'with shared propriety' is exactly the same as in Franconian notation: the two notes following an upward tail are both Ss. Figure 48(e) will illustrate all that has been said about longer ligatures.

Figure 48. Ligatures

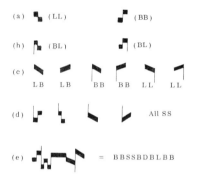

In French notation ligatures can combine with single notes to make up a perfection; they do not necessarily form a unit by themselves, as in Italian notation, although they may of course do so in certain circumstances.

It was noted above that the old 'division of the mode' was gradually replaced *c.* 1280–1320 by the dot of division (*punctum divisionis*). The division of the mode did not entirely disappear: but with the increased use of a sign of perfection on several different levels in French Ars Nova notation, that sign became a mere dot, quicker to write and less liable to be confused with a rest.

To the dot of division, two more types of notational dot were added in the early fourteenth century.

1. The 'dot of addition' (*punctum additionis*). In duple mensuration, a dot after a note adds half the length of the note to its duration: e.g. a dotted S lasts for the duration of one-and-a-half Ss.

2. The 'dot of syncopation' (*punctum demonstrationis*—the dot which 'points out'). It is impossible to give rules for the use of this dot, or to tell a student what to look for: but

(i) if a dot cannot be read as a normal dot of division or addition, and it is not a blemish on the paper or a worm-hole, then it must be a dot of syncopation or a scribal error; and

(ii) the dot of syncopation is really a misplaced dot of division—that is, a dot of division that forces a perfection to start in the 'wrong' place.

Sometimes a single dot is used, and sometimes two: if two, and they are very close together, the device is easy to recognize. Basically, syncopation is caused by the prevention of imperfection and/or alteration (Figure 49(a)): more positively, the dot shows that a 'misplaced' perfection follows it, in which the normal rules must be observed. The effect of a *punctum demonstrationis* is therefore to split a perfection ((x) in Figure 49) and to place another perfection (y) in the middle of it. The same effect can be gained by using a 'split' coloration group (b).

Figure 49. The Dot of Syncopation

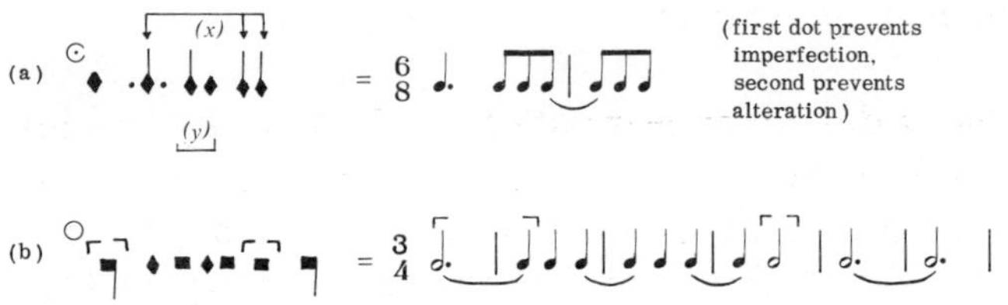

The *punctum demonstrationis* was rare until the late fourteenth century, when it entered a brief period of more regular use in the complex rhythms written in 'mannered' notation (see also Figure 51, below).

Although these different types of dot may seem confusing, there is usually no ambiguity. For instance, a dot following a S in O time will be a dot of division if it comes at the end of a perfection; if elsewhere, it is either a dot of addition (in which case it requires an odd M to make up the duration) or a dot of syncopation (which will be fairly obvious from the immediate context). A S would not receive a dot of addition in major prolation, where it would be kept perfect (if necessary) by a dot of division.

Syncopation caused by a *punctum demonstrationis* was not the only type possible, however. In both the fourteenth and fifteenth centuries use was made of the fixed duration of notes in duple mensuration for this purpose. In C time, any note-values can be made to produce syncopation, but even in other mensurations the effect can easily be obtained as long as the value used is not itself part of a triple mensuration—the M in ○ time, for instance (Figure 50, taken from Dufay's 'Estrinez moi' in the Escorial Ms V.III.24, f. 59v). This type of syncopation causes no problems, because in order to work at all it must give the singer no choice—i.e. it is unambiguous.

Figure 50. Syncopation

pour vous donner ce jour de l'an nouvel

pour vous don - ner   ce_ jour de ____ l'an __ nou –   – vel

Ars Nova notation in England

In England, Ars Nova did not appear out of Ars Antiqua as suddenly as in Italy and France, nor are the old and new arts so clearly differentiated as in those countries. Franconian elements appeared in English music only at the very end of the thirteenth century, and the notation of the following century is derived directly from the Franconian. Despite a number of Petronian elements from about 1300 onwards, therefore, English notation in the fourteenth century was closely related to that of France. There is little reason to refer to 'English Ars Nova notation', then, but as English music of the period has a number of peculiarities it deserves a section to itself.

Until about the middle of the thirteenth century England seems to have shared in a common musical style and notation. Then there appeared a peculiarly English notation, ◤◦◦ , which seems to be a division of the B, just as the universal ◦◦◦ was a division of the L (NOHM II, 368). From the former group was derived a note-shape of exclusively English use, ◢ for a S, and English scribes also favoured a rhombic B, ◆ :[4] but by about 1300 both had been abandoned in favour of the French shapes. At about this time, too, English sources began to use the dot of division to set off Petronian groups of up to six Ss. Various sources of the early fourteenth century also use the new note-shapes for the *semibrevis major* (◆) and the *semibrevis minor* (◆): in addition to these, the early fragment from Fountains Abbey also uses the *semibrevis minima*.[5]

The early Fountains Fragment displays two more notational peculiarities:

1. A very individual use of ligatures, including

(i) the joining together of two or more ligatures 'with shared propriety' (normally separated or included only in longer ligatures of higher note-values); and

(ii) the incorporation into a ligature of a note that would normally be single.

2. The use of a special sign, ♣ , for an altered S in *tempus perfectum*. Other English manuscripts sometimes indicate such alteration by means of a figure 2 above or below the note in question. This latter method of avoiding any ambiguity persisted in England to the beginning of the sixteenth century. Both methods are unnecessary to a singer who knows the rules, and are probably symptomatic of a provincial attitude. Nevertheless, it is likely that the 'swallowtail' S (*per caudam hirundinis*) was used more often than the surviving fourteenth-century sources indicate: both Hanboys and Tunstede reject it as a corruption of the art of music (CS I, 432a, and III, 349a = IV, 271a). Despite the disapproval of theorists the sign was used to show alteration until the early fifteenth century.[6] Every notational sign described here as being found in the earlier Fountains music appears also in the fifteenth-century manuscript usually known as The Fountains Fragment (British Library Add. MS 40011B: see Bukofzer *Studies*, 97): this suggests a consistent use of this rather individual notation over a century or so. (The later source is in void notation, for which see Chapter 6.)

One more notational feature of the fifteenth-century Fountains Fragment seems also to be a specifically English phenomenon (Bukofzer *Studies*, 98): the use of the sign ⌐⊥⌐ to show a perfect S rest in major prolation, which is described only by English theorists such as Anonymous IV (c. 1280), Simon Tunstede (*c.* 1350) and John Hanboys (fifteenth century) (see the table of rests in Wolf HdN i, 336 f). We might regard this sign as an amalgamation of ⌐⊥ and ⊤⌐ in a single pen-stroke. (As before, these rests show absolute values.) The sign is also found in a marginally earlier source, Cambridge University Library Add. MS 5943 (BMS I), both as a perfect S rest in major prolation and with its older meaning of the Franconian *divisio modi,* showing a rest whose value must be determined by the singer.

6. Mannerism and the Fifteenth Century

In the last quarter of the fourteenth century there arose a movement which tended greatly towards complexity in musical notation and in the music itself. A search for rhythmic sophistication engendered subtleties of notation that constitute a real *fin de siècle*. This situation was not maintained for long, and soon after the beginning of the new century music generally became simpler in style. A residual preoccupation with the appearance of the music rather than its sound can be seen in certain types of work up to the beginning of the sixteenth century, running alongside the generally simpler notational and musical styles that became dominant *c.* 1420.

The complicated style, with its exceptional rhythmic subtlety and obvious visual impact, is usually known as 'mannered' notation. Mannerism was primarily a French phenomenon, but there was an Italian form of it which for technical reasons we call 'mixed' notation. Although mixed notation is mannered, the terms 'mixed notation' and 'mannered notation' have always been used as if they were mutually exclusive. It is for this reason that Apel (NPM, chapters VIII and IX) was at first unable to define the two types satisfactorily: only later (ibid., 451 f) did he formulate the geographical definitions that I follow here.

Mixed notation

The phenomenon of 'mixed' notation arose from the Italian use of certain elements of French notation between *c.* 1375 and *c.* 1400. Relations between northern Italy and southern France were probably close: the papal court was mainly at Avignon between 1305 and 1378, and certainly many north Italian composers worked there during the Great Schism (1378–1417). This may by itself explain why Italian composers discarded some of the main principles of their own notation; or perhaps they simply found that the Italian system of *divisiones* was inflexible and notationally clumsy. While Italian music written in mixed notation does progress in 'measures' of a B's duration, the *punctum divisionis* itself is virtually absent (except when it would be required by French notation), and the rhythmic organization within the 'measure' uses the French system. To the occasional dot of division was added the dot of addition, common in French notation but completely contrary to the basic principles of Italian. In general, the French mensuration-signs were used, often in their old forms such as ⊙ and ₵·.

Another set of innovations concerned coloration. To the Italian form (black void) was added the normal French type (full red): and before long red void coloration was also used. Combined with the many and often unstandardized note-shapes of Italian notation, these gave a very wide variety of note-values. To all this, 'mixed' notation added another refinement—half coloration. This is the colouring of one note in a two-note ligature, or of half a note which divides into two. For instance, a S ligature in major prolation, if half coloured, would have the value of a perfect S + an imperfect S = 3 Ms + 2 Ms (or *vice versa*); similarly, a half coloured L in *tempus perfectum* would be equal to 3 Ss + 2 Ss (one perfect and one imperfect B, or *vice versa*) = 5 Ss. On the whole, this was as convenient a way of obtaining unusual note-values as some of the more abstruse note-shapes.

Mannered notation

While 'mixed' notation was confined to sources of Italian derivation, mannered notation proper apparently grew up in the great secular courts of southern France, as well as in the papal court at Avignon. The papal court supplies a direct link between French and Italian mannerist styles: and it must be admitted that the distinction between them is sometimes based mainly on the nationality of the composer.

French mannerism showed itself in strange ways: the use of ♡ to replace the word 'coeur' (heart) in a chanson-text, common in the fifteenth-century chansonniers; a love-song written in the shape of a heart; a completely heart-shaped chansonnier; or a perpetual round in the form of a circle.[1] These, we may think, take whimsy too far and show a somewhat puerile sense of the extravagant. Yet they were an enrichment of medieval life, a symptom of that web of parallels, allegories and other types of hidden meaning which are characteristic of the declining Middle Ages. (This final and fascinating chapter of the Middle Ages is the subject of Johan Huizinga's *The Waning of the Middle Ages*, an excellent introduction to the modes of thought in the fourteenth and fifteenth centuries.)

An obvious technical feature of mannered notation is the increased use of coloration, an affectation (as it often is) that again indicates a concern with the appearance of the sources. To some extent coloration replaced the special note-shapes of Italian notation. The main uses of coloration in the first two decades of the fifteenth century[2] were as follows:

1. For imperfection. As we have seen, this does not affect the value of a note which would be imperfect anyway.

2. For sesquialtera diminution (see below). This reduces *every* note—perfect or otherwise—to two-thirds of its normal (black) value: the most common use of this is for triplet figures (three Ms in the time of two).

3. For the Sm. In both Italian and French notation a Sm could by the end of the fourteenth century be written as a coloured M.

4. For the fusa (F: half a Sm).

5. For passages written proportionally, especially for duple mensuration in diminution (two Ss in the time of one, four Ms in the time of three).

6. Augmentation colour, in which an imperfect note has the value of a dotted note (i.e. $\frac{3}{2}$ of its apparent value).

Some of these uses are illustrated in the opening of 'Un orible plein' from the Chantilly manuscript (Figure 51, in which the dotted brackets, ⦂⁚ ⁚⦂, denote void red coloration).[3] Types of coloration in this figure are identified by the numbers allotted to them above.

Figure 51. Mannerist Coloration

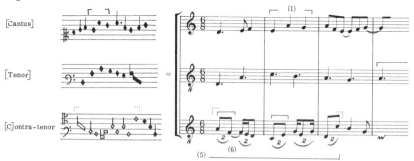

(Chantilly, Musée Condé, MS 564 (olim 1047), f. 13v)

(Text omitted. Mensuration is ₵ in all parts, although no mensuration-signs are given. The dot of syncopation in the cantus is the first of two; both prevent alteration of the M following.)

Until about the end of the fourteenth century only uses 1–3 were known, and there was normally no ambiguity. With the arrival of uses 4–6, however, and especially when two or more types of coloration were used in a single source (and often in a single piece), some notational distinctions were required:

(i) Between the triplet M and the Sm, in such a way that the F would not cause problems.

(ii) Between normal coloration (types 1 and 2) and proportional coloration (5).

(iii) For smaller note-values (3 and 4) when passages of proportional coloration were also included.

The various types of coloration, in chronological order of their appearance, were:

(a) Full red (originally French).

(b) Black void (originally Italian).

(c) Red void.

(d) Other colours, such as the full blue used in the Old Hall manuscript.

It will be as well to discuss here the various uses of coloration (1–6, above) in the light of these possible types.

1. In France, imperfection shown by full red notes (as in the *Roman de Fauvel*) remained normal: in the fifteenth and early sixteenth centuries full red coloration was still used everywhere for this purpose in black notation. In Italy, black void notes were used for this until about the end of the fourteenth century, when full red became normal.

2. For triplets, the situation is as for (1), except that Italy originally used full black tailed notes (Figure 42(b), above).

3. In Italy, the Sm was first written as a flagged M (Figure 42(a)), but later as a black void M (perhaps by analogy with (5)?). For much of the fourteenth century French notation avoided the Sm altogether by using either proportions or *plicae*. (The *plica* is occasionally found in Machaut's music, but then it disappeared from polyphony.) Early in the fifteenth century French sources used the black void form, which gave way to the (full) flagged form by about 1415. The flagged form is mainly associated with major prolation where the M is the beat, but the *void* flagged form had already been used *c*. 1400 in the earliest examples of void notation (which looks the same as black void coloration: see Figure 59, below). Between *c*. 1415 and *c*. 1430 the normal coloured M (full red) came to be used for the Sm. However, when a distinction was needed the void red form was sometimes used instead, leaving the full red M for its previous functions. In the simpler

mid-century style this distinction was unnecessary, and full red coloration remained normal for all of the uses 1–3.

4. The F was largely avoided until well into the fifteenth century, just as the Sm had been previously. Proportions were again used for this purpose; and after *c.* 1415 triple mensuration tended to be ○ with a S beat in music that might previously have been notated in ℂ with a M beat (see Figure 55, concerning the Agincourt Carol), which also made the F unnecessary. When the F became regularly used, its form depended largely on that of the Sm. It was of course vital to distinguish the Sm and F visually, while the distinction of Sm and coloured M was much less important. The same possibilities existed as for making a Sm from a M: viz. the addition of a flag (if none existed already) or the use of coloration of various types. Figure 52 shows the possible forms of Sm, F, coloured M and coloured Sm at this time. It should be noted (i) that a note can carry only one flag at this stage; (ii) that the coloured Sm is derived from the Sm, not from the coloured M; (iii) that there was a sort of coloration hierarchy, void red being of a higher order than full red and its equivalent void black; and (iv) that the various possibilities give a number of potential note-value series, which differ in size and number of ambiguities.[4]

Figure 52. Smaller Note-Values

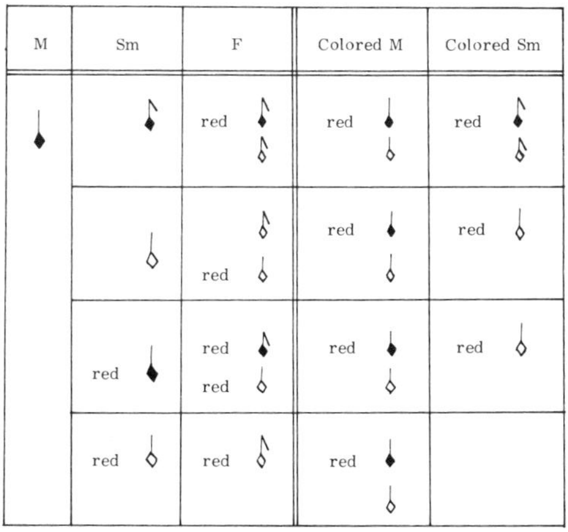

M	Sm	F	Colored M	Colored Sm
♩	♪	red ♪ / ♬	red ♩ / ◊	red ♪ / ♬
	◊	♬ / red ♪	red ♩ / ◊	red ◊
red ♩	red ♩	red ♪ / red ♪	red ♩ / ◊	red ◊
red ◊	red ♪	red ♪	red ♩ / ◊	

(All notes are black unless marked as red)

5. Passages written in proportions are easier to read correctly if they are distinguished by colour. This is the purpose of much coloration in the Old Hall manuscript including the full blue notation (Apel NPM,

432 f). In Italian notation passages in void black tend to be in the proportion shown in the contratenor of Figure 51 (though the Chantilly MS uses *red* void here): in a passage of this sort in Parrish's plates LVI and LVII (NMM), fourth staff of each page, the mensuration-sign ℂ has been written, though it was perhaps strictly unnecessary. It is probably as an extension of this general use of void black coloration that the specific use of it for four Ms in the time of three became common.

6. Augmentation colour is too unstandardized for rules to be given: it is one of those things that have to be kept at the back of the mind in case of need. (For examples, see Figure 51 and Apel NPM, 406). It was apparently responsible for a rhythmic figure that now causes us some difficulty in interpretation. By extension from triplet figures, a coloured B + S in *tempus imperfectum* or a coloured S + M in minor prolation gave a triplet arrangement in the time of an imperfect B or S, respectively (Figure 53(a)). However, after about 1425 this same figure, no doubt by analogy with augmentation colour, became used for the 'dotted' rhythm (b)—that is, 3 + 1 instead of 2 + 1. This use disappeared during the sixteenth century, but for much of the fifteenth it is not always possible to know which rhythm was intended. Note that in (b) the resulting durations are only half of those that augmentation colour would give (cf. Figure 51, start of Contratenor); and that this notation again avoids the smaller note-values.

Figure 53. Uses of Coloration

As will be obvious from our consideration of colour, proportions were also an important characteristic of mannered notation, though they were not always notated by colour. Proportional notation is older than fourteenth-century mannerism, its first exponent probably being Jean de Muris (CS III, 58). Music which might have been notated using proportions—had they existed—is even older: some thirteenth-century clausulae, as well as motets of this and later times, notate the tenor tune in successively shorter note-values as it is repeated. Later composers used proportions to notate these mathematically-related sections of the music in a more concise way. The simplest way of showing proportions was to write a fraction, as if it were a new time-signature, in which the numbers denoted the numerical relationship between the notes before and after it. For example, the proportion sign $\frac{3}{2}$ denotes that three notes following take up the same time as two previous notes (Figure 54(a)). Proportions are normally based (as here) on the S, which is, as it were, the unit of conversion.

The proportion shown at (a) is called *proportio sesquialtera* (= *semiquealtera*, 'a half and one'). The other most common proportions are *proportio dupla* (in which note-values are halved) and *proportio tripla* (in which they become one-third of their notated value): in each case the notated value of any note is reduced, so these proportions are all examples of diminution. The fractional signs for *dupla* and *tripla* are, respectively, $\frac{2}{1}$ and $\frac{3}{1}$ (b). From these it will be seen that any diminution-sign whose 'denominator' is 1 causes a change of the beat to a higher note-value—from the S to the B in these two examples. These fractions are sometimes simplified to a single figure (e.g. 2 or 3).

Figure 54. Proportions

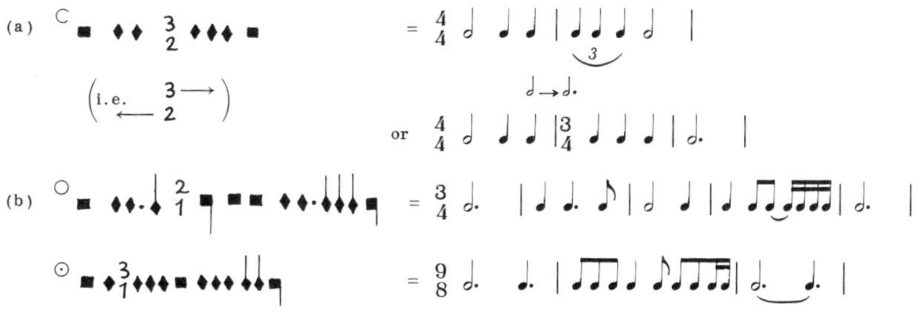

Augmentation, a proportion in which the written note-values are increased in duration, can be notated in the same way, although this is less common. Just as $\frac{3}{2}$ implies that three Ss now take up the time of two previous Ss, so $\frac{2}{3}$ shows augmentation in the same ratio, where two Ss take up the time of the previous three.

Proportional signs are cumulative in their effect. For instance, a section of *proportio dupla* followed by a sign for augmentation by two would result in the original speed and notation, while a triple diminution followed by a sign for duple augmentation would lead to *sesquialtera* of the original metre ($\frac{3}{1} \times \frac{1}{2} = \frac{3}{2}$). (In fact, fractions as signs of augmentation are used almost exclusively for the cancellation of an existing proportion. Pieces which use numerals throughout are rare.) Time-signatures (mensuration-signs proper), on the other hand, are not cumulative: so a mensuration-sign in a proportional section cancels the prevailing proportion, and the process begins again.

Unfortunately, both diminution and augmentation were often shown by means of Philippe de Vitry's *quatre prolacions* (see above, Figure 43), usually modified but not always so. Hence there is some room for ambiguity, and it is occasionally difficult to decide whether a sign is a true time-signature or a proportional sign. Indeed, in many sources of the late fourteenth and early fifteenth centuries ℂ was used as a real time-signature but implying the M, rather than the S, as the beat—*tactus alla minima* (Sachs, *Rhythm and Tempo*, 219). Thus the two versions of the Agincourt Carol in the Trinity Roll (*c.* 1420) and the Selden MS (*c.* 1425–40) are actually identical (Figure 55).[5] (The Trinity manuscript is in void notation.)

Figure 55. Tactus Alla Minima

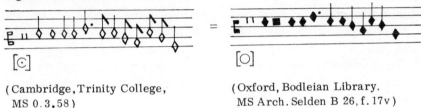

[ℂ]

[○]

(Cambridge, Trinity College, MS O.3.58)

(Oxford, Bodleian Library, MS Arch. Selden B 26, f. 17v)

This is notationally a special case: used with proportional significance, the sign ℂ more often appears as a sign of duple augmentation, not as a time-signature (i.e. at the beginning of the piece) implying augmentation. Another of Vitry's signs, ○, was also sometimes used as a proportional sign, with the meaning of triple augmentation. However, Vitry's signs are almost always modified when used proportionally. Two of the earliest such modifications, *c.* 1400, imply diminution by two (Figure 56(a) and (b)), as do some slightly later ones (c). Similar modifications indicate *proportio tripla* (d). Four of these signs, if appearing as the first modification of the normal S beat, have the usual meanings of the *quatre prolacions*, but written in the next-higher note-values (e). It will be noted that ₵, which is familiar from eighteenth-century music, implies duple time with a B beat: that is, it is a sign of metre *alla breve*. This terminology, indeed, is still used in eighteenth-century music in diminution, even though with the smaller note-values of that century the beat in music notated *alla breve* is actually on the M.

86

Figure 56. Signs of Diminution

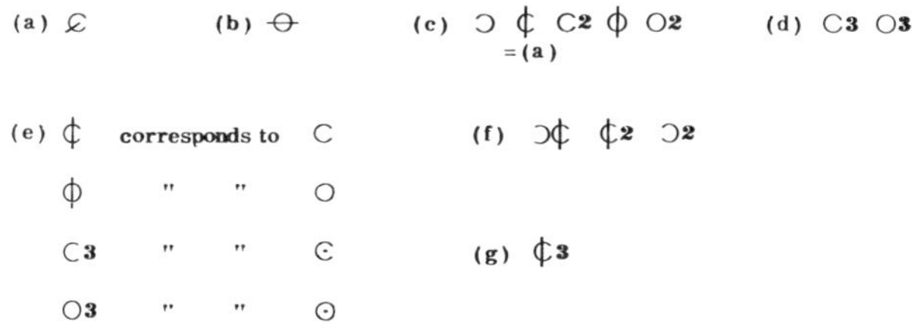

(a) ¢̶   (b) Ꝋ   (c) Ɔ ¢ C2 ɸ O2   (d) C3 O3
             = (a)

(e) ¢   corresponds to   C   (f) Ɔȼ ¢2 Ɔ2

   ɸ   "   "   O

   C3   "   "   Ꞓ   (g) ¢3

   O3   "   "   ⊙

There is no general rule as to whether these modified signs act cumulatively or not: usually they do not, but this varies with the sources. However, when these signs come together (i.e., not separated by music) they act cumulatively to produce a new sign. Two *dupla* signs put together form a sign of *proportio quadrupla*, i.e. diminution by four (Figure 56(f)). There is, however, one common exception to this principle: (g), which should indicate *proportio sextupla* (i.e. diminution by six), normally indicates only *tripla*, or three-fold diminution.

Following the main period of mannerist notation, proportions were used rather less, and generally for one of three purposes:
1. To give an aura of learning. Often the music could have been notated without proportions, but proportions made a notationally more complex piece.
2. To change the speed of a piece from section to section, which is otherwise impossible with a fixed-speed beat.
3. In mensuration-canons.

The third of these brings us to the last major characteristic of mannerist notation. Like proportions, canon is older than the mannerism which used it to excess; also like proportions, it outlived the main movement. The Greek word *kanōn* means a rule or direction. Originally this was a written instruction enabling the performers to derive one or more parts from a single notated part. One of the earliest examples, and perhaps the most famous, is 'Sumer is icumen in', in which the main notated part gives rise to a four-part rota sung above a two-part notated rondellus,[6] a total of six singers being involved. The written instructions are long and in Latin: the notational apparatus, on the other hand, is very small—only the cross in the top part which shows the second and subsequent voices at what stage in the previous singer's part they are to start the tune themselves.

Indeed, canon presupposes no notational apparatus at all:[7] but for most composers, the use of written verbal instructions is not *per se* an acceptable method of making their wishes known, this being precisely what notation avoids. (Any piece of music could, of course, be 'notated' purely by written verbal instructions, but this would be an extremely clumsy way of doing it). Nearly all canons—even those which include fairly precise verbal instructions—therefore make use of notational symbols as a more concise method of giving the necessary directions. Symbols can be used (1) in a fairly normal way to give a specific piece of information, and (2) in an unusual way to hint at a particular method of working that will lead the performer to the correct solution. We shall return to the idea that a 'solution' is necessary.

1. The specific piece of information might be any one of the following:
  the mensuration of both notated and derived parts;
  the starting-pitch of the derived part;
  the ending-note of the derived part.

The mensuration of a canonic part could be shown quite normally by means of a mensuration-sign: but in a mensuration canon (where the same music is sung simultaneously in different metres) more than one mensuration might have to be notated on a single staff, and many notated canonic parts show two or more mensuration-signs together. Normally, the mensuration-signs read from top to bottom in the order of the voice-parts. This notation, with the addition of a repeat-sign, is also used for a single part in which the tune is repeated under a new mensuration.

For showing the starting and ending of a derived part, the sign of congruence (*signum congruentiae*, commonly called simply *signum*) was much used in the fifteenth century, as it was for a number of similar purposes. The sign usually took the form of a narrow 'S' (sometimes reversed), with dots below, .*s*. .*s*. .*ʔ*.; there is also an inverted form, .*ʒ*. . In 'Sumer is icumen in', the cross takes the place of a *signum* for showing the starting-place of the derived voice (in fact, *signa* were not used at all for that purpose so early). Both for the starting-place and for the ending-note of the derived part, all that is needed is a *signum* on or above the staff near the relevant note. In the case of the starting-pitch, however, the *signum* must actually be placed at the correct pitch on the staff.

The last note of a piece was conventionally written as a L until well into the sixteenth century, and the same was often true of main mid-point cadences (e.g. in the middle of one of the medieval *formes fixes*). A performer would therefore be used to holding his final note until all performers reached the end of the piece (it is common for one part to 'arrive' first), and so there is no difficulty in treating any note (marked by a *signum*) as the end of the part.

2. Under the second heading we have fewer examples. Here a normal piece of notation is presented abnormally in such a way as to suggest the basis of the canon. For example, the name of the voice-part may be written as 'Ronet' or 'ɹouǝⸯ' (it is usually the tenor part that suffers this sort of treatment) to indicate that it must be performed in a retrograde or inverted retrograde form. More strictly notational is the use of an inverted clef (in the normal position) to indicate inversion.

Clearly 'canon' meant in the Middle Ages and later far more than in the present century, when it implies only an exactly-imitative texture. It could result in that, of course: but canon usually affected the structure of the music by imposing on it the strictest limitations (often the result of a highly intellectualized approach to composition), presented in a deliberately abstruse or affectedly 'learned' way. Nowhere are the intellectual processes more remarkable than in the extreme examples of mensuration canon, in which the sheer contrapuntal skill of the composer excites admiration.[8] When the work is also of a very high musical quality (as is the case surprisingly often) the result is almost miraculous. In a mensuration canon, incidentally, it is normal for the various voices to begin simultaneously.

Although canon originally implied verbal instruction for the derivation of an additional part or parts, it very soon became something quite different. Many fifteenth-century examples seem to be an elaborate joke played by the composer on his performers, and some are so abstruse that only a prolonged effort of trial and error will provide the correct solution. Of course, a composer was often responsible for his own performances, and could easily suggest the solution verbally. Even so, this deliberate obscurity hid the solution from others, as if there were a necessity to keep music a highly-trained skill to which the uninitiated should not be admitted and whose secrets should not be given away.

Mid-century changes

The foregoing discussions suggest three reasons for the late retention of certain mannerist notational devices:

1. To create an atmosphere of learning. This concerns theorists even more than composers: theoretical treatises included learned discussions of proportions, for instance, when the musical use of

proportions was largely confined to particular types of work (such as keyboard *cantus firmus* settings).

2. More specifically, to foster (or even to create) musical skills which might help to keep music an exclusive profession.

3. Because of a delight in musical puzzles and the visual attractiveness of the sources.

From about 1420 onwards music became rather simpler as mannerism in its most extreme forms disappeared. The new style, apparent in the work of Dufay, is melodically and rhythmically smoother than mannerist music. In fact, the style was not really new at all (it can be seen in much French music of *c.* 1400), but its more general currency allowed a virtual return to the simpler pre-mannerist French notation of Machaut. There are differences, of course, and not only the obvious graphological differences: but in general it is surprising to what extent the later notation can be seen as a direct descendant of French Ars Nova notation.

One example is the use of notational groupings. In the fourteenth century the grouping of notes and rests for rhythmic purposes is seen in both Italian and French sources. Parrish remarks with respect to a piece by Frate Bartholino (NMM, 177 and plates LVI-LVII, fourteenth century) that the necessity for the dot of division 'is obviated by . . . the careful and appropriate grouping of notes by the scribe'. He could have made a similar comment about his plates XLVII (part of the Machaut Mass) and LVIII (Gherardello's *Sotto verdi fraschetti*). In the latter there are no dots of division, as would be normal in Italian notation: instead, a slightly larger space between notes shows where the division occurs. The extra space is obvious in the sections in *senaria imperfecta* and *perfecta*, but is not obvious at first glance in the opening section. As is usually the case, the opening has no mensuration-sign: but the spacing shows it to be in quaternaria (not, as Parrish says, in octonaria).

Grouping may be of rhythmic significance in either of two basic ways:

1. Apel (NPM, 111) formulates a rule for the rests in a 'dead' interval (between phrases or sub-phrases) in ○ time: when a B is followed by two S-rests (i) if they are on different stave-lines, the first imperfects the B and the second belongs to the next perfection (Figure 57(a)); or (ii) if they are on the same line, the B is perfect and both rests belong to the next perfection (b). This rule applies also to M-rests following a S in major prolation. Often the visual separation over the dead interval is so great as to leave the singer no choice (c).

2. The second example at (c)—marked (x)—shows also the other means used, horizontal separation. In some manuscripts the note-groups are separated by spaces, often merely confirming what the rules would dictate anyway (though not invariably so), but making unnecessary even the cautionary use of a dot of division. In (d), for example, the grouping of the notes prevents any possibility of imperfection of the Ss (N.B. this is a void-notation manuscript).

Figure 57. Rhythmic Note-Groupings

(Madrid, Escorial Palace, MS V . III . 24 . f . 59v)

(Cambridge, University Library, Add. MS 5943, f. 163v)

Fifteenth-century sources show these visual groupings more than earlier ones do. There are, I think, two main reasons for their use:
1. it is clearer, and more quickly written, than a more liberal use of dots of division; and
2. it assumes that the singer is less capable than before of reading many notes at a time and deciding their rhythm.

In general, it is probably true to say that fifteenth-century scribes tried to communicate music more directly than before, especially by the application of principles which are visual rather than legalistic. Indeed, 'easy to read' is a modern phrase which describes fifteenth-century notation, a description that is supported by certain new notational ideas in the latter half of the century.

Before these new ideas are discussed, we must see how 'easy to read' applied. A scribe writing a book in the Middle Ages followed certain principles which made the book more easily assimilable by the reader (chapter-heads clearly marked by headings and coloured initials; no two adjacent lines ending or starting with the same word, to avoid confusion), and music scribes had similar techniques for directing a singer's eye and mind. In 'Sumer is icumen in', for instance, the two texts are differentiated by colour (red for the Latin and black for the English, in this case); a three-part piece (e.g. in the fourteenth-century 'Fountains Fragment') might have the middle part written in red (no rhythmical significance here, of course); fifteenth-century sources use red notation to distinguish sections to be sung by soloists, or as an extra warning that proportions are in operation.[9] The use of colour to distinguish a middle part occurs again, strangely enough, in the sixteenth century, both for the voice-part in vihuela-songs (see Chapter 11) and in English keyboard music (where the 'meane' part is sometimes in black coloration).[10] The 'colour for clarity' principle was certainly not in common use, but it was a general principle over a period of nearly three centuries.

I have suggested above with respect to the use of the 'swallowtail' that scribes in the fourteenth century did not assume complete competence in their singers. Throughout the fifteenth century this attitude increased, and it can be seen in a variety of ways: in the continuing use of (strictly unnecessary) numerals; in a number of new notational aids; in the continued use of visual groupings; and in the introduction (or re-introduction) of certain types of notation which facilitate the reading of pitch or rhythm.

The use of numerals to warn the singer of a note's duration is seen throughout the century. The most commonly used are 2 and 3, to show that a note is imperfect/altered or perfect respectively: but higher numbers are also found, particularly in tenor parts, where ligatures and long note-values sometimes caused imperfection by remote values and where the ligatures themselves caused difficulties of evaluation. These numerals, being placed normally above or below the relevant note (see Figure 58), will not be confused with the proportional signs 2 and 3, which appear in the middle of the staff. In the early sixteenth century the same signs were used (normally below the first note) at the beginning of a passage of triplets (3) or duplets (2). Confusion is usually prevented here by the context, or by the use of coloration for such passages.

The writing of void notation (see below) is if anything a more laborious process than that of black, and this is especially noticeable in ligatures. Indeed, the change to void notation probably contributed to the gradual elimination of ligatures. In the vocal music of the period, especially in the non-melismatic settings, only the two-note S-ligature is at all common: this is relatively quickly written, and was often useful in clarifying the underlay, a ligature taking no more than a single syllable. Longer ligatures are of course found, particularly in tenor parts, where there are often no words to be considered and where the use of ligatures was in any case traditional. The 17-note ligature at the beginning of 'O praeclara stella maris' in the Glogauer book (Ringmann ii, no. 5) is by no means unusual even in the second half of the century, and long ligatures are found even from the late sixteenth century. On the whole, however, we may regard these as the results of conservatism—of tradition—and perhaps sometimes of that wish to appear 'learned' which we have noted at various points in this chapter.

We have seen that the problems of musical literacy in the late Middle Ages concern not only the rhythmic interpretation of a group of notes but also the number of notes which must be read before any interpretation can be started; and I suggested that on both counts French notation was found preferable to Italian notation from 1375 or so onwards. The trends under consideration in this section point to the growing need for a notation whose 'signposts' or points of rhythmic reference are close together (more frequent, perhaps, even than the end of adjacent perfections). There is also a growing necessity, at least in keyboard score and in tablatures, to mark the perfections or other 'measures'. Regular bar-lines are found in the early fifteenth-century Faenza manuscript (MSD 10), and in that century became normal for keyboard music. In the Locheimer Liederbuch we find bar-lines in red, perhaps in recognition of their purely practical (rather than strictly musical) function in the vertical alignment of two or more parts. Practicality is characteristic also of the cancellation of accidentals, unnecessary until the fifteenth century, since a singer apparently knew how long any accidental remained in force. The use of the sign $\mathfrak{f}$ (just before a note F) to cancel an F sharp is not uncommon in the fifteenth and sixteenth centuries, and by analogy $\mathfrak{c}$ was used to cancel a C sharp.

In the second half of the century we find some attempts to overcome problems of notating pitch and rhythm by means of more or less radical change. One piece in the Glogauer Song Book (*c.* 1480) uses heighted text-syllables to show the pitch of the lower part: the text is written straight on to a six-line staff, with a C-clef showing the pitch. As the upper part is notated conventionally, it is hard to see what advantage this offered, especially as the rhythm is not notated (Figure 73(b)). Of much more importance is the use of simple orthochronic notations *c.* 1450–*c.* 1550 (see Chapter 7). Figure 58 shows an example of stroke notation from the Locheimer Liederbuch, in which numerals are used for the long notes: this whole page is, however, interesting also because these numbered Ls later give way to groups of six Ss. Here the scribe really seems not to trust the singer at all.

Figure 58. Stroke-Notation and Numerals

(Berlin, Staatsbibliothek Preussische Kulturbesitz, Mus. MS 40613, p. 44)

Void notation

The most obvious notational revolution of the fifteenth century was the use of outline (void) note-forms for normal notation. There is no real notational difference between full black notation and the 'white' notation which eventually took its place. The rests remained the same as before, as did most auxiliary symbols such as *custodes*, time-signatures, etc., while the notes and clefs gave way to exact equivalents (Figure 59(a)). The Trinity Carol Roll (Cambridge, Trinity College, MS 0.3.58), a fairly early example of void notation, used full red coloration, but full black coloration was normal. This disappearance of red notes (no doubt a welcome simplification for the scribes) severely limited the possibilities for the smaller note-values (cf. Figure 52). At first the flagged Sm was used, with an extra flag added for the F (Figure 59(b), upper line). In the end, these forms were superseded by the colored forms (lower line of (b)), which needed only two flags for the *semifusa* (Sf) when that became necessary. When we compare these note-shapes with their modern equivalents (c) it becomes clear

Figure 59. Void Notation

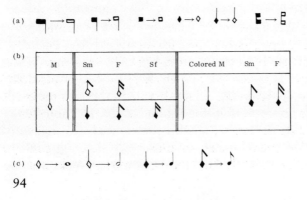

94

that our C is in fact a Sm of the colored M type, with the colored series extended to smaller values.

The circumstances of the change to void notation are still debated. Wolf's theory that the use of paper forced scribes to adopt void notation in about 1450 was discredited as to dating by Bukofzer (*Studies*, 92–6); Brian Trowell has since dated the change from 'the 1420s', ascribing the use of void notation to an attempt to minimize the spluttering effect of a pen writing on a rough paper surface (Robertson and Stevens, *Pelican History* ii, 66 f); more recently, Margaret Bent has concluded that void notation may have been an English innovation and that the earliest examples of it may date from the very beginning of the century ('The Transmission of English Music', 77 f). Both of Bent's conclusions must surely be sound (see the note to BMS 1).

On the question of the reason for the change, however, more needs to be said. It is well known that void notation sources do not always use paper, and that black notation is not invariably on parchment, so that the paper/void, parchment/black distinction is not wholly valid; it is also well known that some void-notation sources are early (e.g. the Cambridge song book and the Trinity Roll), while some black notation sources are very late (e.g. the Eton, Lambeth and Caius choir-books, which are dated *c.* 1500–10; and the Mass 'O Quam Suavis', *c.* 1500, in Cambridge University Library). Further, it is obvious that those manuscripts which are very beautifully decorated are on parchment because that is a better medium for the use of paints, gold leaf, etc., than paper is, as regards both the surface to be worked on and the permanence of the medium itself (paper tears easily). This explains why certain manuscripts using white notation (such as the Trinity Roll early in the century, and the Mellon and Cordiforme chansonniers later) are nevertheless written on parchment. Conversely, the four late choir-books that I cited above use black notation because it is more legible for a large choir gathered round the book; and they use parchment not only because of the decoration, etc., but also because of the page-size. Paper leaves of that size, especially subjected to regular use by a choir, would not survive long. What, then, is the difference between the two groups of manuscripts that I have cited? All are on parchment, all are decorated: but it is the small soloist sources that are in void notation, and the large choir-books that use black. I have, of course, chosen the extremes to make my point, and among the medium-sized manuscripts there are some in white notation that are slightly larger than some in black. But the principle holds, I think: the sources in smaller format require a finely-cut pen for the text, and void notation allows the same pen (or one similarly cut) to be used for the music.

The adoption of black void notation caused no basic change of notational principles. There are, however, some contexts involving coloration in which a mechanical symbol-for-symbol copying from black notation into void will not suffice. An imperfect rest written in red cannot be distinguished as a colored rest when the music is copied into void notation: hence a red B-rest in ○ time must be re-written as two S-rests, and so on (Bent, 'The Transmission of English Music', 78). Figure 60(a) shows this.

With the increasing use of smaller note-values, too, the colored forms of Sm and F caused ambiguities that had not previously been a problem. In (b), an incomplete coloration group is written where we might expect a complete hemiola grouping. Strictly speaking, the two Ms preceding the colored Ss should also be colored, to prevent alteration of the second—a notation which would almost certainly have resulted in the colored Ms being read as Sms. As it is, the singer is unlikely to take all three Ms together as a perfection, thus leaving two colored Ss by themselves: and a dot of division after the first M would invite alteration of the third. On the whole, the scribe's solution here is probably the simplest and least confusing. In the same piece (see BMS 1) we find a coloration group in one voice against an uncolored group in the other (c), as if the latter were synonymous with the colored version that we expect (d). Presumably the scribe decided that the risk of a singer reading the colored Ms as Sms was too great: or (as is more likely in both (b) and (c), I think) he was unwilling to spend time filling in note-heads unnecessarily.

Figure 60. Problems of Coloration

(Cambridge, University Library,
Add. MS 5943, f. 164v)

(Ibid.)

96

7. The Age of Transition

The revolution in durational measurement

It is often dangerous to speak of an historical period as 'transitional'. Nevertheless, the sixteenth century can usefully be regarded as such for our purposes, in that its notation tends towards a radically new concept of durational measurement. This concept, which we may call 'additive mensuration', gave rise to 'orthochronic' notation. 'Orthochronic' means 'showing the correct time': the word was used by Jacques Chailley (in *Les notations musicales nouvelles*), with reference to the period since 1600, to describe notation in which the various symbols correctly represent durations relative to one another. According to orthochronic principles the relationship between, say, a M and a S is constant: that is, any M bears the same relation to a S as any other M. The same is true for other values. It follows that the twin principles of alteration and imperfection are destroyed by orthochronic measurement, since they require each note-shape to have more than one possible value. Consequently, such notational auxiliaries as the dots of perfection and syncopation are no longer necessary. In short, an orthochronic notation solves the rhythmic problems—the real notational difficulty of the Middle Ages—by elimination.

The concept eliminated was that of triple mensuration, which largely disappeared during the sixteenth century, leaving almost all music in the duple measurement that we have used ever since. By 'duple measurement' I mean here that in the new hierarchy of note-values each value could be only twice that of the next value below. Hence there could only be two Ms in a S, two Ss in a B, and so on. There is of course no over-riding reason why an orthochronic notation should be based solely on duple measurement, and it is probably an accident of history that that direction was taken. Medieval rests, after all, are orthochronic (Figures 35 and 47, above). None of the earliest uses of the orthochronic principle relied wholly on duple measurement: all, however, required the general principle of additive rhythm.

Like all historical transitions, this one is not clearly defined at either end: indeed, Chailley's view that the change from mensural to orthochronic notation can be fixed for practical purposes at about 1600 assumes an accuracy of historical definition that is quite impossible. The roots of orthochronic notation go back to the middle of the fifteenth century, and we can recognize some of its important characteristics in much earlier music. At the other end of the transition, the tendency towards orthochronic notation was largely complete by the turn of the seventeenth century (which is one reason why the year 1600 is a convenient dividing-point between Parts I and IV of this book): yet the remains of medieval notational principles were usefully employed as late as the middle of the seventeenth century and, as we shall see, the problems caused by triple mensurations in conjunction with orthochronic principles can be seen as late as the nineteenth century. The transition, then, was not a direct substitution of the new system for the old, but something much less orderly over a long period of time. As a result, notation in the middle of the transition often presents a mixture of old and new features, symptomatic of old and new ways of thinking. Before these features are described, however, we must discuss the abstract concepts of durational measurement that gave rise to them.

Additive and divisive rhythm

In ascribing the rise of orthochronic notation to a new concept of 'additive mensuration' at the end of the Middle Ages I have contradicted the views of Curt Sachs, who believed that the rhythmic revolution *c*. 1400–1600 was due to a change from additive to divisive rhythmic organization (*Rhythm and Tempo*, p. 92). Sachs regarded duple metres, which are essentially regular and symmetrically divisible, as multiplicative or divisive: a $\frac{4}{4}$ bar can be divided by two several times to give smaller (and regular) units, while a $\frac{6}{8}$ bar is demonstrably twice a $\frac{3}{8}$ bar (though the stresses are not equal). Ternary metres occupy a mid-point, though inclining strongly to the additive side: they could be regarded as 3×1 (and so at first sight are divisive), but are nearly always in practice either iambic (1 + 2) or trochaic (2 + 1) (op. cit., 168). Such metres as $\frac{5}{4}$ or $^{3+3+2}_{8}$ Sachs regarded as additive, since they are not susceptible to the halving which he considered the hall-mark of divisive rhythm. When he considered the primary position of ternary metres in medieval music and the change to duple measurement during the sixteenth century, Sachs felt justified in regarding the change as from additive to divisive measurement.

This theory was based on Sachs's work as an ethnomusicologist, in which he used the idea of breathing (asymmetrical, additive) and walking (symmetrical, divisive) as generators of rhythmic principles. Clearly, it has much to recommend it. We need not dispute the additive nature of the asymmetrical groupings which form the metres of Bulgarian folk music, for instance, and his definitions are acceptable as far as they go. But one cannot help being suspicious of the assumption that a theory developed in relation to the monodic (though often polyrhythmic) music of various eastern peoples can be usefully applied to the polyphony of western Europe. Sachs considered most music to have elements of both additive and divisive principles, but he did not adequately explore the relations between them in the various rhythmic levels to be found in complex medieval polyphony (op. cit., pp. 168 f.). Instead, he quickly turned to non-musical examples of supposed additive thinking in an attempt to support his thesis by means of analogies. Unfortunately, these examples confirm the logical inadequacy of his thesis as applied to western culture. In discussing the west front of Notre Dame cathedral in Paris, for instance, he noted the rows of statues ('which the French so aptly call *registres*') and remarked that they 'all add up to sets and rows'. This is perfectly true at one level of perception: but if we are talking about the *construction* of the building then the verb 'add up to' is inaccurate and begs the important question (and the same is true of '*registres*'). For if this were really an example of additive organization, we must suppose the dimensions of this west front to have been decided by the number of statues to go on it, and that if there had been more kings of Judah the whole building would have been larger in consequence. This is clearly nonsense, and it stems from a confusion of structure with decoration. Those responsible for the statues knew the dimensions of the proposed west front and, knowing also the number of statues to be accommodated on it, accordingly disposed those statues in orderly ranks across it. The west front decoration of Notre Dame is organized divisively, not additively.

Now, the relation between structure and decoration in music could indeed be explained as an analogy to that shown by the west front of Notre Dame: but Sachs does not give such an explanation, and in any case, as we have seen, the direct analogy that he assumes leads him to a false conclusion in this non-musical example. In view of this, we must ourselves explore the uses of additive and divisive organization in medieval and immediately post-medieval music. We shall take into account that the existence of written music and a related body of theoretical writings may indicate a different mental approach to rhythmic organization from that found in unwritten traditions, even when the musical result is similar. We can use Sachs's basic definitions, but we must examine different levels of mensural organization as independent systems. On the other hand, it seems reasonable to ignore multiplicative rhythm altogether as a type distinct from divisive and additive rhythm. Sachs first treated it as synonymous with divisive rhythm: later it was dropped altogether, although his discussion of ternary metres had suggested that his theory would require it as something separate. No doubt it would be possible to develop an argument along the lines of Sachs's discussion in which all three types were used, but a consideration of western notation indicates that for our purposes, at least, it would be better to discuss additive and divisive rhythm without considering the third category.

We shall begin by examining the rhythmic structure of music notated modally, *c.* 1180–*c.* 1250. At the level of the L and above, the organization seems to be additive: it is normal for the Ls to group themselves in twos, but it is also quite possible for an extra L to be added in, causing a $\frac{9}{8}$ bar in a modern transcription predominantly in $\frac{6}{8}$. At this stage there was no theoretical discussion of the D as a divisible unit: and moreover, as Sachs himself pointed out (op. cit., pp. 170, 162), the strict rhythmic organization by *ordines* is additive. (This constitutes something of a weakness in his theory, since he insisted on the divisive nature of duple metres.) On the other hand, those modes requiring a two-beat pattern (III and IV) do presuppose a fixed duple unit broken up into Ls and Bs, and therefore a divisive organization.

The relationship between L and B is a less straightforward matter. Odington, writing *c.* 1300, states that the L originally had the value of two Bs, the perfect L being a later development (*De Speculatione Musicae*, ed. Huff, p. 8). The reason for this, apparently, was that musical rhythmic theory paralleled poetic metrical theory. In origin, then, the perfect L would result from grouping a L (two *tempora*, for a long syllable) and a B (one *tempus*, for a short syllable), an additive process. One way of regarding poetic metres would indeed be to see the individual foot as composed of a grouping of long and short syllables. But, looked at from a higher organizational level, it is more likely that accentuation was the primary constructional force with a subsequent division of each foot. In music, in any case, there is good evidence that this latter, divisive, view is the correct one: for as soon as we reach those modes that require two Bs together (III and IV) we find that the second B of the pair must be altered. Now, it does not make sense to regard as additive the organization of elements which depend on division for their existence, and the altered B certainly owes its existence to its context in the three-*tempora* unit as a whole. Thus the relationship of L to B must be divisive. Odington took the same view, apparently, for he speaks of resolving a perfect L into three Bs ('Longa igitur perfecta potest resolvi in tres breves': CS I, 235; translated by Huff, p. 9).

In the later Ars Antiqua period, *c.* 1250–*c.* 1320, some of these features are repeated. Again, Odington speaks of 'resolving' the B into Ss (loc. cit.), and a comparison of Master Lambert's work (*c.* 1275) with that of Franco (*c.* 1280) supports Odington's statement that the B was at first divided into two Ss and only later into three. Once more the question of alteration arises. Is it reasonable to regard the B-S relationship as additive? Surely not.

With Ars Nova rhythmic theory, *c.* 1320 onwards, we are conscious of a strongly divisive approach. In French music, the alternative duple and triple components of the L, B and S suggest divisive organization, as does the extension of the principle of alteration to the M (seen in an early form in the writing of Odington, as noted at the end of Chapter 4). Indeed, the extension of this system of dual measurement also to the higher levels brought both the L-B relationship (modus, not wholeheartedly either additive or divisive in Ars Antiqua theory) and the D-L relationship (maximodus, certainly additive) into an organization that could be described only in divisive terms. In theory, even the highest metrical levels acquired the same flexibility as the lower levels (Jean de Muris starts his system with a triplex L: GS III, 295, and Strunk SR, 177). In practice, however, maximode was rarely perfect, and it mattered little that the triplex L was hardly more than a theoretical value (see Apel NPM, 124 and 404). The concept of divisive organization is at the heart of the use of coloration-groups for hemiola rhythms, etc. Practically, this concept would have been preserved by the choir-master's technique of beating a regular *tactus* against which any irregular rhythms (such as might be notated by coloration) would be sung. The remains of this divisive concept can be clearly seen as late as the English madrigalian repertory: Figure 61 shows the opening of Tomkins's 'See, see the shepherds' queen' as edited by E. H. Fellowes (a) and as felt according to the tactus (b) (and how much more subtle is Tomkins's accentuation heard to be when sung according to the stresses that (b) implies).

Figure 61. The Divisive Concept

Obviously, the Italian system of *divisiones*—the metrical organization of notes within a unit valued at a B—is also a divisive one.

At the same time, the deliberate and comprehensively speculative nature of Ars Nova theory should warn us not to take all this quite at face value. A more careful consideration shows that Ars Nova theory did not in fact eliminate additive features entirely. As we noted earlier, maximodus was hardly more than a theoretical metre. Although the musical result of it could be obtained, the triplex L was rare and this metrical level was normally reached additively, through a succession of Ds and Ls. In practice, this meant that a whole perfection in maximodus would not be expressed by a single note, but only by a D plus a L-rest, or by two or more notes. Thomas Morley's inclusion of a triplex L in the metrical scheme set out in *A Plain and Easy Introduction* of 1597 (ed. Harman, p. 25) is far too late for any practical usage.

More important, however, was the increasing use of low-level additive techniques in the notation of the fourteenth and fifteenth centuries. In late fourteenth-century Italian music we find an additive use of note-stems (Figure 42(c)), which suggests a change of outlook. But the Italian method does in any case have a built-in additive element. Since the S (i.e. one half or one third of a B) is the unit of equivalence, the B is longer in perfect time than in imperfect time: hence the B-unit which is to be divided up is itself a variable unit, the ternary B being produced by adding a S to the binary B. A strong feeling of this additive relationship would be experienced by a singer performing Figure 39, for example, where the B in quaternaria is followed by one in senaria perfecta which looks the same but is in fact half as long again.

102

In French notation, too, there are additive elements. As we have already seen, the note-by-note addition of small and invariable values could create a syncopation not only within the 'measure' of a B but actually crossing the boundaries between B-groups. This results in syncopation across the modern bar-line, which in perfect time could be effected in larger note-values only by means of coloration or dots of syncopation (cf. Figures 46(d), 49 and 50). Small-value syncopation depends on the duple mensuration of the values concerned. Indeed, this additive type of syncopation is possible at any level governed by duple measurement, and therefore at all levels in C -time: it is the ambiguity of values in ternary measurement—those values that can be either perfect or imperfect—that may make it impossible.

All of the foregoing suggests that divisive rhythm and predominantly ternary measurement go together, as do additive rhythm and duple measurement. This being so, it is natural that some of the most interesting manifestations of the additive principle are found in the music of the period 1450–1600, when ternary measurement disappeared. These symptoms of additive thinking fall into two broad categories: first, minor notational features and the special orthochronic notations; second, certain experiments in metrical organization. As regards the former, the orthochronic notations known as 'stroke' and 'strene' notation merit separate discussion in the next section. The two-tailed idea of Italian Ars Nova notation was revived (or re-invented), and can be seen in the tablature of Fridolin Sicher, *c.* 1525 (see Apel NPM, 31 f). In this manuscript two stems on the same note-head signify a note of double length (Figure 62(a)): the stems both point upwards at an angle, in contrast to those of Italian usage (Figure 42(c)). Sicher's use of this principle is deliberately orthochronic, for he uses a different notation (b) for the perfect S.

Figure 62. An Additive Note-Shape

In the sixteenth century the principle of additive rhythm made readily available a number of metres that had been hardly more than theoretical possibilities before. Alwood's quintuple rhythms in the mass 'Praise him praiseworthy' is a good example, as is the $\frac{11}{4}$ In Nomine of Bull. Such devices could be used in conjunction with proportional metres, and Bull's piece uses a different metre for the last section. The designation '$\frac{11}{4}$' is not, as a matter of fact, very accurate for this work: it is not really in $^{4+4+3}_4$, as appears at first sight, but in $^{2+2+3}_2$, for the beat is the M, not the C, as the time-signature ₵ shows. In the final section the beat is changed to the dotted M and the metre altered accordingly to the corresponding composite metre, $^{6+6+9}_4$. The result of additive thinking, indeed (Figure 63(a)).[1]

Figure 63. Additive Metres

(Cambridge, Fitzwilliam Museum, Music MS 168, p. 220: the Fitzwilliam Virginal Book. See FWVB ii, 38–9)

Voy - ci le verd et beau may

(Jacques Mauduit; from Expert, *Maitres musiciens* xi, p. 16)

Additive rhythm could equally well be used to form metrical patterns less regular even than what I have called the 'composite metre' of Bull's In Nomine. There is no reason, in fact, why the rhythms should not be so variable as to make the word 'metre' irrelevant. This is the main characteristic of the *musique mesurée* written by members of Baïf's academy *c.* 1570–1600, in which the long and short syllables of the text are set to long and short notes, respectively, the long being twice the short (Figure 63(b)). The poetic quantities are thus allowed to determine the music's rhythm, creating a metrically flexible line in which no one metre can be seen as the basis of the construction. This approach was not new: it went back at least as far as the settings of Horace published by Peter Tritonius in 1507,

104

and the idea was taken up by Senfl, Hofhaimer and Celtes, among others, before Baïf's time (Reese MR, 705 and 747). It is hardly necessary to point out that *musique mesurée* proceeds additively not only from one measure to the next but even from note to note. At the beginning of a measure we do not know whether the grouping will be ternary or duple: and if the second note is a M, we do not know until the third note whether that second note is the end of a group of four Cs or the start of a group of three (Figure 63(c)).

Early orthochronic notations

The early orthochronic notations known as 'stroke' and 'strene' notation are found in the very middle of the orthochronic revolution: stroke notation was most used in the second half of the fifteenth century, strene notation in the first half of the sixteenth. They have in common that they are both, apparently, deliberate attempts to devise an orthochronic method at a time when triple mensuration and its attendant problems could still cause difficulties to singers with limited experience or training. Other features that they have in common are:
1. They are related to the notation and repertory of chant, though in ways not yet fully explored;
2. They are often found in sources (and even pieces) which also use conventional notation;
3. They depend on duple measurement; and
4. Both fell out of use when general acceptance of duple measurement in conventional notation made them unnecessary.
As will become apparent, however, there are also some important differences between them, and they deserve separate study.[2]

'Stroke notation' strictly speaking refers only to a few late fifteenth-century pieces in which pitch is shown on a staff by means of short vertical strokes rather than notes. Duration is represented on a wholly additive basis. Each stroke stands for a S, the beat: two strokes together at the same pitch are to be performed as a single note of double length, three such strokes as a note of triple length, and so on (Figure 64(a)). This principle was also used, however, in music notated with normal note-heads, either black or void. These latter forms are now included in the term 'stroke notation', even though they do not use strokes. For convenience, the three types may be referred to as 'true', 'full' and 'void stroke notation', respectively. All three are especially suitable for the notation of long notes, and therefore of tenor parts, since it is in the higher note-values that triple metre caused problems. The smaller note-values had to be expressed in normal notation, of course, so that music which uses stroke notation may be written this way in the tenor but in conventional notation in the upper part, or a mixture of the two notations may be found throughout the texture.

The full and void forms of stroke notation are older than true stroke notation. The notes of the full form often bear a marked graphic similarity to the distropha and tristropha of fifteenth-century chant notation. As a matter of fact, it is very likely that the interpretation of the plainsong distropha and tristropha had changed by the fifteenth century, the continued use of a simpler notation (square or Gothic) having resulted in a simplified performance in which these neumes were sung as a single longer note. If so, the relationship between neumes and stroke notation is indeed close. This is supported by a very interesting item discussed by More ('The Performance of Plainsong', 131 and plate 4), a version of Credo IV, the Credo Cardinale, from a Dutch gradual of the late fifteenth or early sixteenth century. The manuscript is notated in Gothic neumes (i.e. with rhombic puncta): but this one piece is fully mensural, with the punctum (semibreve) as the beat and a double-length note shown by a distropha (Figure 64(b)). Shorter notes are written as minims.

Figure 64. Stroke Notation

(See also Figure 58)

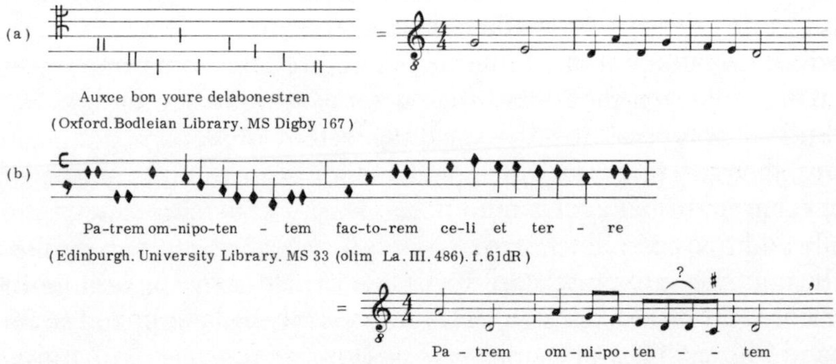

(a)

Auxce bon youre delabonestren

(Oxford. Bodleian Library. MS Digby 167)

(b)

Pa-trem om-nipo-ten - tem fac-to-rem ce-li et ter - re

(Edinburgh. University Library. MS 33 (olim La. III. 486). f. 61dR)

Pa - trem om - ni-po - ten - - tem

It is too early in the study of stroke notation to rely very much on speculation, however. One type of notation might very easily borrow the graphic forms of another without there being a closer relationship.

Moreover, there is some evidence for the stroke-notation principle early in the fourteenth century, using mensural symbols entirely. The Robertsbridge manuscript (for which see Chapter 10) uses a strange grouping in which one or more void Bs follow a normal black B at the same pitch. Opinion is divided on the meaning of this, but it is certainly possible that notes of double and triple length are intended (Parrish NMM, plate LXI and p. 184; Apel NPM, 38–40; Caldwell, *English Keyboard Music*, p. 8). If so, then this, the earliest known example of the stroke-notation principle, distinguishes graphically between the first beat of the sounded note and its continuation. This distinction is not made in fifteenth-century stroke notations, and it is one of the problems in transcribing them: for unless the notes are carefully grouped it is impossible to decide whether a single long note is intended, or two shorter notes of the same pitch.

Margaret Bent has pointed out that this potential (and usually actual) ambiguity may be responsible for some variant versions between concordances ('New and Little-known Fragments', p. 149). It may also have been partly responsible for the notation's disappearance: but the main reason for stroke notation's failure is probably that it is inflexible compared with the conventional notation on which it relies (and in which it usually finds itself embedded) and, used by itself, cannot notate the more complex rhythms. My own view of its origins is that the fifteenth-century interpretations of the bistropha and tristropha were transferred to mensural notation proper. It is almost a necessary corollary to this that the Robertsbridge notation is not an early example of stroke-notation principles, though this could certainly be argued separately.[3]

'Strene' notation takes its name from one of its note-shapes, a plica form with two downward tails. The sources using it are few and, as far as is known at present, exclusively English.[4] 'Strene' was apparently the English vernacular term for a plica as used in chant in the fifteenth century, but in strene notation this note-shape represents only a single note.

The notation is explained by Merbecke in *The booke of Common praier noted* (1550: R/1979): it uses particular shapes to signify the B, S, M and a note with a pause which 'is a close, and is only used at the end of a verse' (Figure 65). The S may be followed by a dot which 'is halfe as muche as the note that goeth before it' (Merbecke BCPN, sig. Aii[r]). This use of the dot of augmentation suggests that strene notation is truly mensural even when (as here) it is used in chant.

Figure 65. Strene Notation

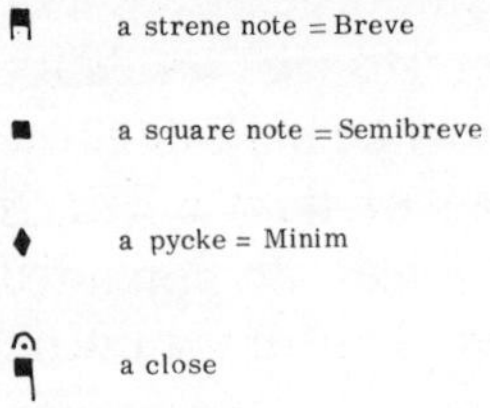

◨   a strene note = Breve

■   a square note = Semibreve

◆   a pycke = Minim

⌒
◨   a close

The characteristics of strene notation may be tabulated as follows:
1. It is fully mensural.
2. It is orthochronic.
3. It uses duple measurement.
4. It relies on value-substitution, the note-shapes being interpreted in diminution.
5. It has a very limited range of note-values.
In respect of the last of these, it is interesting to note that the strene notation in the Ritson Manuscript version of the Power/Dunstable 'Salve Regina' transmits a *simplified* version of the chorus sections (Benham, 'Salve Regina'). As regards no. 4, a comparison of Figure 65 with Figure 13 will show that the diminished notation of the former actually coincides with the note-values of chant apparently performed in a stylized speech-rhythm.[5] Although these characteristics raise many interesting questions that cannot be discussed here, the characteristics themselves are clear. Strene notation is a simple orthochronic notation that can have had little to recommend it after the middle of the sixteenth century.

Ternary metres

The change to wholly duple measurement greatly simplified notational practice. The elimination of the possibility of there being three of any note-value contained in the next higher value gave to the entire mensural system all the advantages of the old Ars Nova metre of C -time.[6] The dots of perfection and syncopation being unnecessary, the dot could be used freely and exclusively as a dot of addition; and additive syncopation was available at all levels. Any wholly duple metre could be notated precisely as before.

With the simple metre that grouped beats into threes—that is, what we should now transcribe as $\frac{3}{4}$ time—the situation was hardly more difficult. The division of the beat caused no problems. The grouping of beats was done additively, and required only one new idea: that was, that a complete 'measure' of three beats would be notated by a dotted note (two beats + (half of two beats)) standing alone. (From now on, 'dotted note' refers to a note with a dot of addition attached.) Until that time a dotted note had always implied a following note or group of notes which would complement the dot. It took some time for the dotted note standing alone to be acceptable. Even quite late in the sixteenth century the undotted note was often preferred as the notation for three beats (or indeed for any 'perfection'), and in this way the old idea of perfections and perfect notes was continued. Figure 66(a) shows the end of 'Divinum mysterium' from *Piae Cantiones*, 1582, R/1967. The metre is ○ —the given time-signature is 3 —so that both of the asterisked Bs are three-beat notes. According to the principles of duple measurement both should be dotted, but they are easily read as 'perfect' notes in the old system. The final L, too, should be dotted, according to the newer practice. Its immunity at this stage might be due partly to its conventional (and therefore extra-metrical) use at the end of a piece: but in fact the L is elsewhere used undotted at the end of a mid-piece phrase ((b), from 'Autor humani').

Figure 66. Triple Mensuration in the Sixteenth Century

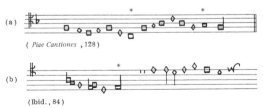

(a)

(*Piae Cantiones* , 128)

(b)

(Ibid., 84)

At the next mensural level down, however, this new use of the dotted note standing alone demanded a much greater mental adjustment. In the medieval system the dotted note had always represented a multiple of three beats, or $1\frac{1}{2}$ beats, or $1\frac{1}{2}$ times some fraction of a beat that could be notated as a single note. (I ignore ligatures, for my present purpose: they bring nothing new to this discussion.) The beat itself had always been an undotted note. This, however, could no longer be the case for a beat which was itself ternary: since the undotted note would represent only two-thirds of a beat, a dot of addition was needed to make up the full beat. This meant that ₵, ⊙ and their later equivalents (i.e. using the M, C or quaver (Q) as the beat)—the metres that would now be transcribed as $\frac{12}{8}$, $\frac{6}{8}$ and $\frac{9}{8}$—had to use a dotted note as the beat. This solution was eventually accepted, but the clumsiness of our 'compound metres' is such that they are rather awkward in use. Indeed, various notational conventions were used at different times to avoid notating compound metres: the later examples of this belong to Part IV, and will be described there, but there is also a feature of early seventeenth-century music that is relevant here.

Coloration survived well into the seventeenth century. With its old function of notating a hemiola rhythm it no doubt continued to be useful, if only as confirmation of the rhythm shown by undotted notes. Probably performers needed such an assurance for many years after the undotted 'perfect' note had ceased to be used. However, it would be only fair to ascribe to early seventeenth-century musicians some sensitivity above that to mere duration: if coloration had previously implied a change of stress, then it would no doubt carry accentual implications in the early baroque, too.

This is certainly the case with minor color. Composers at the turn of the seventeenth century enjoyed playing with related metres, and not least with the proportional relationships to be found in triple metres. Until the new system should be fully formed, some of the old-system notational techniques would serve them best. In particular, use of color to show three in the time of two would allow an undotted note as the beat, and would also imply a slightly faster speed. Donington (IEM, 655) discusses an example from *Parthenia In Violata* (c. 1614), but he misses these two points. The Fitzwilliam Virginal Book is full of this notation, which Tregian often used for music in a fast triple time. Both frontispieces to the edition show this notation, and it occurs at two levels. Figure 67(a) shows the opening of an anonymous jig (no. CCXI: ii, frontispiece and 274): the notation of the tied Ms is found throughout the manuscript.

Another example of minor color appears in the Turpyn Book version of Dowland's 'Can she excuse my wrongs' (BMS 2, f. 1v). Here the colored notation does not imply a faster metre, but is used simply to distinguish a *change* of metre ($\frac{3}{2}$ to $\frac{3}{4}$, in modern terms) from syncopation. There is also hemiola rhythm, giving the feeling of $\frac{3}{4}$. Figure 67(b) shows the main $\frac{3}{2}$ metre (*), syncopation (†), hemiola (**) and the new metre (‡): the rhythm-flags of the lute part are given under the vocal line. The barring is original.

This last use of color is of course strictly unnecessary, for the rhythms could be notated orthochronically without recourse to

Figure 67. Late Coloration

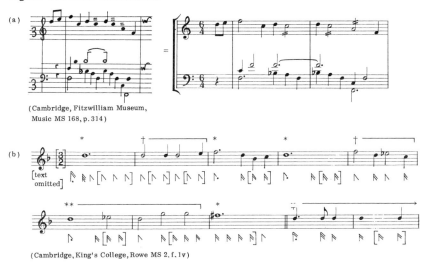

(Cambridge, Fitzwilliam Museum,
Music MS 168, p. 314)

(Cambridge, King's College, Rowe MS 2, f. 1v)

coloration: indeed, the rhythms of the lute part are entirely orthochronic, and concordances do not use coloration (the piece survives elsewhere both as a song and as 'The Earl of Essex's Galliard'). The difference is between *duration* and *metre*. An orthochronic, additive notation can represent durations, but the metre must be decided on other, harmonic, grounds (in Figure 67(b) the white notation defines no particular metre, and the bar-line is able to disguise the hemiola); but a divisive notation, such as we have with this use of coloration, can both notate a metre and, incidentally, give some indication of speed. In the change to orthochronic methods, notation largely lost the ability to show metre rather than rhythm.

The features of staff notation

The staff notation of the age of transition causes few problems to the transcriber, and in many cases it is quite possible to perform from the original notation. The staff, which had four or five lines in modal notation and increased as necessary to as many as seven or eight in the fifteenth century,[7] settled at five in the sixteenth, except in Italy and for keyboard scores, where six was normal. The clefs were the G, C and F-clefs, though not always in immediately-recognizable forms and capable of appearing on any line of the staff. The gamma-clef is sometimes found, for low G (Figure 68(a)), and occasionally two clefs

111

together (see Figure 98(a)). 'Key-signatures' sometimes help in identifying the clefs, and the flat sign is often modified to the double-bulbed form to distinguish E flat from B flat and one octave from another. A typical disposition of flats (in both 'key-signature' and 'accidentals') is shown in Figure 68(b).

Figure 68. Clefs and 'Key-Signatures'

(a)

(b)

The sharp sign was not used as a key-signature until the seventeenth century. In the sixteenth, however, one occasionally finds a natural sign used as a key-signature on f″, apparently as a warning not to sharpen the f by *musica ficta* (see Chapter 9) in the higher octave.

It is convenient to mention here a matter related to key-signatures. As we have seen, Bb and B♮ (♭ and ♮) were early regarded as separate, though alternative, notes. To these were added the chromatic notes in due course: E flat, A flat and the sharpened notes first supplied by *musica ficta* and then notated—F♯, C♯ and G♯. A table in the Board Lute Book, *c*. 1626 (BMS 9, f.[i]v), shows the notes available in staff notation: they are, working upwards, C, C sharp, D, D sharp, E flat E, F, F sharp, G, G sharp, A flat, A, B flat, B natural, C. Hence, although the full chromatic compass is available, chromatic notes cannot all be used in both forms—C sharp is available, for instance, but not D flat, which makes it impossible to notate music in the keys of A flat major or F minor. Since this table was perhaps written out by John Dowland we need not regard it as ultra-conservative, at least for England: his view is supported by Morley (P & E, 261 f), who thought that the vocal parts should be notated in a key with few sharps or flats, and that the accompanist should transpose as necessary. Certainly, English music of the early seventeenth century tended to use the keys of C major, A minor, F major, D minor and G minor most (the minor keys usually notated with one flat fewer than we should use in the key-signature, the last flat being added as an accidental): more remote key-signatures were relatively rare. In Italy, however, the chromatic experiments of madrigalists such as Luzzaschi and Gesualdo resulted in a much freer use of chromatic notation, and this clearly had an effect elsewhere.

Campion, in his most forward-looking collection, used the key of F minor, for example, notating the music in three flats in all parts, with D flat as an accidental (Campion, *The Third and Fourth Booke*, sig. Dv: 'Shall I come, sweet love'). Besides, solo instrumental music in *Griffschrift* had no such limitations: its tablatures did not observe the difference between (for example) C sharp and D flat, so that in theory they could notate any key at all. Lute music in A flat major or F minor is common enough.

Many of the medieval time-signatures and proportional signs were retained in the sixteenth century, though not always with their original meanings. Proportions themselves were little used, and some proportional signs came to stand on their own as time-signatures: hence ₵ is often found at the beginning of a piece, acting as a true time-signature for two Ss in a 'measure', 3 ₵ for three Ss in a 'measure', and so on. The *tactus* throughout the sixteenth century was the M, giving way to the crotchet (C) in the first thirty years of the seventeenth.

Regular bar-lines were still not used except in scores and instrumental tablatures. In single parts, whether in part-books or in *cantus lateralis*, bar-lines were used, as before, to mark off main sections of the piece. An innovation during the sixteenth century was the use of a double bar-line to mark the end of a repeated section (Figure 69(a)). This was especially used in tablatures, although some later tablatures placed a figure 2 above it to make sure that the repeat was not missed (b). At least as early as 1529 (in Attaingnant's lute prints) we find also the form with two or more dots on either side of a single or double line (c), (d), (e).

Figure 69. Repeat-Signs

Another way of showing a repeat was to place a *signum congruentiae* or a direct on the staff at the pitch of the first note of the repeated section, referring back to a *signum* placed over that first note. In concerted music such as lute-songs or instrumental consorts with lute it is quite usual to find two of these methods used simultaneously in different parts, or even in the same part.

We have previously discussed the use of the *signum* in canons, and it is time to describe its more normal functions. Its principal use throughout the fifteenth century was, as its name implies, to mark those points of congruence, or coming together, when the various voices land on a chord together after a period of intricate part-writing, or when a voice joins in with a new section after a long series of rests. Such a reference-point is of course very useful to individual singers if their music is written in *cantus lateralis* or in part-books: but the *signum* probably served also as a reference-point for the *rector chori* or director in rehearsal, just as rehearsal-numbers in a modern orchestral score are used. The use of *signa* to show the last note of a canonic part or the first note of a repeat (the coming-together at the start of a repeated section) can be regarded as an extension of this main use. At the end of a piece a *signum* would *inter alia* imply a pause, and indeed the pause sign took over this function entirely in the seventeenth century.

To return briefly to the subject of bar-lines, two comments need to be made. First, the use of bar-lines in printed scores and instrumental parts of the sixteenth and early seventeenth centuries was far more consistent than in manuscript sources even as late as the middle of the eighteenth century. Secondly, the regular barring of instrumental pieces paradoxically kept alive well into the seventeenth century a way of writing keyboard music that is very much a product of divisive rhythm. In early keyboard music the small notes for the florid right-hand part are distributed evenly across the bar, whereas a single note in the left hand is placed in the centre of the space between the bar-lines: this is very noticeable in the Faenza manuscript,[8] and can be seen in many other keyboard sources, where each bar is considered as a metrical unit within which the notes of individual voice-parts should be distributed about the centre. Even as late as the middle of the eighteenth century we find examples of keyboard music in which the alignment of chords is very far from the vertical. There may of course be obvious reasons for this, such as the need for clarity in closely-spaced part-writing:[9] but it nevertheless shows that vertical alignment was not felt as a necessity for a considerable time.

The effects of music printing

It is instructive to see how notation in the sixteenth century was affected by the recent invention of printing. 'Recent' is only partly a false description: for although Gutenberg's first print had appeared in 1457, it was not until 1501, with the publication of Petrucci's *Odhecaton*, that the invention was used for polyphony. Meanwhile, beginning *c.* 1473, printing had been used mainly for service-books, in both Gothic and square notation, plus a few examples in treatises and didactic works.[10] The effects of printing on the notation of the sixteenth century can, I think, be regarded in three different ways: as conservative, as simplifying, or as innovatory. Over all, the most important effect was perhaps the result of the first two: that is, a standardization in which the individual quirks of scribes tended to be subordinated to a general 'house-style' of the printers. In music this perhaps mattered more than with printed text: and although collaboration between composers, arrangers and publishers was often very fruitful indeed, the type of difficulty sometimes experienced by nineteenth-century composers in dealing with their publishers could perhaps have been foreseen in the sixteenth century.

It is suggested below (Chapters 10 and 11) that printing was partly responsible for the continued use of German keyboard and lute tablatures. Elsewhere, the conservative effect of printing can be seen most obviously in the actual shape of note-heads. In manuscript, rounded note-heads were normal at the beginning of the seventeenth century, and have continued to be so except in plainsong (where square notation continues) and in formal, archaic hands of the sixteenth and early seventeenth centuries. But both in woodblock cutting and in movable type (where a note had to be cut in metal before a mould could be made) the tools used resulted in straight-edged and therefore diamond-shaped note-heads (or square, for the B and L). Moreover, since printing long continued to reproduce the look of manuscripts, the thicks and thins of pen-strokes in different diagonal directions continued to be observed in printing. It was not until engraving came to be used, early in the seventeenth century, that printed music took on the look of the then-current (round-headed) style of manuscript. Printing also tended to be conservative in preserving symbols such as the direct, which might have fallen out of use in manuscript music much earlier than it in fact did had it not been for the regular and consistent use of such signs in printed music.

There were, however, certain signs which gradually disappeared from printed music, for which there were probably three main reasons:

1. A symbol which is somehow inconvenient to use in print will be replaced by one which is less so.

2. Printers prefer to use the smallest number of pieces of type that they conveniently can. In text, for instance, the thorn (Þ) was replaced by the y: hence 'ye' for 'the', 'yᵗ' for 'that', and many other examples in the

seventeenth century. In music, we see the elimination of different types of repeat-sign, for example.

3. Printers prefer not to use symbols that are rare, going out of use anyway, or which may be misunderstood by potential buyers.

For all of these reasons ligatures disappeared from printed music, while still fairly common in manuscript. Similarly, the *signum congruentiae* is much less common in the sixteenth century than in the fifteenth, although there may also be other reasons for this.

The innovatory aspect of printing is a little more difficult to pin down, but perhaps not of great importance. For some strange reason, the use of ties is first found in a printed source, Marco Antonio Cavazzoni's *Recerchari, motetti, canzoni* of 1523. In that this source seems to have been printed from metal plates, the use of ties here is no different from that in a manuscript: and perhaps one or more manuscript sources antedating Cavazzoni's print used ties but did not survive. More important, in a way, is the fact that Cavazzoni's print is a keyboard score. Here, where regular bar-lines are used, is a situation calling for ties which is not found in unbarred music. Nevertheless, a note tied across a bar-line could also, until the late seventeenth century, be written as a complete note on the bar-line itself (Figure 70).

Figure 70. The Tie

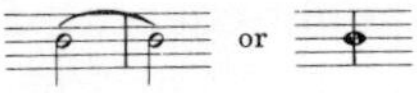

Another example of innovation is really only the hastening of a change that was already taking place. When the M was first used its upward tail was probably intended to signify shortness, just as the downward tail of the L signified length, and until well into the sixteenth century all M-tails normally went upwards. This was not always convenient, for it wasted space if the scribe was not to run the risk of allowing a M-tail to collide with the text above it, and such a collision made the text difficult to read. On the other hand, an inverted M could not be mistaken for some other note-value, and there could be no ambiguity at all if the note concerned were in the middle of a group of normal Ms. So from the beginning of the fifteenth century we find a M-tail occasionally going downwards when the note is at the top of the staff. Single-impression printing hastened this process and quickly made a downward M-tail quite standard: for downward stems also greatly reduced the necessary type, since the inversion of a piece of type could be used for a note on another part of the staff

116

(Figure 71). For the same reasons, it became possible for L-stems to point upwards (cf. Figure 66) and for rhythm-signs in tablature to be inverted.

Figure 71. Dual Use of Type

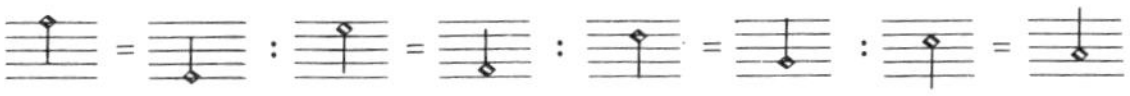

The following are therefore unnecessary:

The sources of the period

For this period, little need be added to our previous discussion of format (see the Introduction). Choir-books survived into the early sixteenth century, but by *c.* 1510 only the smallest choirs could have sung from a single copy. Part-books, known as early as *c.* 1460 (the Glogauer Liederbuch),[11] were the usual format from the beginning of the sixteenth century, both in print and in manuscript. From *c.* 1570 table-layout was used for consorts in which there was only one performer per part, though this was restricted to purely instrumental music or consorts including instruments. A modified table-layout for two or three solo singers was largely a product of the seventeenth century. Collections of lute-songs from the mid-sixteenth century onwards were written in score, the vocal part on a five-line staff and the lute-part on six lines. Although a five-line staff was normal for all music (unless in tablature), Italy continued with a six-line staff for some time: hence 'Italian keyboard tablature'—that is, keyboard score—was also written on six-line staves, in England, France and Germany as well as in Italy. Keyboard music did not finally discard the six-line staff until the end of the seventeenth century.

Part II
Didactic Notations

8. Early Didactic Notations

The notations discussed in this chapter form a disparate group of isolated examples with few real connections between them (the sources are listed in Spiess, 'Early Polyphony', and Wolf HdN i, 214, n.3). They are concerned with heighting, with the use of letters as note-names, or both. All appear to attempt to fulfil basic notational needs for a specific purpose. In most cases that purpose can be shown to be a didactic or at least an explanatory one. These notations can therefore be regarded as attempts to notate pitch simply and accurately for the purpose of teaching music or of illustrating points of musical theory.

Systems of note-naming

The method of giving to individual notes letter-names by which they could always be identified was used by the Greeks and known to Boethius. Boethius himself used the Latin letters from A onwards: but the letters referred only to convenient notes in particular musical examples, there being no lasting correspondence between pitch and letters. The term 'Boethian notation' is still occasionally used for early systems of note-naming, but this is misleading.

Figure 72 shows the main letter-systems in use during the Middle Ages, compared with the modern nomenclature (see Apel NPM, 21, and Parrish NMM, 29). They show no clear chronological pattern, although a single series of letters over two octaves or so generally ante-dates the series A-G repeated in each octave. These systems are divided as to the starting-note at the lower end: some use tenor c, the lowest note likely to be needed for short examples, while others begin at the A below it, the lowest note normally required in chant. However, the application of polyphony to the chant may demand an extension of the range at either end. At the lower end, extension of one note from bass A is given the Greek form Γ , to distinguish it from the G above, where octave-distinctions are made (VI); where the A-G

121

series is used without distinction (V), a lower repetition of some of the series is all that is needed. At the upper end the solution is similar: either a simple repetition of the series (V) or a lower-case Greek equivalent ɑ (VI), though in the latter case an alternative of doubled letters was sometimes used for a further extension of the range.

Figure 72. Letter-Nomenclature

(Top of figure: "Modern equivalent" — a bass- and treble-clef musical staff showing the ascending series of notes corresponding to the columns below.)

		G	A	B	c	d	e	f	g	a	b♭	b♮	c'	d'	e'	f'	g'	a'	b'(b)	c''
I	Modern (Helmholtz)	G	A	B	c	d	e	f	g	a	b♭	b♮	c'	d'	e'	f'	g'	a'	b'(b)	c''
II	Daseia — *Musica Enchiriadis*	*(Daseian glyph)*	*(Daseian glyph)*	*(Daseian glyph)*	*(Daseian glyph)*	*(Daseian glyph)*	*(Daseian glyph)*	*(Daseian glyph)*	*(Daseian glyph)*	*(Daseian glyph)*	*(Daseian glyph)*	*(Daseian glyph)*	*(Daseian glyph)*	*(Daseian glyph)*	*(Daseian glyph)*	*(Daseian glyph)*	*(Daseian glyph)*	*(Daseian glyph)*	*(Daseian glyph)*	*(Daseian glyph)*
	B.N. Latin MS 7369	*(Daseian glyph)*	*(Daseian glyph)*	*(Daseian glyph)*	*(Daseian glyph)*	*(Daseian glyph)*	*(Daseian glyph)*	*(Daseian glyph)*	*(Daseian glyph)*	*(Daseian glyph)*	*(Daseian glyph)*	*(Daseian glyph)*	*(Daseian glyph)*	*(Daseian glyph)*	*(Daseian glyph)*	*(Daseian glyph)*	*(Daseian glyph)*	*(Daseian glyph)*	*(Daseian glyph)*	*(Daseian glyph)*
III	*Scholia Enchiriadis* (9th cent.)				A	B		D	E	F	G	H	I	K	L	M	N	O	P	
IV	Anonymous II, Montpellier MS H 159, Bodley MS 572 (Also called 'Boethian' notation)				A	B	C	D	E	F	G	H	I	K	L	M	N	O	P	
V	Notker, Hucbald, Bernelinus	(E)	F	G	A	B	C	D	E	F			G	A	B	C	D	E	F	(G)
VI	Odo of Cluny (double letters also used by Guido of Arezzo)	Γ	A	B	C	D	E	F	G	a	♭	b	c	d	e	f	g	α (or aa)	♭♭ (or ♭♭)	c (or cc)

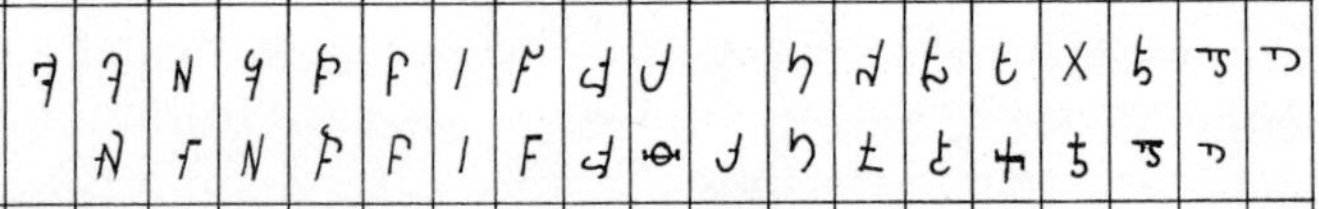

N.B. I = J. It should be stressed that there are many variants of the methods shown here: more detailed descriptions can be found in the works listed in the notes to this chapter.

The Daseia system (II) is essentially the oldest of these notations, for it derives from a Greek system. It had no general use in the Middle Ages, perhaps partly because of the complexity of its forms, partly (and more importantly) because it relied closely on the Greek tetrachord system. 'Daseia' means 'breathing', and the basic symbol of the notation is the Greek 'rough breathing' aspirate, ⊦. In the second tetrachord the first, second and fourth notes consist of the basic symbol plus an s, reversed c and c, respectively, on top. The lowest tetrachord reverses these symbols, the third inverts them, and the fourth inverts and reverses them. In each tetrachord the third note is the upper note of a semitone interval, and is shown by an alphabetic symbol, easily distinguishable by the eye.

Unfortunately this tetrachordal system is really incompatible with a system using the octave as a basic unit. The *Musica Enchiriadis* ('The

Textbook of Music', *c.* 900) uses these symbols, plus two versions laid sideways, for the scale from G to c″: but, as is seen in Figure 72, the special signs no longer invariably show the semitones.

Three solutions present themselves:

1. Another set of symbols can be used to show tones and semitones. *Musica Enchiriadis* uses the letters t and s (see below) in some examples, written between the Daseia symbols used as 'clefs'.

2. Another set of letter-names can be used to give pitch-references. One example in the *Scholia Enchiriadis* ('Notes on the Textbook') uses the letters A, H and P to indicate the starting-notes (GS I, 185). Strunk transcribes these as A, a and a′ (SR, 127), although the starting-note often assumed is c (as in Figure 72, III rather than IV). Neither of these tunings is entirely satisfactory.

3. The whole set of symbols can be redistributed so that the special signs (with additions as necessary) again show the semitones. This solution is found in a (?)fifteenth-century example discussed by Parrish (NMM, 29 and plate XI). In this case (also shown in Figure 72, II) both B flat and B natural are notated in the middle octave.

Notations using heighted symbols

As we saw in Chapter 2, letters were placed at the beginning of the staff during the eleventh century, and from this stems the use of clefs. It is perhaps worth noting here that, although eleventh-century notation sometimes gave the pitch of all four stave-lines, either by colour and/or by clefs, later notation has normally used only one clef per staff, this being considered sufficient to fix the pitch of all the lines and spaces (for exceptions, see Figure 98(a)).

The early notations under consideration here actually seem to have anticipated the basic idea of a staff as early as the ninth century. However, for reasons which are not wholly clear (a tentative suggestion will be made presently) the idea was dropped and later had to be re-discovered by the process discussed in Chapter 2: or perhaps the slightly confused chronology of that development should be allowed to suggest to us that someone quite early on thought of placing neumes on the horizontal lines used as pitch-indicators in letter-notations.

Be that as it may, these earliest didactic notations tend to use a series of horizontal lines (sometimes imaginary, but usually drawn) as pitch-indicators for some form of heighting, with letters at the beginning to show what pitch each line represents. Only the lines are significant, not the spaces between them: and the symbols heighted may be placed across the lines or 'on' them as in text on a base-line. The letters at the beginning may be one of the various series shown in Figure 72 (usually VI), or they may show intervals, rather than pitches, according to a system described (and probably invented) by Hermannus Contractus (d. 1054). In this system the intervals are shown as follows (GS II, 149):

e	(equaliter)	= the same pitch
s	(semitonum)	– a semitone higher or lower
♀ or t	(tonus)	= a tone higher or lower
♭	(= t + s)	= a minor 3rd higher or lower
♯	(= t + t)	= a major 3rd higher or lower
∫	(diatesseron)	= a perfect 4th higher or lower
Δ	(diapente)	– a perfect 5th higher or lower
∆̊	(= Δ + s)	= a minor 6th higher or lower
∆̧	(= Δ + t)	= a major 6th higher or lower

The oldest didactic notation which has survived is that used in the *Musica Enchiriadis*, where the actual syllables of the text are themselves heighted, the precise pitch being given by the relevant Daseia letters arranged vertically at the beginning (Figure 73(a)). The syllables are joined by lines which guide the eye. This system is remarkably unambiguous, and is found in several copies of the treatise, one of which has the letters s and t of Hermannus's system added for further explanation (GS I, 166). Rather remarkably, this notation also occurs in the Glogauer Song Book, for the lower voice of 'Alga iacet humilis', the upper voice being in conventional staff notation. In this very late case, of course, the pitch is shown not by the Daseia symbols but by the normal alphabetical series (Figure 73(b)).

This notation is rather wasteful of space, and in addition may make the text a little difficult to read. Two notations were designed apparently to minimize these disadvantages. The first appears in the work of Hucbald (*c.* 900), and is very close to staff notation. Instead of heighting the syllables of the text, Hucbald placed flattened circles at the correct pitch above the text, again using the Daseia letters as 'clefs'. Just as the syllables of the previous notation had been joined by guide-lines, so were Hucbald's symbols; but in addition he also gave vertical guide-lines between notes to be sung simultaneously. (The heighted syllables do not need this—in fact, do not need any vertical alignment—because the text is sung simultaneously by the various voices.) The result is, as Apel remarks (NPM, 207), rather like an engineer's drawing (Figure 73(c)).

The second alternative to syllable-heighting is to write the text as usual below the music, indicating the notes of the music above it by their letter-names, heighted as if on a staff. There is of course no need for clefs in this case. The guide-lines between the notes are again used, and syllable-division in the music is sometimes shown by a dot following the last note of a group. This notation has an advantage over syllable-heighting

1. in that a staff and accurate heighting are not vital (indeed, are strictly unnecessary), and

2. in that there is usually enough space to indicate liquescence should the music require it—for instance, by means of a sign such as ꙇ or ꙉ after the relevant letter (Figure 73(d)).

Notations without heighting

The notation shown in Figure 73(d) is still unnecessarily wasteful of space, for if the letters are enough to indicate the pitch, then the heighting is not needed. The logical result of such thought is a notation which is found in a number of manuscripts of the tenth and later centuries, either by itself or as an added explanation under neumatic notation (usually Norman notation, as we noted in Chapter 2). The letters are placed on a line immediately above the text: occasionally the second and subsequent letters of a melisma may be slightly heighted to help visual separation, but this is not usual. The dots between note-groups remain, as do the signs of liquescence: only the guide-lines between notes disappear, since they are now superfluous (Figure 73(e)). The letters used are normally those of series VI or VII (Figure 72), but the Daseia symbols are also known.

The last early didactic notation is closely related to that just described. In the same way that Hermannus's interval-signs could be used in place of 'clefs', so they can be used in this purely phonetic way (GS II, 149). Letters with a dot below signify falling intervals; those without, rising intervals. In the example (of which a different copy from Gerbert's is shown in Parrish, plate XII) Hermannus gives the starting-note of each piece as an upper-case (capital) letter at the beginning (Figure 73(f)).

Figure 73. Early Didactic Notations

(a)

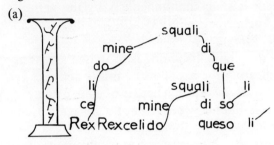

(Paris, Bibliothèque Nationale, MS lat. 7211,
f. 9v: see Parrish NMM, plate XXa)

(b)

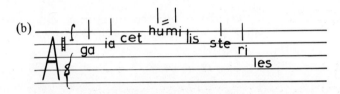

(Glogauer Liederbuch (formerly Berlin, Preussische
Staatsbibliothek, Mus. MS 40098, but now lost), no. 140:
see Ringmann ii, XI and 4–5)

(c)

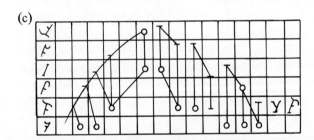

(From *Musica Enchiriadis*: see CS II, 77)

(d)

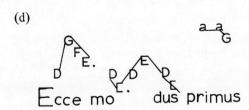

(Paris, Bibliothèque Nationale, MS lat. 7211,
f. 128r: see Parrish NMM, plate V)

(e)

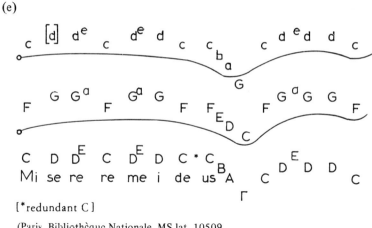

[*redundant C]

(Paris, Bibliothèque Nationale, MS lat. 10509,
f. 89r: see Parrish NMM, plate XXb)

(f)

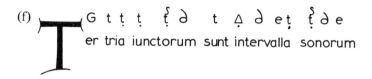

(Vienna, Österreichische Nationalbibliothek,
MS 2502, f. 27v: see Parrish NMM, plate XII)

These didactic notations represent in some measure an exploration of the possibilities of phonetic and diastematic means. Used in conjunction on equal terms, these means duplicate each other. The choice was, therefore, between the two: the result is *Griffschrift* on the one hand and staff notation on the other.

9. Later Didactic Notations

Guido of Arezzo and 'Ut queant laxis'

In referring to the innovations of Guido of Arezzo previously (Chapter 2) I said that his third innovation was not really a notational one. Nevertheless, Guido's system of solmization may make clear a few notational matters that cannot be explained in other ways: and eventually the system was turned into a true phonetic notation.

Guido's system was intended to help choir-boys to sing new chants at sight, and especially to make it easier to sing the semitones in the right place. For this purpose the available scale was divided into hexachords, or groups of six notes, the hexachords overlapping as necessary. Overlap was needed because each hexachord had precisely the same structure of intervals, viz., a semitone with two whole tones on either side. The notes of the hexachord were named as follows:

tone
tone
semi-tone
tone
tone
ut
re
mi
fa
sol
la

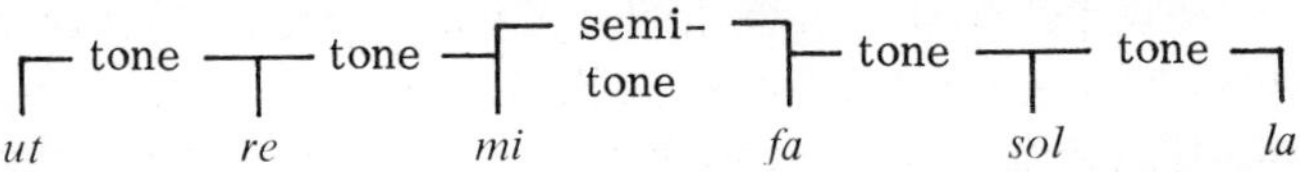

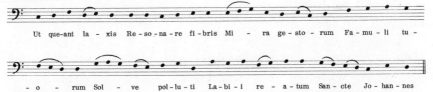

These names, or solmization-syllables, were the first syllables of each line of the stanza given below: the stanza itself is the first of the vesper hymn for the feast of St John the Baptist (Figure 74).[1]

Figure 74.

Ut que-ant la - xis Re - so - na - re fi - bris Mi - ra ge - sto - rum Fa - mu - li tu -
- o - rum Sol - ve pol - lu - ti La - bi - i re - a - tum San - cte Jo - han - nes

The verse may be translated as follows: 'That your servants may with relaxed throats sing the wonders of your deeds, take away the sin of their unclean lips, O holy John.'

As can be seen, each line except the last starts one note higher than the previous line, thus connecting each note of the scale with one of the syllables. Some lines also end on the starting-note of the next, which helps in the memorizing of the tune as a whole. (Rodgers and Hammerstein used the same method in 'Doe, a deer': they adapted the system to the complete octave (tonic sol-fa), but it is otherwise the same as Guido's.)

Bearing in mind that chant uses B flat as well as B natural, we see that there are three starting-notes on which hexachords of the required interval-structure can be based: G, C and F. Starting at the lowest available singing-note, therefore, the syllables are given to the notes of the scale as in Figure 75.

Figure 75.

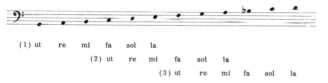

That beginning on G and containing B natural is called the 'hard' (*durum*) hexachord; that beginning on C the 'natural' (*naturale*) hexachord; and that beginning on F and including B flat the 'soft' (*molle*) hexachord. Of course, it may also be necessary to sing B natural in the upper octave, in which case hexachord (1) is transposed up an octave to begin on the note g. Boys' voices will also require the transposition of at least one more hexachord, and a medieval diagram of the gam looks as on page 130 (I have added modern note-names). The solmization-names deriving from the diagram of the gam, obtained by reading the syllables from left to right, were the normal way of referring to notes until the eighteenth century. For instance, tenor C is 'C Fa Ut', while middle C is 'C Sol Fa Ut' and the C above 'C Sol Fa'. Scribal compression often made these into 'C solfaut', etc., and the reader must be ready for such odd-looking 'words'.

Guido apparently first taught his choristers to sing 'Ut queant laxis' using a monochord to give them the notes (GS II, 43–61; Strunk SR, 121–5). When they could sing it from memory he then made them sing any individual line he chose, starting on the correct note: that achieved, they could sing any required note in that one hexachord. After that, they had to be taught to sing the complete scale, or gam (the name derives from *gamma*, Γ, its lowest note), from 'Gamma ut' upwards. Apparently they were required to give each note all its solmization-syllables. As a test and exercise of this ability, Guido

129

HEXACHORDS

Note	hard	nat.	soft	(hard)	(nat.)	(soft)	Old Name
c″						sol	The names of the octave below are repeated here, on the assumption that another hard hexachord begins on g′
b♮′							
bb′						fa	
a′					la	mi	
g′					sol	re	
f′					fa	ut	
e′				la	mi		
d′			la	sol	re		D la sol re
c′			sol	fa	ut		C sol fa ut
b♮				mi			[B fa B mi]
bb			fa				[B fa B mi]
a		la	mi	re			A la mi re
g		sol	re	ut			G sol re ut
f		fa	ut				F fa ut
e	la	mi					E la mi
d	sol	re					D sol re
c	fa	ut					C fa ut
B♮	mi						B mi
A	re						A re
G	ut						Gamma ut

allotted each note of the gam to a joint or knuckle of his left hand: when he pointed to a part of his hand the boys had to sing the correct note (Cole, *Sounds and Signs*, p. 100: a modernized Guidonian hand is shown in Abdy Williams SN, 87).

The only problem remaining is that of mutation, or changing from one hexachord to another. In Guido's time (and always in chant) this probably posed no great difficulties: the hexachords overlap a good deal, and the change from the syllables of one to the syllables of the other could be effected easily at any point of overlap. As to whether one changed to the hard or soft hexachord from the natural, that was decided by the absence or presence of the ♭ sign shortly before the note B.

Once Guido's choristers could sing a chant correctly, using the solmization-syllables, they then probably learnt it by heart before singing it to its own text.

The developed solmization system

The demands of chant required only a relatively simple system of solmization. When the system continued to be used for polyphony, however (as it was until the early seventeenth century), something more was required of it. A need for more chromatic notes led to transpositions of the soft hexachord up a fourth and then up another fourth, making first E flat and then A flat available (Figure 76(a)). The second of these transpositions was rarely needed, even in the late Middle Ages, for in practice the A flat was available by means of a rule that a single note above La and returning to La should be sung as Fa a semitone above La. Allaire cites medieval writings showing that this rule was in common use, though it does not seem to have been formulated as such until Maximilian Guilliaud's *Rudiments de Musique Pratique* of 1554 (Allaire in MSD 24, pp. 45 f). The rule is best known in a later version: 'Una nota super la/Semper est canendum fa', or 'one note above la [returning] is always to be sung [a semitone above] as Fa'. Because of this, a semitone above the top of a hexachord is always available without the necessity of notating it (b). Transposition of (b) down a tone (i.e. to the hexachord beginning on B flat, the first transposition of the soft hexachord) will give the sung note A flat, although it would not be notated.

Figure 76. The Hexachords

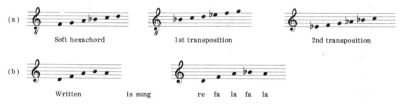

131

In other circumstances, it is a notated flat-sign that forces mutation to the flat side. The flat-sign is a direction that the note to which it applies is to be sung as 'Fa'. Were the sign to be placed only just in front of the note the singer would often already have changed to the wrong hexachord: so the flat-sign sometimes appears in advance of the relevant note, and we may take it that the flat shows the point at which the mutation should be effected (Figure 77).

Figure 77. Point of Mutation

(Cambridge, University Library, Add. MS 5943, f. 169r)

If a part begins in the soft hexachord or one of its transpositions, then one or more flats appear as a 'key-signature' at the beginning of the piece. If that hexachord continues in force, the 'key-signature' also continues. This use of the flat-sign, however, does not really constitute a key-signature, and we should not regard it as one: it is a hexachord indication, and if in any line of music it is not required, it is usually omitted. Its use may therefore vary among different copies of the same piece, according to the positions of the line-ends in the music.

In mutation away from the flat side, it is the third degree of a hexachord (mi) which forces the change. Again, it is the positioning of the Mi-Fa interval that decides the hexachord. When a ♯ or ♮ is used to cancel a ♭ the result is usually to return the music to a hexachord that it had previously left (notationally, ♯ = ♮ at this time: see Chapter 13). When ♯ is used on a note that cannot be flattened, however (see Chapter 7), the effect is to force the music into a 'fictitious' or auxiliary hexachord—i.e. a hexachord which starts on a note other than those we have so far mentioned, and which cannot exist except for this one purpose. For instance, a cadence in G minor requires certain notes from an auxiliary hexachord on D if the 7th of the scale is to be sharpened (Figure 78(a)). The auxiliary hexachords account for some apparently inconsistent notation in the sixteenth and seventeenth centuries, such as (b), which must plainly be performed as (c):

Figure 78. Use of Auxiliary Hexachord

(a)
        sol   fa mi re (-)   re
                        mi   fa
(Allison, *Psalmes*, sig. M2v: text omitted)

(b)
(Dowland, *Lachrimae*, sig. D2v)

(c)
       mi fa   mi re mi

Using the hexachord system, the interval G sharp to F natural is manifestly impossible, and the performer automatically sharpens the F according to the intervals of an auxiliary hexachord starting on F. (At least, it is certainly sensible to *think* of it this way: but see under rule (8), below.) In the earlier part of our period such cadential accidentals were not notated at all, and the singer mutated to an auxiliary hexachord according to certain rules well known to him (but not to us). This is not, however, a suitable place to discuss the problems of *musica ficta,* and for an introduction to the subject the reader is referred to Parrish's excellent résumé (NMM, 197–200).

Although notational symbols are concerned in only a part of the medieval system of solmization, I am convinced that a student of notation should be able to solmize much medieval and later music if he is to understand its notation fully. This is largely a matter of practice for us, as it was for both singers and instrumentalists until—at least in some parts of western Europe—the early seventeenth century. Such a system must be worked strictly according to the rules, however, and I therefore set out here some rules which may be found helpful.[2]

1. Use Ut only for the lowest note of a part.

This rule comes from Morley (*Plain and Easy Introduction*, ed. Harman, 13): it seems to be part of a general trend to discard Ut and Re. Earlier music is often solmized more efficiently if Ut and Re are allowed for the bottom notes of a *musical phrase.*

2. All three main hexachords can be transposed an octave, either up or down.

3. Once in any hexachord, stay in it until forced to move. One may be forced to move

    (i) by going outside the range of the hexachord,
    (ii) by moving up or down a 4th or 5th from 'fa' (see rule 7), or
    (iii) by means of an 'accidental' ♭.

In this rule I discount the La-Fa-La movement (rule 5) and the use of auxiliary hexachords forced by a ♯ (rule 8).

4. When leaving any hexachord (unless an auxiliary one), move to an *adjacent* hexachord: the 'key-signature' or lack of it determines which.

5. A single note above La, returning, should be sung as Fa: return immediately to the former hexachord (see Figure 78). (If the scale continues upwards, a new hexachord is introduced by either Mi or Fa, according to the 'key-signature' or lack of it).

6. Hexachords can be transposed to the flat side: e.g. an E flatted must be sung as Fa in a hexachord beginning on B flat. These hexachords, too, can be applied in any octave.

7. A leap up or down of a 4th or 5th must be a perfect interval. If the leap is from Fa the second note must often be flatted to avoid a melodic tritone, in which case it, too, will be sung as Fa in a new hexachord.

8. A leading-note sharpened at a cadence by *musica ficta* is to be solmized as 'Mi', the sub-mediant (sharpened if necessary) as 'Re'; these are from an auxiliary, hypothetical, hexachord, and make no difference to the basic Mi-Fa relationship of the main hexachord. This rule may have been little used: Sol-fa notation (see Figure 78(a)) used F[a] for an F, even when sharped. See also Morley, ed. Harman, the last example on p. 18.

Of course, any given set of notes will often have two possible solmizations, because of the overlapping of hexachords.

Later variants of solmization

As an aid to the correct reading of staff notation, the medieval solmization system continued in use during the sixteenth century. With the simpler musical and notational styles of that century, and with the growth of amateur participation, solmization became for the first time a truly popular teaching system, used in musical treatises and teaching-aids aimed at a much wider readership than those being trained for the musical profession. In particular, the growing popularity of metrical psalms required some musical knowledge in those who would sing them, whether in church or in the course of domestic devotions. From the 1560s onwards metrical psalters in England tended to have prefaces in which solmization was explained in conjunction with the basics of staff notation. This gave rise to the use of letters—the initials of the solmization syllables—on the staff next to the notes in printed Protestant psalters, on the continent as well as in England (Figure 79(a)).[3]

The medieval system had two serious disadvantages by the turn of the seventeenth century, however. First, the methods of mutation were ill-defined and complicated to learn. Second, the growing feeling for key-structure in music made a hexachordal system unsuitable: complex music, at least, required the octave as the repeating unit. In the popular use of solmization, the effect of the first of these was to some extent minimized by the simplicity of the music itself. Even so, the two reasons together were no doubt instrumental in bringing about a simplification of the system. In detail, there were different versions of the simplified system. In all, however, the regularity of the octave scale was allowed to suggest a simpler method of mutation, in which the key-note and subdominant of the major scale were sung as Fa. Some versions at first retained the renaissance rule, using Ut for the key-note if it was the lowest note of the part, and Re for the supertonic; but in practice the first of the rules given above virtually prevented both Ut and Re from being used.

The most widespread of these modifications was known as Lancashire Sol-fa or (more appropriately, since it became common all over England) Old English Sol-fa. In this system the ascending major scale was solmized as

fa – sol – la – fa – sol – la – mi – fa

The relative minor took the same syllable for each note, so that the minor scale became

la – mi – fa – sol – la – fa – sol – la

This four-note system travelled to North America, where its use became general under the name of Fasola. In the late eighteenth century a modification was made to staff notation so that there should be a visual connection between each note and the relevant syllable. This connection had of course been missing since the letter-plus-note notation of the sixteenth century, since the solmization syllables were not otherwise notated. In the American notation known as 'Patent-note' or 'Buckwheat' notation, different note-head shapes were associated with the four syllables used (Figure 79(b)). The series shown here is that first used by William Little in *The Easy Instructor* (1801): two years later Andrew Law used the same shapes, but with Fa and La exchanged. On a staff, as in Little's publication, these shapes do of course duplicate information already there. Law stressed that the advantage of the shapes was that they made a staff unnecessary, and he used the shapes without a staff, but with the notes slightly heighted, in *The Art of Singing*. (On Law and Little, see Lowens, 'Andrew Law', especially pp. 218–20.)

Figure 79. Notations Using Solmization Principles

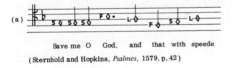

(a)

Save me O   God.   and   that with   speede

(Sternhold and Hopkins, *Psalmes*, 1579, p. 42)

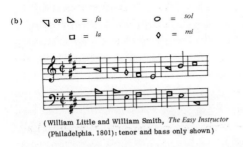

(William Little and William Smith, *The Easy Instructor*
(Philadelphia, 1801): tenor and bass only shown)

The shapes, used in this notation for pitch-designation, do not show rhythm, which is notated by the presence or lack of a stem. In the psalms, fugueing-tunes and religious songs for which shape-notes were used, rhythm was probably a less important element than pitch. Buckwheat notation was extended in the nineteenth century, under the stimulus of the 'movable-Do' system which became Tonic Sol-fa in England. The first seven-note series, with new shapes for Do, Re and Si, was introduced in 1846: alternative series were later offered, but the earliest survived in general use. The elimination of the repeated shapes (Fa, Sol and La) within the octave gave 'Shape-notation' an exact graphical parallel to the Tonic Sol-fa system. Shape-notation is still in use in parts of the United States.

Phonetic systems derived from solmization

The hexachord series was extended to an octave towards the end of the seventeenth century, when the French added a syllable for the 7th of the scale, Si (suggested by 'Sancte Iohannes'). The series then ran:

ut – re – mi – fa – sol – la – si – ut.

At about the same time Ut gave way to Do. Out of this extension of the Guidonian system arose several closely-related phonetic notations used for teaching purposes, virtually the vocal equivalents of instrumental tablatures.[4]

The seven-note syllable-series, by its representation of a complete diatonic scale, eliminated the problem of mutation between hexachords. Mutation would now be from one key to another: that is, transfer between complete diatonic scales. This idea was put into systematic form by Sarah Glover in her *Scheme for Rendering Psalmody Congregational* (1835) and other works. In the *Scheme* Glover called the notes of the diatonic scale Doh, Ra, Me, Fah, Sole, Lah and Te.[5] For the ascending minor scale, starting on Lah, the syllables Fah and Sole were replaced by Bah and Ne, representing the sharpened 6th and 7th of the scale. The substitution of Te for Si, and the use of Bah and Ne, gave her a non-repeating series of initial letters, which could then be used in place of the syllables. An acute accent on a letter indicated the octave above the unaccented letter, a grave accent the octave below: thus a range of three octaves was available in any one key. The change of octave took place between Sole and Lah. Chromatic notes took the vowel 'oy' added to the initial for a semitone below and 'ow' for a semitone above. Mutation from one key to another was effected by means of a double syllable for one note—i.e. the syllables for that note in both the old and the new key.

Glover's rhythmic notation consisted of marking the beats and their divisions. A strong beat was shown by a bar-line; a weak beat by a comma; and a secondary accent by a semicolon. A half beat was shown by a hyphen, a quarter beat by an 'equals' sign.

The Norwich Sol-fa system, as it was usually called, is illustrated in Figure 80(a): this example comes from *The Sol-fa Tune Book* of 1839, in which Sarah Glover incorporated some minor improvements to the rhythmic notation. 'Column H', referring to her table of all the notes and syllables, places the music in A major; 'Foot .ı. ' shows the metre (i.e. up-beat, stress, weak beat); a metronome marking and the length of pendulum required (in inches of string) show the speed; and the letter V at the beginning, referring to the same table of notes and syllables, shows the starting-pitch of each part to be the note e″.

Figure 80(b) is an example of John Curwen's system, which he evolved during the 1840s. As will be seen by comparing it with (a), Curwen's system owed much to the Norwich Sol-fa method, a fact that he readily acknowledged. Miss Glover's rather cumbersome method of pitch-reference via her table of notes and syllables has given

Figure 80. Norwich Sol-fa and Curwen's Tonic Sol-fa

(a) 149th PSALM. *Spirited and Dignified*

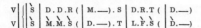

Column H. Foot . | .   Metronome 88.
Pendulum 18.

(Sarah Glover, *The Sol-fa Tune Book* , 1839, p. 18)

YE SPOTTED SNAKES.

KEY **A**.   *Andante*. M. 96.   *R. J. S. Stevens*.

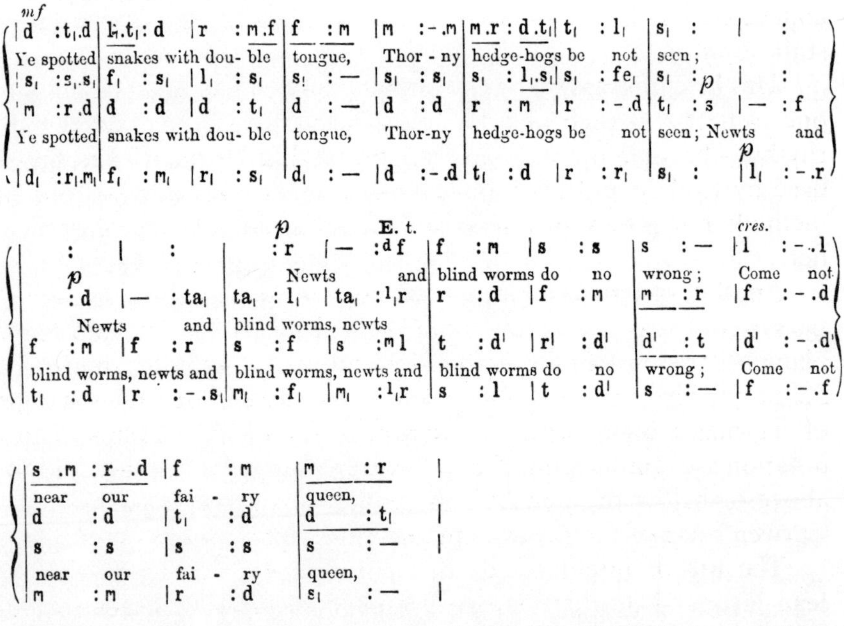

mf

| |d | :t₁.d | l₁.t₁: d | |r | :m.f | |f | :m | |m | :-.m | m.r: d.t₁| t₁ | :l₁ | s₁ | : | | : |
Ye spotted snakes with dou- ble | tongue, | Thor - ny | hedge-hogs be | not | seen ;

| |s₁ | :s₁.s₁| f₁ | : s₁ | |l₁ | : s₁ | s₁ | :— | |s₁ | :s₁ | s₁ | : l₁.s₁| s₁ | :fe₁ | s₁ | :*p* | | : |

| |m | :r.d | d | :d | |d | :t₁ | d | :— | |d | :d | r | :m | |r | :-.d| t₁ | :s | |— | :f |
Ye spotted snakes with dou- ble | tongue, | Thor-ny | hedge-hogs be | not | seen ; Newts and
p

| |d₁ | :r₁.m₁| f₁ | :m₁ | |r₁ | : s₁ | d₁ | :— | |d | :-.d| t₁ | :d | |r | :r₁ | s₁ | : | |l₁ | :-.r |

p   E. t.   *cres.*

| : | | : | |:r | |— | :d f | |f | :m | |s | :s | s | :— | |l | :-.l |
p   Newts and| blind worms do | no | wrong ; | Come not

| :d | |— | : ta₁| ta₁ | :l₁ | |ta₁ | :¹₁r | r | :d | |f | :m | m | :r | |f | :-.d |

Newts and | blind worms, newts
| f | :m | |f | :r | s | :f | |s | :m l | t | :d¹ | |r¹ | :d¹ | d¹ | :t | |d¹ | :-.d¹ |
blind worms, newts and | blind worms, newts and | blind worms do | no | wrong ; | Come not

| t₁ | :d | |r | :-.s₁| m₁ | :f₁ | |m₁ | :¹₁r | s | :l | |t | :d¹ | s | :— | |f | :-.f |

| |s .m | :r .d | |f | :m | |m | :r | |
near | our | fai - ry | queen,
| d | :d | |t₁ | :d | |d | : t₁ | |
| s | :s | |s | :s | s | :— | |
near | our | fai - ry | queen,
| m | :m | |r | :d | |s₁ | :— | |

(John Curwen, The Standard Course . . . in the Tonic Sol-fa Method (new edition, 1872), p. 81)

way to a plain statement of key, and for similar reasons the apparatus of mutation is simpler, although in principle the same. As in Glover's method, a change of vowel is used for chromatic notes not covered by a change of key: a sharpened note takes the vowel 'e' (e.g. 'de' is a semitone above Do) and most flattened notes take the vowel 'a' (pronounced 'aw'), though Do and Fa become 'du' and 'fu'. Lower-case letters take the place of capitals, while superscript and subscript strokes take the place of acute and grave accents, respectively. The middle octave for male voices is assumed to be an octave lower than that for female voices.

In the notation of rhythm, Curwen followed Sarah Glover quite closely, with the pulse, half-pulse and quarter-pulse marked by colon, full stop and comma, respectively. For two or more notes sung to a single syllable of text, underlining takes the place of the slurs used by Glover. It is an important characteristic of Curwen's notation that the horizontal spacing is proportional to the duration of the note, so that the rhythm is visually recognizable. By Curwen's time, of course, equal spacing for equal duration was at least a theoretical ideal of staff notation. Indeed, Curwen used the normal auxiliary signs of staff notation much more than Glover did, probably a deliberate choice connected with his basic aim to provide a step towards the learning of staff notation.

This brief discussion of Glover and Curwen has touched on only one aspect of their work. Such matters as the teaching of rhythm—brought out very clearly in the modified form of Tonic Sol-fa used by Kodály and his followers—is of enormous interest in their methods, but as they are not notational aspects I shall not discuss them here.

Another system to which Curwen was indebted—also a movable-Do system—was that developed in France by Pierre Galin, Aimé Paris, Nanine Paris and Emile Chevé. Instead of the letters standing for Sol-fa syllables, they used the numerals 1–7, ascending from the tonic of the major scale, with 0 as a rest. Many of the features of this notation are familiar from Curwen's adaptation: for instance, the dot above or below the numeral, to denote the octave, is paralleled in Curwen's use of the superscript and subscript stroke.

The use of numerals for this purpose was not new. In 1742 Jean-Jacques Rousseau had read a paper before the Académie des Sciences in which he proposed a movable-Do notation using numerals, dots above and below showing the octave. Bar-lines and punctuation-marks showed the main metrical divisions, while the smaller divisions were shown by single or double horizontal lines over or under the numerals. The Académie des Sciences were unimpressed, not least because they knew that the system had already been used by Jean Jacques Souhaitty in 1677. Even this cannot have been a new invention but a rationalization of an old idea. William Braythwaite's

Siren coelestis (1638) had set out a movable-Do notation using the numerals 1–7, in which four octaves and all the note values from *maxima* to *semifusa* were graphically distinguished (Krummel, *English Music Printing*, 98–102). This extraordinarily cumbersome system cannot often have been used in performance, and certainly not as an aid to sight-singing. In this, Braythwaite's notation can be contrasted with its probable ancestor, Henestrosa's keyboard notation discussed in the next chapter.

With this example we may remind ourselves that for more than two centuries the movable-Do idea derived from solmization gave rise to phonetic notations using letters and numerals. It would be wrong, however, to assume that the movable-Do notations had the field to themselves: the fixed-Do principle was strongly supported on the continent and in Curwen's time had influential adherents in England. The fixed-Do principle is at the basis of the pitch-learning aspects of Italian *solfeggio* and French *solfège*. As a phonetic system, it simply substitutes the Sol-fa syllables for note-names. That is why the French and Italian names for the notes of the C major scale are still those of the sol-fa system: Ut Re Mi Fa Sol La Si Ut in France, and the same in Italy but with Do for Ut. With a fixed-Do system, however, vowel-modifications are necessary as soon as one moves away from C major, because of the chromatic alterations: and so the system becomes progressively harder to use as the music modulates to remoter keys. This is not a matter of notational principle, however, and it need not be discussed further here.

Part III
Tablatures

10. Keyboard Tablatures

Considerations of chronology make it appropriate to discuss instrumental tablatures at this stage. Tablatures belong principally to the sixteenth and seventeenth centuries, although there is an important body of keyboard sources in the fifteenth and many more for various instruments from the eighteenth century onwards. In so far as instrumental tablatures provide some parallel with staff notation—in their measurement of duration, for example—they belong, therefore, to the period that was reached at the end of Part I. The earliest examples of keyboard tablature, however, take us firmly back into the Middle Ages.

German tablatures

German keyboard tablature is a letter-notation, related to those discussed in Chapter 8 but adapted to the keyboard. It is often referred to as organ tablature, although it was used also for other keyboard instruments. With the exception of the earliest manuscript, its sources are exclusively German: and apart from a few pieces in the Ileborgh tablature all German keyboard music of the fifteenth and sixteenth centuries is written in this notation. In the seventeenth century German tablature was used mainly in north Germany, not exclusively for keyboard music (Winternitz MA ii, plate 7). As late as *c.* 1720 J. S. Bach used it in the *Orgelbüchlein*.

From the middle of the sixteenth century onwards German organ tablature used letters for the whole texture of the music: this is usually called 'new' German organ tablature. Before that time the top line of music was almost invariably notated on a staff (one short piece in Ludolf Wilkin's tablature-book is written entirely in letters), a system normally referred to as 'old' tablature. The staff-notated part shows strong Italian characteristics in the sources up to *c.* 1460, especially in the use of tailed Ss. The earliest source of all, the Robertsbridge manuscript, dates from the 1330s and is almost certainly English.[1] It is therefore the only non-German example of this notation known at present. Despite its date, it is notated in a pre-Ars Nova fashion, with Petronian dots of division separating note-groups valued at a B.

Like other letter-notations, the earliest examples of German organ tablature show great differences among themselves and little sign of a settled, standardized notation. The Robertsbridge manuscript has no rhythm-signs for the letters, the alignment of each letter under the staff notation showing when each note should be played. The letter s (*sine*, 'without') indicates a rest in the lower part. The tablature-books of Ludolf Wilkin, 1432, and Adam Ileborgh, 1448,[2] both use the note-shape shown in Figure 81(a) to indicate a long note, not the short one that we should expect. In the Ileborgh tablature other note-shapes are also of uncertain meaning, and the manuscript cannot be transcribed with certainty. The Wilkin and Ileborgh tablatures are unusual, too, in their letter-notation: the single line of letters must be read in pairs, each pair being played together, so that the music is in three parts, not two. This may be an indication of double pedalling, the first letter of each pair being for the left foot and the second for the right. Ileborgh's indication 'with pedals or with manuals only' (*pedaliter sive manualiter*) is the earliest known indication of the use of organ-pedals: but the piece concerned is one of those in keyboard score, with two parts notated on a staff.

The Ileborgh tablature also shows an interesting feature regarding chromatic alteration that illustrates a general truth in German organ tablatures: namely, that ♯ and ♭ need not necessarily be differentiated notationally, C, F and G always being sharpened, E and B always being flatted. In the upper parts Ileborgh added a tail to show chromatic alteration, probably always sharpened: but in those pieces notated in score, a tail added in the lower voice (which is in breves) always flattens a B or E. These tailed breves, of course, look like Ls, but their duration is not affected. Chromatic alteration shown by a downward tail occurs also on smaller note-values, and was normal from this time onwards.

In the letter-notated parts the Ileborgh tablature uses the Latin -is abbreviation-sign (ꝯ) for either sharp or flat, according to the context: thus Aꝯ = G♯, by an extension of the principles just outlined. The scribal -is sign was later used consistently to denote a sharp (Cꝯ = C♯, Fꝯ = F♯, etc.) and flat notes were then written as their enharmonic equivalents (e.g. Dꝯ for E♭). As a matter of fact, Fis, Cis, etc., are still the German names for F♯, C♯ and the rest: and organ-builders and tuners still use only the sharp designations for

144

organ-pipes. Bb and Bᵇ were normally distinguished as before—b and h, respectively.

Figure 81(b) shows the opening of Ileborgh's 2nd *preambulum*: durational values are largely conjectural.

Figure 81. The Wilkin and Ileborgh Tablatures

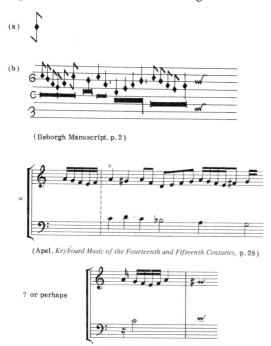

(Ileborgh Manuscript. p. 2)

(Apel, *Keyboard Music of the Fourteenth and Fifteenth Centuries*, p. 28)

? or perhaps

Conrad Paumann's *Fundamentum Organisandi*, 1452,[3] is the earliest of the sources displaying all the main features of the notation as it remained thereafter:

1. In the staff notation, both chromatic alteration and ornaments are indicated by descending stems (ascending stems having durational meaning). This method of notation, specifically connected to an individual note, seems not to allow any prolonged validity. This is usual, of course, for ornaments, which always apply to a particular note: but it seems that we must accept as a general rule that chromatic alteration too, in this notation, applies only to the note concerned.

As these stem-shapes are confusing, it will be simplest to tabulate those of the main sources (Figure 82(a)).

Figure 82. Note-Stems in German Tablatures

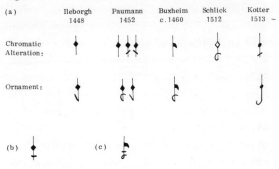

In the *Fundamentum Organisandi* the note-shape at (b) should not be mistaken for chromatic alteration—it is simply the cancellation of a stem written in error. In the Buxheim Organ Book,[4] that at (c) indicates both an ornament and chromatic alteration (of the main note). In the Schlick tablature[5] a note with a plain descending tail sometimes occurs: this is only at the very top of the staff, and it is a M. Buchner's *Fundamentum*, *c.* 1520,[6] says that to play an ornament (a shake, w in modern terms) the player should hold the main note and repeatedly strike the auxiliary. Obviously, this applies principally to the organ, in which there is no decay of the held note.

2. The letter-notation of Paumann's *Fundamentum Organisandi* has rhythm-signs in the shape of red notes placed above the letters. These occur only when necessary, however, and are omitted if duration is clear without them (e.g. because of alignment with notes on the staff). In the Buxheim Book we find a more complete system for notating rhythms, which was taken up by later sources. The time-values are given as dots or stems, thus:

Perfect B	Imperfect B	S	M	Sm	F
. . .	. .	.	|	↾	↾

The Buxheim Book also has rests, given as in Figure 83(a); and a complete bar's rest is marked 'vacat'. In the tablature of Johann Kotter, 1513,[7] the rhythm-signs for consecutive Fs or *semifusae* (Sfs) in the letter-notation are written as a sort of grid which really consists of connected flags (Figure 83(b)): this grid became normal for German tablature from then onwards. In the staff notation of Kotter's tablature the reverse is true, and only the first of such a group has a stem (c).

146

Figure 83.

(a) ⊥ ⊤ etc.   (b) ⫯⫯ or ⫯⫯   (c) [musical notation] for [musical notation]

3. The increased ranges of voices in the *Fundamentum Organisandi* require that the octave be specified in the letter-notation. The lower octave is written as plain letters up to b (i.e. Bb below middle C), while the upper octave, starting with ᵂₕ, has a single scroll-like dash over each letter. Arnolt Schlick's tablature of 1512 uses a lower dash— e.g. h—for the lower octave still, and other sources use the same symbol or else a capital letter. Kotter's tablature and later sources use the octave above the highest used in the Schlick print, and this is given two dashes, thus: c̄. In Kotter's manuscript, the letters are also doubled in this octave: c̄c̄.

The staff-notated part is regularly-barred in the Paumann source, a feature found also in the Buxheim Organ Book. In Schlick's tablature and in the manuscript tablature of Regina Clara Imhoff, 1629,[8] there are no bar-lines, a space between groups of notes or letters serving the same purpose. In the Schlick source this may be a good solution to the technical problem of printing a bar-line on the staff: in the case of the Imhoff tablature (which is in 'new' German organ tablature) a gap no doubt helps to guide the performer's eye. In 'new' tablature, however, no such indication is normal; indeed, without staff notation regular barring is probably unnecessary. Most sources do divide up the notes into groups that the eye can take in easily, however, and this acts as a guide to the rhythmic and metrical structure of the music.

One notational problem of the *Fundamentum Organisandi* should be mentioned here: the value of the note ♪. It is certainly a short note, as one would expect: but the music does not make clear whether the group ♩♪, for example, should be transcribed ♪̄ or ♪ (a problem sometimes encountered in normal staff notation). The grouping • ♪ seems to indicate a remnant of imperfection by a remote value (cf. Figure 45, above), and—with the same uncertainty in mind—should presumably be transcribed as either ♪̄ or ♪ .

Before leaving the subject of double-stemmed notes, the reader should be reminded of the tablature of Fridolin Sicher, *c.* 1525,[9] discussed briefly in Chapter 7 (see Figure 62).

Finally, the sources of 'old' German tablature, from Kotter's tablature onwards, sometimes have the bass part as the top line of letters. The order of parts is, therefore—from top to bottom—discant, bass, alto, tenor. The reason for this is not known for certain. Otto Kinkeldey's explanation (*Orgel und Klavier*, p. 190) was that it reflects the order of the parts in the book from which the tablature was made (i.e. discant and bass on the left-hand page, facing alto and tenor). He may have been right, but this would be an unusual disposition of parts.

For the understanding of 'new' German tablature, little need be added to the description of 'old' tablature: the only difference in principle is that the notation of the top line changed from staff notation to letter notation. This may seem a strange and anachronistic change, but a brief discussion of the advantages of the old and new tablatures may explain it. The old notation was a great saver of space if the top, staff-notated, part was the faster-moving. This was especially the case if there were two very slow-moving lower parts that could be notated as a single line of letters, as in the Wilkin and Ileborgh tablatures. In this respect two facts are significant: first, that the score-notated pieces in the Ileborgh tablature are written on a single staff (a second staff just for a part entirely in Bs would have been a great waste of space); and second, that the one piece in the Wilkin tablature that is in rhythmically equal parts—the little two-part 'Kyrie'—is notated entirely in letters.

In the sixteenth century, however, this advantage was lessened. Keyboard music might be more florid in the lower, rather than the upper, part; and vocal writing, even when not imitative in texture, tended towards equal movement in all parts. Moreover, by the second quarter of the century the process of printing music was clearly about to become (and actually did become) a viable proposition: and although there was an expanding market for printed music in the middle of the sixteenth century, it was not an easy matter to print music for some time after that. But, on the other hand, there was no problem with letter-press. On both of these counts, the 'new' German notation had great advantages. The saving of space is illustrated well by those pages of the *Orgelbüchlein*[10] where Bach used it because he did not have space to finish a piece without turning to a new page if he continued in staff notation.

Spanish tablatures

No Spanish keyboard music survives from a date earlier than the mid-sixteenth century, so we do not know what notation was used at that time. Apel suggested (NPM, 47) that earlier keyboard music in

Spain may have been notated like Italian music, i.e. in staff notation. He probably based his reasoning on the title of Hernando de Cabezon's edition of his father's music, which suggests that Hernando had transcribed staff-notated music into tablature:[11] and indeed the two earliest-known Spanish keyboard notations, which appeared soon after the middle of the century, were apparently being described for the first time.

Spanish keyboard notation uses numerals to indicate particular notes on the keyboard. The three variants of this notation raise between them two main issues:
1. whether to treat the 'black' notes as subsidiary to a main series of 'white' notes, or to regard the chromatic scale as a unified series; and
2. whether to treat the octave as a recurring pattern or to deal with the whole keyboard as an indivisible series.
It is perhaps worth noting here that, because of the letter-nomenclature of notes, German organ tablature
1. treats the black notes as subsidiary to the white (except for B♭); and
2. treats the octave as a repeating pattern of letter-names, to be distinguished at its various appearances.

The first Spanish notation is described by Juan Bermudo in his *Declaración de instrumentos musicales* (Ossuna, 1555, R/1957). His instrument has a range of C–a″, with a short octave at the bottom tuned as follows:

$$\begin{array}{cccccc} & D & E & & B♭ & \\ C & F & G & A & & B♮. \end{array}$$

There are thus 42 notes in all, which Bermudo numbered 1 to 42 starting from the bottom.

1	2	3	4	5	6	7	8	9	10	11	12	...	42
C	D	E	F	G	A	B♭	B♮	c	c♯	d	d♯	...	a″

This is a logical way of numbering, and one that uses the potential of the tablature system in taking no account of octaves, tuning-structure, or the subsidiary nature of the black notes as placed on the keyboard. On the other hand, Bermudo's numbering of the short octave is illogical since he numbered the note-names and not the keys; the numbering takes account of the *sound* of each note, not its position on the keyboard. Thus the player must remember the following series for the short octave:

$$\begin{array}{ccccc} & 2 & 3 & & 7 \\ 1 & 4 & 5 & 6 & 8 \end{array}$$

Logically, the short octave should have been numbered thus:

1	2	3	4	5	6	7	8
C	F	D	G	E	A	Bb	B♮

Bermudo's example of this notation uses a four-line 'staff', on each line of which are placed the numbers referring to the notes of a certain voice-part. The voices are cantus, altus, tenor and bassus, reading from top to bottom. Hence the lines do not constitute a staff in the usual sense, and their purpose is the purely practical one of separating the parts of a polyphonic composition: this we have seen before (Figure 73(e); and see also Parrish NMM, plates XXI, XXII and XXIII). The music is barred regularly, the numbers being more or less carefully spaced through each bar: however, there are no rhythm-signs, and the rhythm is not invariably clear. Tied notes are indicated by ties between the numbers concerned. The text, for the cantus part only, is printed below the 'staff' (Apel NPM, 48).

Bermudo elsewhere mentions another notation, in which only the white notes are numbered, the semitone above being notated by a *croix* above the numeral. This notation is used in an Italian publication, Antonio Valente's *Intavolatura de Cimbalo* (Naples, 1576: for a page of this work, see Apel NPM, 51. It uses a printed form of the *croix*, ⚹). Because the black notes are not numbered as part of the main sequence, fewer numerals are employed, so that the system is easier to memorize. The numerals are allocated as follows (the short octave is not the same as Bermudo's):

1	2	3	4	5	6	7	8	9	10	11	...	23
C	F	G	A	B	c	d	e	f	g	a	...	f″

In Giovanni Picchi's *Intavolatura di balli d'arpicordo* (2nd edn, 1620) the range is increased to c‴ and the numerals, therefore, to 27. The short octave is the same as Valente's, with the three bottom black notes tuned to D, E and Bb respectively. In this case, however, the tablature is entirely logical in its treatment of the short octave: indeed, there is no other way of allocating the numerals. The three black notes are therefore treated as F♯, G♯ and A♯ respectively. Chromatic alteration is shown only by sharps, so in the short octave the notes D, E and Bb are numbered $\overset{⚹}{2}$, $\overset{⚹}{3}$, and $\overset{⚹}{4}$, respectively.

Use of the sharp-sign above the numerals virtually prohibits the use of the 'staff' representing the voices, which would make the music cluttered and unreadable. Instead, the numerals are *in campo aperto* (if one may use the term in this context), although still ranged horizontally as if the lines were there. A single line separates the numerals belonging to the player's right hand from those to be played by his left. (This, too, awakens echoes. See Parrish's reproductions of early twelfth-century polyphony: NMM, plates XXI–XXIII.)

Rhythm-signs appear at the top of the score. Only the shortest time-values are indicated, and only for the first of a group: a sign applies until cancelled by another (cf. German Organ Tablature, above). The signs, beginning with the *battuta over semibreve* ('beat, or semibreve'), are:

S	M	Sm	F	Sf

In addition, there are a few special durational signs for single notes:

$$; \ = \ 1\tfrac{1}{2}\,M \quad : \ = \ 2\,M \quad : \ = \ 3\,M$$

$$? \ = \ 4\,M \quad \iota \ = \ \text{trill or mordent}$$

These follow the numeral concerned, except the ornament, which is placed above it.

A third notation is first found in Luys Venegas de Henestrosa's *Libro de cifra nueva para tecla, harpa y vihuela* (Alcalà 1557), a work which includes several pieces by 'Antonio'—presumably Cabezon. This notation is simpler than the earlier two: it uses the same series of numerals for each octave from F to E, with the different octaves distinguished graphically.

```
C – E:    5   6   7

F – e:    1   2   3   4   5   6   7

f – e':   1 – 7

f' – e":  1·  2·  3·  4·  5·  6·  7·

f" – a":  1' – 3'.
```

(The notations of Braythwaite, Souhaitty and Rousseau, mentioned in Chapter 9, are perhaps direct descendants of this one.) In later sources the notes BB and b" are found, with the numerals 4 and 4', respectively.

This notation again uses a horizontal line for each voice-part; chromatic alteration is accomplished by either sharps or flats, below or following the relevant numeral; and rhythm-signs are used only as necessary. In the posthumously-published edition of Antonio de

Cabezon's work (see n.11) it appears that his son Hernando has collected the music and transcribed it into tablature ('recopiladas y puestas en cifra'), so the music may originally have been composed in staff notation. The accidentals are again either below or following the relevant numeral; in this case the rhythm-signs—again sparingly used—are complete notes, not rhythm-stems. The figure 4 can denote either B flat or B natural, depending on whether a B or a natural is placed at the beginning of the piece: this is, therefore, a unique case of a 'key-signature' being used in a phonetic notation—a slightly illogical usage, although neat and unambiguous. There are two special signs: 1. a comma, , shows that the note preceding it is tied over, and 2. a stroke, ⧾ through the 'stave'-line indicates a rest.

This last notation has obvious advantages over the other two, and it continued in use—though rarely—until about 1700.

11. Lute Tablatures

The basic notation

The earliest lute tablatures, dating from the late fifteenth century, are for a five-course instrument. Some English tuning instructions show the instrument to be tuned to c, f, a, d' and g': this, with the addition of one more course tuned to G, gives the six-course tuning which was most commonly used for the tenor lute during the sixteenth and early seventeenth centuries.[1] The repertory for the six-course instrument is written in tablatures apparently conceived for a five-course lute and later adapted for six courses: the adaptation is very clearly seen in German tablatures, and in some of the earliest French sources.

The G tuning for tenor lute is, of course, only the written tuning: the actual pitch—which was decided by the lutenist, and no doubt partly depended on his instrument and the singer if there was one—varied. The six courses were not all strung alike. The top course consisted of a single string, the 'chanterelle', until *c*. 1600: thereafter it was a double-string course, at least in England (Robert Spencer in the *Lute Society Journal* 15 (1973), 51). The lower courses normally had two strings each, those of the second and third courses being in unison and those of the lowest three being tuned in octaves.[2] This arrangement gives the maximum resonance to the instrument throughout its range, while allowing the top course to sound with great clarity and penetration.

All but a few of the earliest tablatures are written on a six-line 'staff', each line of which represents a course. On these lines are placed symbols, either letters or numerals, which refer to the fret on which the player's finger is to be placed. Since the frets of the lute were placed at intervals of a semitone, the notes obtained by playing the full series of symbols is the full chromatic scale. Most lutes had eight frets, but in some tablatures further fret-positions are indicated. Probably the player simply fingered the note on the plain finger-board: in the seventeenth century a ninth fret was often used, but the player sometimes had to finger a semitone higher still.

Rhythms are shown by any of the means that we have seen used for keyboard tablatures. Each musical event, whether a single note or a chord, is of a certain duration before the next event happens: it is this duration (which may or may not be the same as the note-value in a staff-notation transcription) which is notated. Most French tablatures show only the changes in this durational unit, but some, especially amongst English sources (which use French tablature exclusively), indicate the durations of all the separate events. In this latter case, a characteristic 'grid' pattern often results, as in Figure 83(b).

The beauty of this system is its simplicity and legibility. As will presently be seen, in all but the German system a total of 54 or more finger-positions are indicated by only nine or ten symbols; the music takes up only one 'staff'; and as it is read from left to right, it can be used in conjunction with staff notation.

French tablature

In the French system, the top line of the 'staff' represents the 'chanterelle'. On the various lines of the 'staff' are placed letters which indicate the fret to be played: later tablatures place the letter above the lines, not over them, but this makes no difference to the system. The letter a represents the open course on any line; letter b represents the first fret, a semitone above; letter c the fret above that; and so on. The notes to be obtained from the 'chanterelle' by playing the series of letters on the top line of the 'staff' are shown in Figure 84(a), and a short musical extract (b) will illustrate the system.

Figure 84. French Lute Tablature

(John Dowland, Fantasie: Robert Dowland, *Varietie of Lute Lessons*, p. 29)

154

It should be noted here that lute tablature differs in one vital respect from tablature for organ. In a lute tablature the different voice-parts of a polyphonic composition are not distinguished visually, since any single part may be shared between two or more courses. In fact, much lute-music is not polyphonic in any case, and a florid prelude (for example) which was originally conceived for the lute is best served by a strict transcription. But much lute-music is transcribed part-music, in which case a strict transcription back into staff notation may not show all the musical qualities that a good performance would allow one to hear: and the same is true of music in that pseudo-polyphonic style to which the lute was so well suited (Figure 85). ('Pseudo-polyphonic' is not intended to disparage the style. It implies that an illusion of part-writing can be maintained even when strict polyphony cannot—an idiomatic style for the lute. See also Figure 88.)

Figure 85. Polyphonic Writing for Lute

(Anthony Holborne. Pavan: Robert Dowland. *Varietie*, p. 34. from 1st strain)

The earliest sixteenth-century examples of French tablature were printed on a five-line 'staff', showing the notation to have been devised for a five-course instrument. By this time (1529, the date of Attaingnant's *Dixhuit basse dances* and *Tres breve . . . introduction*) the lute did have six courses, however, and the letters for the lowest

155

course are printed below the 'staff' on separate pieces of line rather like leger-lines. The six-line 'staff' of Italian sources was used in the anonymous *Livre plaisant* printed at Antwerp in that same year, but five-line tablature continued in use for several decades. However, six lines were normal from about 1584 onwards, after the publication (also at Antwerp) of Emanuel Hadrianus's *Pratum Musicum*. Towards the end of the century the lute acquired one or two extra bass courses, and more were added later. The symbols for these are placed under the 'staff'. These various additional courses are distinguished by lines above the letters: /a for the seventh course, //a for the eighth, and so on. The seventh course was apparently normally on the fingerboard, so that its frets are shown as /a (open string), /b, /c, and so on. The other additional courses appear to have been unstopped, and only the letter a is used. The tuning of these additional bass courses varies with the source. In some, the seventh, eighth and ninth courses are tuned to F, E and D respectively, only the open strings being played; in others, the seventh course only is used, tuned to D and stopped to produce notes from E♭ to F♯. The tuning can always be decided by transcribing the tablature. As more bass courses were added, the letters /////a, etc., were used: but a simplification soon occurred, by which the four-barred letter ////a was designated 4, the next (five-barred) 5, and so on.

By the late sixteenth century certain additional signs were in use:
1. A short vertical stroke. In the earliest prints and in manuscript this showed alignment between notes to be played simultaneously, but it is also found in later and very clear prints where no such alignment is needed. Here it seems to indicate a rest, the course being damped.
2. Dots below the letters indicated the fingerings for the player's right hand: usually, one dot meant that he should pluck the course with his index finger, two dots with the second finger, and three dots with the third. Undotted letters between were to be played with the thumb.
3. A long diagonal line beneath several letters indicated 'covered play'. Each note was to be held as long as possible, the finger being lifted only when needed to play another note. The result is a more sustained texture than would otherwise be achieved.

Around the turn of the century, the increase in numbers of bass courses (up to seven by about 1620) began to necessitate some instructions for tuning. Such instructions are usually given at the end of a piece and show two notes aligned vertically, to be tuned either in unison or at the octave (Figure 86(a)). These instructions were often included in seventeenth-century sources, since various other ways of tuning the lute began to be used. Several new tunings were in use by about 1620, and others appeared during the course of that century. One of the most important was the 'new tuning' (*nouveau ton*, to distinguish it from the *vieil ton* or 'old tuning' of the sixteenth century) introduced by Denis Gaultier *c.* 1640: this remained in use until the eighteenth century. The purpose of these tunings was to facilitate the use of certain chords and keys. Some of the most frequently-used tunings are shown in Figure 86(b).[3]

Figure 86. Baroque Lute Tunings

In the seventeenth century the flexibility of tunings was extended to the bass courses: as before an *accord* or tuning-instruction might be included, though often at the beginning of a piece rather than at the end.

The two earliest prints do not use bar-lines, except to show repeats at the end of each phrase. Thereafter, French tablatures are normally barred regularly, although—as in staff notation—the barring tends to be for visual convenience, not to show the real metre of the music (see Figure 88; also Apel NPM, 65 ff).

The subject of ornamentation on the lute is a difficult one, since the few tutors that describe ornaments and their notation do not agree. Indeed, the discovery of the Board Lute Book (BMS 9) has actually made the subject more confused as regards English music (Robert Spencer in the *Lute Society Journal* 15 (1973), 52), and adds nothing to our knowledge of the French. The most common ornaments are:

1. The shake: this may be a simple upper mordent, but a 'long shake' may be a candential trill. Its most common notations are apparently , in French sources and later English ones, and # in English sources up to the mid-seventeenth century.

2. The fall: from the diatonic note below, this seems often to be notated as ℓ, + or × : these signs for the fore-fall may sometimes imply also that the ornamented note is shaked. In continental sources (and English sources after the mid-seventeenth century) a fall is often notated by writing tablature-letters for both notes concerned (c.f. the Capirola book, below) with a 'slur' under them: a ͜ c.

Spanish and Italian tablatures

Lute tablatures in Spanish and Italian sources have much in common with the tablatures just described. All use a six-line 'staff', and their auxiliary signs—such as rhythm-signs and fingering-dots—are easily recognizable by anyone conversant with the French tablatures. There are two principal differences:

1. Spanish and Italian tablatures use numerals instead of letters to indicate the fret to be played. The open course is indicated by 0, the first fret by 1, the second by 2, and so on: in some sources the fret-positions go up to 10, 11 and 12, while in the earliest Italian sources these higher frets are indicated by the roman numerals x, ẋ and ẍ. (This early system saves space and helps legibility. The superscript dots should not be confused with dots *under* the numerals showing right-hand fingering.)

2. With a single exception, Spanish and Italian tablatures are 'upside-down'—that is, the top line of the 'staff' represents the lowest course, and the order of the other courses is also reversed. It has been argued that since the player holds his instrument with the 'chanterelle' next to his lap, this is the logical way to write the tablature (Apel NPM, 61): but it should be said in objection to this that the player sees the instrument in this position relative to his own head only if he watches himself in a mirror.

The exception to this second difference is the earliest of the Spanish sources, Luis Milan's *El Maestro* (Valencia 1536): this, alone of the sources in Italian tablature, has the 'chanterelle' line at the top of the 'staff'. It may be asked, then, if 'Spanish Lute Tablature', implying as it does a distinction from the Italian notation for lute, is a term with any meaning. Certainly we are hardly justified in regarding *El Maestro* as the single example of a peculiarly Spanish tablature. On the other hand the term might be admissible as implying 'Spanish sources of Italian lute notation', and for this meaning there is some other justification:

1. Several Spanish tablatures, including the prints of Milan and Fuenllana, show an ingenious system for notating lute-song: the text is printed underneath the 'staff', and those symbols in the tablature which indicate notes to be sung are printed in red. These red symbols should be played by the vihuelist: the case is something of a parallel to that of the coloured mean in contemporary English keyboard music (see Chapter 6, especially n.10).

2. As the titles of the Spanish books say, the instrument for which these books were intended was the *vihuela de mano*, which is really a guitar, not a lute. The vihuela was, however, tuned in the same way as the tenor lute. Hence, although the Spanish books use the same notation as the Italian lute-sources, they should be treated separately because of the different instrument involved.

One more difference between the Italian and Spanish sources may be noted here: generally, although not exclusively, the Spanish sources use complete notes as rhythm-signs, while Italian sources use only flagged stems. As in French tablature, the stem of longest duration denotes the S, the beat (Figure 87(a)). The Italian sources also have stems of unusual duration, dividing the beat into thirds or fifths (b).

Figure 87. Italian Rhythmic Signs

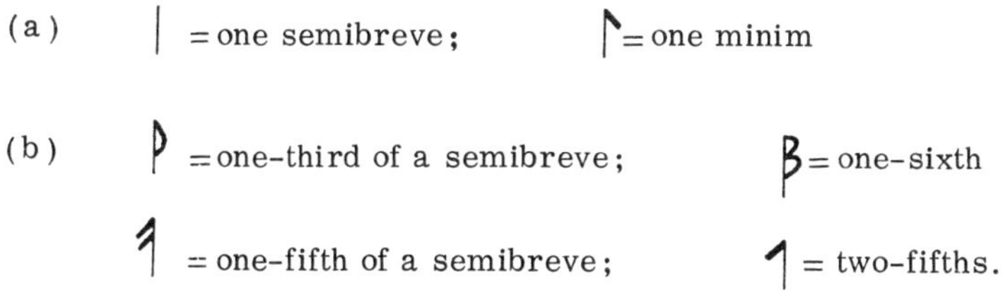

(a) $|$ = one semibreve; $\wedge$ = one minim

(b) $\wp$ = one-third of a semibreve; β = one–sixth

$\wedge$ = one-fifth of a semibreve; $\uparrow$ = two–fifths.

Regular barring is a feature of sources in Italian tablature, beginning with Petrucci's *Intabolatura de lauto, Libro primo* (Venice 1507). A warning is necessary, however, especially in respect of the Spanish sources, that the barring is often used to divide off a S's length—i.e., a beat, not a bar. This method can often hide the true metre of the piece: for example, a triple-time metre may be brought out by smaller note-values and fewer bar-lines (Figure 88).

Little need be added here to what was said concerning ornamentation in French tablature. However, the Capirola Lute Book is especially interesting not only because of its marginal decorations and its use of different colours for rhythm-stems of different values,

Figure 88. Barring in Lute Tablature

Original:

(Milan, Fantasia 6: from *El Maestro*, 1536)

Literal transcription:

Musical transcription:

but because of its notation for ornaments. Here the auxiliary note is indicated as a numeral written in red dots next to the main (black) numeral: the graphic effect of this is very striking.

German tablature

According to Sebastian Virdung (*Musica getutscht*, 1511) German lute tablature was invented by the blind organist Conrad Paumann (*c.* 1410–73). Although this attribution was not queried at the time, commentators in the present century have often suggested that a blind man could not invent and would not use a notational system of such complexity, requiring at least 41 different symbols to be distinguished visually. Reasons for accepting the attribution to Paumann, however, have been argued convincingly by Rudolf Henning ('German Lute Tablature'). Henning's reasons may be summarized as follows:
1. German tablature is ideal for dictating to an amanuensis (as Paumann would need to do).
2. It does not use a 'staff', which would be a source of mistakes and confusion in copying—mistakes which a blind man could not rectify.
3. Other types of lute tablature are graphic in so far as they offer a representation of the fingerboard itself: this would certainly be rejected by a blind man.
Henning also suggests that the necessary date of invention, some time before 1473, is about right. Certainly this notation was originally designed (like French tablature) for a five-course instrument, and the

dating of the Königstein song book at *c.* 1470–3 is compatible with an attribution to Paumann. We should note, too, that the real difficulty of dealing with German tablature stems from its adaptation to a six-course instrument: for a five-course lute the notation is perfectly logical and can easily be used by any player with a good memory. Indeed, its advantages and the demands it makes on the performer are almost exactly those of Bermudo's first keyboard tablature (Chapter 10: Bermudo, too, was blind).

It will be convenient to discuss the basic five-course notation to begin with, since this is universal, whereas the notation for the sixth course varies. The original five courses are numbered 1–5, starting from the bottom course: these numbers represent the open courses. Starting from the bottom again, the first fret begins the letters of the alphabet, a–e, the second uses f–k, and so on: the alphabet has 23 letters (i = j, u = v, and there is no w), so the fifth fret can be allocated letters only with the help of two additional symbols. For this purpose, the abbreviation-signs for *et* (ꝫ) and *con-* (9) are used. For the sixth and subsequent frets, the alphabet is started again, with modifications: each letter is either doubled (aa, bb, etc.) or is given a superscript bar (ā, ƀ, etc.). The following is a diagram of the fingerboard:

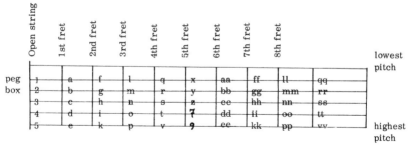

Clearly, this is a very different notation from those for lute found in France, Spain and Italy. The numbering is carried across the courses, not along them, requiring a separate symbol for each intersection of fret and course. There is thus no need to write the tablature on a 'staff' representing courses. Indeed the music can, if desired, be written in horizontal lines according to the voice-parts, an advantage that it shares with keyboard tablatures.

For a five-course instrument this notation is logical and not difficult to use. With the addition of a sixth course, however, the system breaks down and produces a very clumsy notation. All the other lute tablatures have the advantage that the symbols used are the same for each course, so that the addition of another course raises no

161

basic problem. But in German notation a new series of symbols must be devised for each additional course, and this was never managed satisfactorily. Various methods of notating the sixth course were tried (all of them cumbersome), but little attempt seems to have been made to devise symbols for the seventh and subsequent courses when they became normal in the early seventeenth century. There are a few examples of German tablature later than 1600 (Wolf HdN ii, 49), but most German composers by then used French tablature. Probably it was only the ease with which German tablature could be printed that kept it in use even so long (Henning, op. cit., 9 f).

Five main ways exist of notating the sixth course (Wolf HdN ii, between pp. 40 and 41; Apel NPM, 76): I give them here in chronological order of their first appearance.

1. Sebastian Virdung, *Musica getutscht* (Basel 1511). This series follows the designations for the course above, with capitals instead of lower-case letters and a scrolled numeral 1 for the open course:

$$\tilde{1} \quad A \quad F \quad L \quad Q \quad X \quad AA \quad FF$$

Arnolt Schlick also used this series in *Tabulaturen etlicher lobgesang und lidlein* (Mainz 1512), but only as far as the fifth fret. He used a barred numeral 1 for the open course.

2. Hans Judenkunig, *Ain schone kunstliche underweisung* (Vienna 1523). This series, perhaps derived from French tablature (although no source of French tablature survives from so early a date), allocates letters up to the sixth fret:

$$A \quad B \quad C \quad D \quad E \quad F \quad G$$

3. Hans Newsidler, *Ein Newgeordnet künstlich Lautenbuch* (Nuremberg 1536). This series uses the normal eight frets: but it neither corresponds to French tablature (being one fret out because of the ⊥ used for the open course) nor connects much with the notation of the upper courses:

$$\mathrm{⊥} \quad A \quad B \quad C \quad D \quad E \quad F \quad G \quad H$$

4. Wolff Heckel, *Discant Lauttenbuch* (Strasburg 1552):

$$\mathrm{⊥} \quad \bar{a} \quad \bar{f} \quad \bar{l} \quad \bar{q} \quad \bar{x} \quad \bar{a}\bar{a} \quad \bar{ff} \quad \bar{ll}$$

Heckel presumably uses aa, bb, etc., for the sixth and subsequent frets of the other courses, not $\bar{a}$, $\bar{b}$, . . . This, obviously, is a modification and extension of Virdung's system (1), and has the same advantages.

5. Hans Gerle, *Ein Newes sehr Künstlichs Lautenbuch* (Nuremberg

162

1552). The only one of these early systems to use numerals: it does not correspond to Italian notation:

$$\bar{1} \quad \bar{2} \quad \bar{3} \quad \bar{4} \quad \bar{5} \quad \bar{6} \quad \bar{7} \quad \bar{8} \quad \bar{9}$$

Later systems use much the same principles as these five. Despite the demands made on the memory in performance, German lute tablatures show few features that would prove difficult to a transcriber. The main problem is the time taken in transcription, due both to the allocation of symbols across the courses and to the Gothic lettering normally used. The music is usually barred regularly.

Rhythm-signs are much as should be expected. In Hans Judenkunig's work the use of the index finger for plucking is shown by the addition of a vertical bar to the rhythm-stem, thus: ↾ or ↿ . The plain stem, ↾ or ↾ , indicates that the thumb is to be used. Newsidler and Gerle show right-hand fingering by means of dots more comprehensively than French sources do: one dot is used for the index finger, two for the middle finger, three for the ring-finger and four for the little finger (Wolf HdN ii, 42).

Normally, the most common tuning for the tenor lute, in G, will be suitable for all pieces in German tablature. However, in the pieces for lute and voice in Schlick's *Tabulaturen* (1512) it is clear from the vocal part that the lute must be tuned in A (i.e., A d g b♮ e' a'), and Judenkunig also used this tuning (Apel NPM, 56 and 77). In a piece for voice and lute, a transcription of the final chord will of course provide the answer if there is any doubt: in a purely instrumental piece, the transposition up a tone may bring the music from an awkward key (in staff-notation terms) to a simpler one. Various *scordatura* tunings are found in the German lute sources, verbal explanations being given rather than an *accord*.

12. Miscellaneous Tablatures

The various tablatures discussed in Chapters 10 and 11 show between them several notational principles that could be used for instruments other than the keyboard and lute. As we have remarked before, German keyboard tablature uses the principle of certain earlier vocal notations, and so is not basically an instrumental notation at all but simply a phonetic method of writing music. This is also partly true of the Spanish keyboard tablatures, a fact that is underlined by what I called the illogicality of the notation for the short octave. Phonetic notations using numbers are found also in music written for flute, for musette, and for accordion, as well as in a number of vocal notations (Wolf HdN ii, 244–8 and 387–419, passim), while many experimental notations, as well as other instrumental tablatures, have used letters. Although the basic principles of these notations are often those which we have already seen, the precise application of them in any particular case may require detailed discussion, for which the reader is referred to Johannes Wolf's excellent descriptions.

Although I propose to deal with two graphic notations for instruments, most of the tablatures to be discussed here are for stringed instruments (bowed as well as plucked) which use the basic principles of the French and Italian lute tablatures. These principles are:

1. (a) The music is written on a 'staff' whose lines correspond to the principal courses or strings of the instrument, (b) additional bass courses being notated above or below the 'staff'.

2. Each line bears letters or figures corresponding to the frets on the fingerboard, which direct the player to stop the relevant course at a particular fret with his left hand.

3. Rhythm-signs above the 'staff' show the duration of each musical event.

Clearly, there are two possible differences between these tablatures and those for lute. First, the correct transcription of pitch will depend on the tuning of the instrument. Second, the incidental features of the notation, such as indications for ornaments, fingering, articulation, etc., may or may not be the same as for lute. They are frequently different: but, since the lute repertory was the largest, most important musically and therefore the most influential notationally, the incidental symbols in other tablatures are usually at least closely related to those used for lute music.

Close relatives of lute tablature

It is convenient to discuss first the group of instruments for which the tablatures are very similar to those for lute. This group includes the viol, bass lute, theorbo and chitarrone.

The Italian tablature for viol found in Ganassi's *Regola Rubertina* (1542) is closely related to Italian lute tablature in using numerals on the lines of a reversed 'staff'. Two things are notable: first, that the rhythm signs can be reversed to keep them on the staff (cf. the question of M-stems in the fifteenth century); second, that there is a system of dots to show fingering, the upper finger-positions above the frets, and the bowing. The fingering is shown as follows:

A dot above the line and to the left of the symbol : index finger.

,,	below	,,	,,	,,	,,	: 2nd	,,
,,	above	,,	,,	right	,,	: 3rd	,,
,,	below	,,	,,	,,	,,	: little	,,

The finger-positions are shown as follows: the numerals 0–9 are used (as in lute tablature) for the open string, the eight frets and the semitone above; then the higher positions (10–15 inclusive) are shown by a series obviously derived from that used in lute tablatures (Figure 89(a)). Finally, a dot placed well above the symbol shows a forward bow, while one placed well below shows a back bow. One could therefore have a symbol such as that shown in (b), indicating the eleventh 'fret', to be fingered with the third finger and played with a back bow: intellectually a satisfying notation, perhaps, this is not ideal from a practical point of view.

The normal tuning of viols was the same as that for lutes:

treble	:	d	g	c′	e′	a′	d″
tenor	:	G	c	f	a	d′	g′
bass	:	D	G	c	e	a	d′

These are the main tunings used by Ganassi: Figure 89(c) shows the opening of a piece, with a transcription as of performance on a bass viol.

Figure 89. Tablatures for Viol

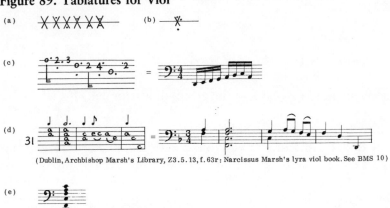

(Dublin, Archbishop Marsh's Library, Z3.5.13, f. 63r: Narcissus Marsh's lyra viol book. See BMS 10)

Tablature was used for viols played as solo instruments, with the possibility of chords—that is, played 'lyra-way'. The usual instrument for this in England was a small bass viol called a 'lyra-viol', but in fact any viol could be played lyra-way. French tablature was used, as it was for the lute: in the seventeenth century there were various tunings comparable to the contemporary lute-tunings. Figure 89(d) shows the opening of a Courant by William Lawes, notated in harp-way sharp tuning. It is transcribed for a bass viol, and I have interpreted the tuning as at (e). The slurs in bar 2 are bowing-marks, the notes governed by any slur being played with a single bow-stroke. As with any bowed instrument, all of the strings must be accounted for between the top and bottom notes of a chord, even if this means resorting to note-doubling.

In Chapter 11 we dealt exclusively with the tenor lute: the treble lute was fairly rare, but a small repertory exists for bass lute. Figure 90(a) will show that its notation is the same as for a tenor lute, but the instrument is pitched a fourth lower. In this manuscript the singer's first note is sometimes shown (as here) in the lute-part, presumably so that the lutenist can play the note quietly to give the pitch to the singer before they start.

Tablatures for the theorbo are also comparable to those for lute, the French notation using letters, and the Italian numbers on a reversed 'staff'. In both cases the 'staff' is of six lines, corresponding to

Figure 90. Tablatures for Bass Lute and Theorbo

(a)

(Cambridge, King's College, Rowe MS 2, f. 14v: see BMS 2)

(b)

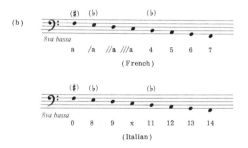

(Accidentals in parentheses are used in certain keys)

the principal courses of the instrument, which are tuned like those of the tenor lute. The difference is in the notation for the various unstopped bass courses, of which there are usually eight and which made the theorbo suitable as a continuo instrument. Their tuning and the notations for them are shown in Figure 90(b) (Wolf HdN ii, 115 f, gives examples). The relationship with the French and Italian lute-tablature is obvious. The chitarrone, a development of the theorbo with the same tuning, and also used as a continuo instrument, had the same sort of tablature.

Tablatures for the cittern

With tablatures for lute and the instruments already discussed in this chapter, the lines of the 'staff' go in order of pitch, whether from top to bottom or *vice versa*. It is thus possible to play from such tablatures at the keyboard, the principal difficulty being the duration of individual notes, for which some skill at keyboard harmonization is necessary. Tablatures for instruments with re-entrant tunings have an added difficulty, in that the tablature-lines follow the courses of the instrument in not being in order of pitch. Such tablatures therefore need special practice for transcription, although there is of course no added difficulty for the performer playing from this notation on the instrument for which it was written.

The cittern has a large repertory dating from the mid-sixteenth century to the eighteenth, mainly for a four-course instrument. For this there are four lines to the tablature, and the instrument has no additional bass courses. French tablature, as before, uses letters: sources of French origin are for an instrument tuned to a g d' e', but the English sources also use a slightly different, Italian, tuning, b♮ g d' e'. If there is doubt in any case as to which tuning is in use, the transcription of a final chord or cadence will give the answer. The sources of Italian tablature, as we should expect, use numbers. However, there is the same division here as we found in Italian and Spanish lute-tablatures: Sixt Kärgel used a 'staff' in which the top line represented the highest course, while David Sammenhammer used the reversed tablature that we might expect.[1] An eighteenth-century Spanish manuscript which came to light in 1973 uses an unreversed tablature on four lines.[2]

The tablatures for five- or six-course cittern, dating from the mid-sixteenth century to the late seventeenth, present no problems. They use either letters or numerals, the latter on a reversed 'staff', and they have five or six lines as appropriate. The five-course instrument is tuned c e g b♮ e' (that is, not a re-entrant tuning), the six-course B♮ G d g d' e'.

A single source of music for a thirteen-course cittern is of more interest.[3] The tablature is basically for a four-course instrument, but nine bass courses are notated below the 'staff', using the numerals 1–9 in descending order. Although the tablature uses numbers, the order of courses is not reversed. The tuning, with the numbering of bass-courses, is shown in Figure 91(a). The music is a collection of

168

chorale-settings, and a feature of the tablature is a system of rhythmic notation by which little more than the main beat is shown in the usual way, beat-divisions in the bass-line being shown separately. A single line under two or more numerals indicates the first division (i.e. into Qs), a double line the second division (into Sqs): these lines no doubt derive from beams (b).

Figure 91. Cittern Tablatures

(Berlin, Deutsche Staatsbibliothek, Mus. MS 40145, no. 103)

Tablatures for guitar

Notation for guitar falls into two main categories: (1) tablatures proper, such as were used for other stringed instruments, and (2) a phonetic notation in which letters stand for certain chords. Of these, the second is related to certain other harmonic notations, and will be discussed in Chapter 15 (see Figure 107).

The earliest guitar-tablatures date from the middle of the sixteenth century, the latest from the eighteenth. At the beginning of this period a four-line tablature was sufficient, for an instrument tuned c f a d'. The tablatures are of the usual French and Italian types: as in the Spanish vihuela-songs, the Spanish songs with guitar are notated on a reversed tablature with the vocal part in red. Seventeenth-century Italian tablatures for five-course guitar (tuned G c f a d') are also reversed, but in the eighteenth century Italian notation was brought into line with the French, resulting in an unreversed number-tablature on six lines for a larger instrument tuned D G c f a d' (and then up a tone to its present tuning, E A d g b e').

169

The guitar can also be played from the 'pop' graphic tablature associated with the ukelele (see Figure 92(c)).

Graphic tablatures

Finally I wish to discuss two graphic tablatures. Thomas Greeting's notation for the flageolet[4] uses a six-line 'staff' whose lines correspond to the six finger-holes of the instrument. A short vertical stroke on any line indicates that the hole is closed; on the top line, half-closing with the thumb-nail is shown as a small cross; absence of any sign shows that the hole is open. A beat or shake is shown by a comma-like hook on the appropriate line, and slurring is indicated by a slur under the symbols. The latter cannot therefore be confused with ties in the rhythm-signs, which appear as notes (tied when necessary) above the tablature. Figure 92 shows (a) the fingering of the scale, and (b) the opening of 'Parthenia' (from Wolf HdN ii, 243 ff). The advantage of

Figure 92. Tablatures for Flute and for Ukelele

(Thomas Greeting, *Pleasant Companion... for the flageolet* (London, ?1672))

('All the Things You Are' from *Very Warm for May* : music by Jerome Kern, words by Oscar Hammerstein 2nd.© 1939 T.B.Harms Co.)

this notation is, no doubt, that it shows such things as cross-fingering, together with a certain amount of expressive detail such as trills and slurs, without cluttering the page with too many visual distractions. Even so, it is a little wasteful of space, and any more information (e.g. dynamics) might well make it unusable.

The twentieth-century 'pop' notation for ukelele is also a graphic tablature, with the same sort of advantage to the unskilled player. The grid which appears for each chord is literally a picture of the fingerboard up to the 4th fret, and the dots show the positions of the fingers. The frets (which are of metal) are shown by the horizontal lines. As long as only the first four frets are needed, therefore, this notation is a more direct one than any system requiring numbering or lettering of the frets. The ukelele has a re-entrant tuning of g' c' e' a' (Figure 92(c)). Obviously, this tablature could be used for any other plucked-string instrument: it is, in fact, used for the guitar, in which case the tablature has six vertical lines.

Part IV
Staff Notation Since 1600

13. The Perfection of the System

The symbols of pitch and duration

At the beginning of the seventeenth century staff notation was recognizably that which is still in general use. This appearance is deceptive, however, for—as we shall see in Chapter 15—an underlying problem concerning the notation of triple mensurations remained until the nineteenth century, and at its most difficult still causes us interpretative problems in performing music of the eighteenth and nineteenth centuries. But on the surface, seventeenth-century notation seems to offer no problems other than small graphological ones. The remnants of medieval notation—coloration, the six-line staff for keyboard music, the non-alignment of scores—largely disappeared in the course of the century, so that much seventeenth-century notation could normally be used for present-day performance. In this, the increasing use of the G-clef for upper voices in the seventeenth century is an important factor. For some way into the century the old founts of music type ensured that diamond-shaped note-heads were still known, but the increased use of engraving for music eventually made round note-heads the norm in printed music as in manuscript.

In a similar way, movable type tended to preserve the use of single notes in long groups of Qs and lower note-values (Figure 93(a)). The joining of rhythm-flags into beams had been known well back in the sixteenth century, and its general use in staff notation may have been in imitation of the 'grids' of rhythm-signs used in tablatures. The scribal advantages of beamed groups over single notes must have commended the former very strongly, and this was no doubt confirmed in printing by the use of engraving.

One characteristic of early beaming survived throughout the seventeenth century, namely, the retrospective flagging of a group of Sqs. (Incidentally, this was not characteristic of tablature rhythm-grids.) Ganassi's notation (Figure 93 (b)) gave rise to such groups as (c): and well into the eighteenth century we find that in beamed groups with dotted rhythm the secondary flag may be either retrospective or drawn across the stem (d). (The modern rule is that the broken secondary beam should face into the rhythmic unit of which it is a part: Read, *Music Notation*, 84 f.)

Figure 93. Beams

(a) (Monteverdi, *L' Orfeo* (1615, R/1972), sig. H4v)

(b) (Ganassi. *Fontegara*, 1535: see Wolf HdN ii, 243)

(c)

(d)

In instrumental music, beaming was recognizably metrical, the advantage being—as in lute tablatures—that the eye is drawn to note-groups which have some rhythmic significance in the prevailing metre. In vocal music, however, beams were used until quite recently only for a group of notes sung to a single syllable. In syllabic settings this graphic way of showing the underlay is very clear as long as the rhythms are simple: otherwise, it can be difficult to see what the real rhythms of the music should be.[1]

As we have previously noted, the C became the beat by the beginning of the seventeenth century. With this further, and final, shift of time-values (although the Q was later used as the beat for some types of music) some smaller note-values were needed. Decorative lute-music had for long been adding flags to rhythm-stems and further beams to rhythm-grids, so that rhythm-signs using three or four flags or beams (notating Qs or Sqs in lute music) were quite familiar. Thus the notation for demi-semiquavers and smaller values in fact existed even before the need for it arose, and staff notation simply took over the idea from lute-tablature. Monteverdi's *Orfeo* already used Dsqs (Figure 93(a)), and hemi-demi-semiquavers (four beams) are found in the Fitzwilliam Virginal Book. Such an easy transition to smaller time-values is of course a mark of the simplicity of duple measurement organized additively.

176

The notation of irregular groups such as triplets was a less simple matter. Coloration proved adequate to composers' needs for a considerable time, and a numeral could always be used if necessary; beaming was a possible help, if only as a warning to the performer, but it was with a numeral placed directly over the notes concerned that a neat and unambiguous solution was eventually found (Figure 94(a)). From the eighteenth century onwards a slur was often used to define the area affected by the numeral (b), although in early examples the slur may notate *legato*. (See Winternitz MA ii, plate 43, however, for an example in which Handel is inconsistent.)

Figure 94. Notation of Triplets

(a)

(Arne, *Sonatas,* 1756, p. 2)

(b)

(Ibid., p. 28)

Accidentals

The seventeenth century and most of the eighteenth present us with a use of accidentals that is transitional and not always easy to interpret. Until about the middle of the seventeenth century only the ♯ and ♭ were used, either cancelling the other, as had been the case since the middle of the previous century. After about 1650 Italian composers began to use the old alternative form ♮ to restore a B natural, then to cancel any flat, and then by analogy to cancel sharps as well. In this way the 'natural' sign came into being. Eventually this made it possible for accidentals to define pitch absolutely rather than relatively. For instance, a notated D sharp would previously have been a semitone higher than the previous notated D, whether that had been a D natural or a D flat: but with the use of all three accidental signs a D sharp would always be the semitone above a D natural, which in turn would

177

always be a semitone higher than D flat.[2] In England and elsewhere the natural sign was not much used until the eighteenth century. A general conservatism in this respect may have been due partly to the unambiguous use of ♯ and ♭ alone to show the major or minor 3rd in figured bass (see Chapter 15), and partly to the rules on which this usage was based: namely, that a major 3rd may not be sharpened (i.e. made into an augmented 3rd) and a minor 3rd may not be flattened (i.e. made into a diminished 3rd). Against this conservatism must be set the increased need for precise chromatic notation as the tonal system developed to its logical conclusion. We can see this need in contexts where ♯ and ♭ also had to suffice for the double-sharp and the double-flat, this being one of a number of methods used prior to the acceptance of ✗ and ♭♭ as the standard notation during the first half of the eighteenth century (chromatic signs are discussed by Donington, IEM, 127 f).

For a while, then, during the second half of the seventeenth century, the sharp sign did duty for a double-sharp, a sharp, or the cancellation of a flat, while the flat sign was similarly used for a double-flat, a flat, or the cancellation of a sharp. The *croix* form of the sharp, ✗, was generally abandoned in favour of the upright form (although 'upright' is a relative term, for considerable variation from the vertical is common): but the *croix* continued in limited use quite late (for instance, in the print of Arne's *Sonatas*, 1756), and its persistence may be one reason for the late acceptance of the double-sharp, with which it could have been confused.

The duration of an accidental's effectiveness depended on a number of circumstances. In sixteenth-century music an accidental that forced a hexachord change need not be repeated for subsequent appearances of the note in the same phrase, as long as no further mutation took place. In general, such an accidental was cancelled after a 'dead' interval between phrases caused by a rest or a bar-line (Figure 95(a)). In practice, the accidental was often repeated, for safety's sake: even when the note appeared two or more times consecutively, it was sometimes considered wise to repeat the accidental with the note. In the early seventeenth century, with the disuse of the hexachord system in all but the most conservative music, the rules changed slightly. Without a hexachord structure, it followed that an accidental could refer only to a single note. Thus in general each appearance of a chromatically-altered note required an accidental: only when the note was immediately repeated was a second accidental sometimes thought unnecessary, and the intervention of a rest or another note nearly always made the second accidental a necessity if the chromatic alteration was not to be cancelled. The musical sense could sometimes be relied on to prevent the performer from going astray, but even so it is remarkable that Monteverdi, for instance, evidently preferred not to take the slightest risk of ambiguity (Figure 95(b)).

Figure 95. Validity of Accidentals

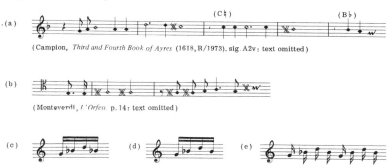

(Campion, *Third and Fourth Book of Ayres* (1618, R/1973), sig. A2v: text omitted)

(Monteverdi, *L'Orfeo* p. 14: text omitted)

To some extent the metrical grouping of notes made the interpretation of accidentals plain, in that the second appearance of a chromatically-altered note did not necessarily require an accidental if it appeared in the same beat or in a recognizably repeated context. Hence, although Figure 95(c) was normal, (d) or (e) would not be misunderstood. Until about 1700 the rather irregular use of this principle occasionally results in ambiguities, thereafter rather less so. The situation was made clearer by the use of regular bar-lines in the music of some eighteenth-century composers, marking metrical units which affected the period of validity of accidentals. Only in the nineteenth century, however, do we find the modern convention regularly at work, in which an accidental affects the rest of the bar in which it occurs (unless cancelled), but not the bar following.

In discussing solmization (Chapter 9 and Figure 78) I cited a cadential figure in which one note which had to be sung sharp never in fact needed a notated accidental. The nature of the hexachord is such that an augmented interval is not possible unless very carefully and deliberately notated, and such intervals were indeed extremely rare prior to the seventeenth century. From then on they were not uncommon, but habit preserved the old notation. Hence the notation of an augmented interval remained a deliberate matter in which both notes were given appropriate accidentals. Without this specific directive a performer always assumed normal scalic intervals, so that

179

in many contexts a single accidental automatically presupposed an accidental also for the following note (Figure 96(a)): and the principle could also work retrospectively (b). In the case of (b), however, the asterisked note would in any case be sung as a C natural because of the intervening notes.

Figure 96. Accidentals Assumed

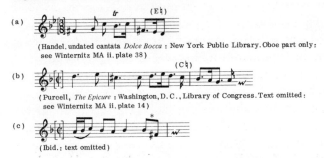

(a)

(Handel, undated cantata *Dolce Bocca* : New York Public Library. Oboe part only: see Winternitz MA ii, plate 38)

(b)

(Purcell, *The Epicure* : Washington, D. C., Library of Congress. Text omitted: see Winternitz MA ii, plate 14)

(c)

(Ibid.; text omitted)

With diminished intervals ambiguity is less likely, and composers did not feel the same need to notate the interval deliberately. Such intervals invariably descended, only the second note (if either) being chromatically altered. No performer then or now would query intervals such as that shown at (c).

The tonal system

As we saw in Chapter 7, the range of notes generally available at the end of the sixteenth century was small. The keys in general use were C major, D minor, F major, G major, G minor and A minor. The system still owed much to the Middle Ages, including the remnants of the hexachord system, and one result of this was a rather inconsistent set of key-signatures. The minor keys, in which the sixth and seventh of the scale are variably inflected, tended to be notated with one flat too few in the key-signature, the last flat—that for the sixth of the scale—being supplied either by the composer/scribe as a notated accidental or by the performer acting according to the principles of solmization.[3] In Italy, however, experiments in chromaticism tended to destroy this reliance (conscious or subconscious) on the hexachord system, and to substitute a real feeling for tonality, while tending also towards an extension of the tonal system. This extending of the tonal system continued for another century or more: but notation was more

180

conservative, and for a long time the minor keys on the flat side were often notated with a flat fewer than we should expect in the key signature (this is very noticeable even in Bach's music) while some of the new keys on the sharp side had one sharp fewer than we should expect. Until the middle of the eighteenth century, too, the nomenclature was not our normal one: composers usually referred to 'the key of G with the minor (or major) third', for instance.

Of the keys just listed G major was a newcomer. Its usual guise had been as a plagal form in which F sharp was not required as often as F natural, and consequently the question of a key-signature for it arose only at a time when the feeling for tonality was growing. Prior to 1600 key-signatures including sharps did not exist: thereafter, they appeared at intervals as they were required by a growing tonal system. In general it was vocal music that showed most conservatism in this respect, as indeed has remained the case. Keyboard music kept mainly to the same keys as vocal writing did, although such a work as Bull's *Ut re mi* III shows that keyboard instruments could be tuned by at least one method that made some very unusual keys acceptable to the ear (Caldwell, *English Keyboard Music*, 77 f).

Of course, an enharmonic excursion to G flat major or F sharp major (Bull notated it both ways) in the middle of a piece in G is one thing: the composition of an entire piece in F sharp major, with the appropriate key-signature, is quite another. The latter did not happen for a century after Bull's piece. It was with those solo instruments whose intonation could be easily adjusted that music in distant keys was possible as a matter of course, and of these the lute was the most influential. As we have already noted, the key of F minor was quite possible in lute music long before it is found elsewhere. The lute can be made to sound acceptably in any key because its frets are adjustable, and a certain amount of adjustment is also possible during performance by altering the position of the stopping finger against the fret. A wider variety of keys was available to the lute than to other instruments, therefore, and this must have affected composers' attitudes towards tonality. We may add that the late sixteenth century's fondness for transposition must also have had its effect, and not only in lute-music: a good deal of music was transposed in order to make it more suitable for a different medium (Dowland's *Lachrimae* in G minor for lute and A minor for strings is only one of many examples).

The result was a gradual extension of the use of both major and minor keys, with their key-signatures, in all music throughout the seventeenth century. D major, B flat major and E minor were followed by B minor, C minor, F minor and A major soon after the middle of the century: by the end of the century E flat major and E major were in general use. In the first half of the eighteenth century it was a logical extension to try other keys, and the move towards equal temperament via modified mean-tone tuning made all keys theoretically possible. With Bach's *Wohltemperierte Klavier* (1722 and 1744) there was for the first time practical proof of the theory that the same key-structure could be started on any note of the chromatic scale. Only then was it vital to have analogous notations for all keys, to be entirely consistent and to avoid the notational imprecision of the seventeenth century.

The results were as follows:

1. The regular use of ♮ to cancel either ♯ or ♭.

2. The introduction of 𝄪 and ♭♭ as standardized forms. Quite apart from the need to avoid the ambiguity caused by the multi-purpose use of ♯ and ♭, noted above, the double-sharp and double-flat signs are notationally very important. Only by using these signs is it possible properly to notate the scales ('ladders') of all the available keys *as scales*, i.e. as a series of notes written on adjacent lines and spaces of the staff. This is necessary for two reasons:

(i) The performer's eye would otherwise see in the notated scale a gap that his ear did not hear.

(ii) Two distinguishable uses of the same notated pitch would otherwise be necessary in some keys (e.g. G♮ and G♯ for the leading-note and key-note of G♯ minor).

Either of these circumstances would be notationally confusing, besides failing to show indentical interval-structures in all keys (we must remember that the intervals C–C sharp and C–D flat, for instance, are identical only on an equally-tempered instrument). Major scales can all be notated in the same way: but enharmonic equivalents are used where necessary, so that double-sharps and double-flats do not appear in key-signatures (Figure 97(a)). Minor keys differ only in their accidentals (b).

Figure 97. Notation of Scales

3. The cancelling of one accidental before the introduction of another: this involved the double accidentals ♮♯ (to negate and reinflect after a ✕ or ♭)and ♮♭ (after a ♭♭ or ♯).

Incidental symbols and directives

From the seventeenth century onwards the use of incidental symbols and directives greatly increased, and continued to do so until the present century. In the seventeenth and eighteenth centuries they can be classified as follows:
1. symbols and directives concerning aspects of the music that had previously been notated, but which became notated slightly differently or whose notation became stabilized and standardized;
2. symbols and directives concerning musical parameters that had not previously been notated.
The classification cannot be an exact one, but for the purposes of this book (2) includes those parameters—dynamics, tempo and articulation—that are discussed in Chapter 14. (1) will be discussed here.

Clefs became rather less mobile than in the Middle Ages, as regards both the stave-lines on which they were commonly found and the changing of clefs from one line to another in the course of a piece. The C clef on the top line of the staff (C^5) was not used again (plainsong continues to use C^4 on a four-line staff): C^1, C^2, C^3 and C^4—such as we should now call the soprano, mezzo-soprano, alto and tenor clefs—were all common. The first two were mainly vocal clefs after the mid-eighteenth century, and although they stayed in use on the continent until the middle of the nineteenth century (England favoured the G^2 clef), their eventual disappearance was inevitable. C^3 and C^4 finally fell out of use as vocal clefs in the early twentieth century, but have remained in use for certain orchestral instruments—C^3 for the viola, and C^4 for the higher registers of cello, bassoon and tenor trombone.

The G clef became more or less standardized on the second line (as the treble clef), and indeed was something of a newcomer that had not normally been used on other lines: its common use as an alternative to C^1 or C^2 dates from the end of the sixteenth century, although the C clef continued in use during the eighteenth century even for some keyboard music—Bach's, for example. The only alternative line for the G clef was the first, where it was used for the *violino piccolo* (which is tuned a 3rd or 4th higher than the violin).

The F clef is normally found only as F³ (baritone) and F⁴ (bass clef) from the seventeenth century onwards: F⁵ is found for specially low bass-parts. The gamma clef disappeared altogether, but it had never been much used in any case, and offered no real alternative to the F clef unless in exceptionally low *tessitura*.

Keyboard music continued to use the Italian six-line staff until after the middle of the seventeenth century. Usually, the two innermost lines are c'. For this larger staff English musicians occasionally felt the need for more than one clef, resulting in the use of C¹ and G³ for the upper staff and C⁵ and F³ for the lower. These were often written together, as a sort of combined clef (Figure 98(a)).

From the rather varied use of repeat-signs at the beginning of the century, usage settled for Figure 69(e) quickly and almost unanimously in the seventeenth century. However, the instrumental music of that century often needs adjustment at the repeats, especially in dance-movements where the music requires first- and second-time bars, the continuation into the second half of the music being different from the return. This notational laxity about the repeat, where the performer must use his musicianship and common sense, sometimes gives trouble to us who are not familiar with traditions of performance, but the problem is never insuperable. First- and second-time bars are found in the late seventeenth century, and of course they offer no difficulties.

Figure 98. Doubled Clefs

(a) Upper staff   Lower staff

(b)

An older symbol that found a new use was that which from the mid-sixteenth century indicated the repeat of parts of a text (Figure 98 (b)). In the eighteenth century it was transferred to music (usually without the dots), where it did service for the repeat of a rhythmic unit, be it a beamed beat or a bar. (The various uses of different forms of this for different units are discussed in Read, *Music Notation*, 223 ff.)

Another old symbol, the *signum*, had by the early seventeenth century lost most of its various functions, being used only for repeats and to show the beginning or end of a canonic voice (above, Chapter 6). In the second half of the century it retained only the first of these functions and it changed its shape from *.S.* to the less overlookable 𝄋. This sign appears at the starting-point of a repeat, the end of the previous section bearing the directive *Dal Segno* ('from the sign'), sometimes shortened to *D.S.* or 'Dal 𝄋'. A parallel directive, *Da Capo* ('from the beginning'—literally, the head), was often shortened to *D.C.*: this gives its name to the *Da Capo* aria, the normal aria-form in opera, cantata and oratorio throughout the late Baroque. Later examples of the *Da Capo* aria often have a modified lead in to the repeated first section, so that the notation is actually *D.S.* with the *signum* just after the beginning of the movement. The directives *Dal Segno* and *Da Capo* give rise to a situation in which the end of the notated music is not the end of the movement: they are therefore accompanied by the directive *Fine* ('the end'), to show where the music stops.

14. The Notation of Expression

Expression and expression-words

In the Introduction I defined 'expression' as 'the deliberate variation of musical parameters for expressive purposes'. Any musical parameter can be varied expressively: variation in pitch, for instance, gives rise to a number of expressive devices, of which vibrato and portamento are obvious examples. But we do not regard pitch as primarily an expressive parameter. Those that we do so regard—tempo, intensity and articulation—are the subject of this chapter.

We have seen (Chapter 1) that special circumstances were responsible for the notating of these parameters in plainsong. Tempo (speed), intensity (dynamics) and articulation (which includes accentuation) otherwise remained generally unnotated until the turn of the seventeenth century. Until then the expressive parameters either were not varied or—as was generally the case—were chosen and varied by the performer according to known conventions. A dance-band played as fast or slow as was consistent with the physical possibility of performing the steps, as loudly as was necessary for the dancers to hear, and with such articulation as made rhythm, tempo and style of dancing obvious. Similar considerations applied to other types of performer (a singer, for instance, was expected to choose a speed, etc., appropriate to the words sung). In these circumstances it was often unnecessary for the composer to indicate how loudly or how fast the music should be performed, or what sort of articulation was required.

During the sixteenth and early seventeenth centuries composers sometimes discussed expression in treatises on performance or in prefaces attached to their compositions. In these works we first find some of the words that later became the common verbal additions to notation. Apart from Romanian letters and the 'tocca pian piano' found in the Capirola Lute Book of *c.* 1515–20 (Gombosi *Capirola*, 85), the history of expression-words used in close conjunction with notation may be said to start with Gabrieli's famous use of 'pian[o]' and 'forte'. Although the notational use of words probably indicated the composers' dissatisfaction with (or distrust of) the conventions, the conventions were themselves at first a necessary context for the words. 'Piano' (and 'echo', with which it was largely interchangeable until the eighteenth century) was to be understood as a departure from a prevailing dynamic, the return to which was marked by 'forte': even until late in the eighteenth century it is fairly safe to assume that a movement should begin *forte* if no dynamic is marked. Similarly, 'lento', 'tarde' or 'adagio' indicated a speed slower than the prevailing tempo, the return of which is marked by 'allegro' or 'presto'.

To begin with, then, several words might have the same meaning (even in the late eighteenth century one could refer loosely to a slow movement as 'an Adagio', whatever its actual marking). It is late in the seventeenth century before we find attempts to arrange verbal indications in hierarchical orders, and the results were often conflicting. Indeed, the study of the precise meanings of tempo-terms, especially, becomes a large, complex and rather frustrating one for the eighteenth century. Also, many of the earliest terms referred to the mood of the music, and only later took on more or less precise tempo-meanings. Some of these terms will be discussed at various points in this chapter.

Because it was Italian composers who used expression-words first (and for a long time most freely) Italian became the language universally accepted for the purpose. True, both English and French composers used in the seventeenth century a very limited vocabulary of words in their native tongues. But early in the century it was already necessary to define Italian terms for the benefit of non-Italian speakers (for instance, Praetorius, in *Syntagma Musicum*), from which we may assume that Italian had a head start which it has never lost. However, German composers developed in the nineteenth century a vocabulary of German terms that successfully competed with the Italian vocabulary, and which German composers still tend to use. The Italian terms being prone to much misunderstanding and mistranslation by those who do not speak the language, there has always been a feeling that use of the composer's native language will help to avoid ambiguity. But, of course, it can only do so for other speakers of that language: and in general composers have recognized the need for internationally-understood terms, and have therefore continued to use the Italian words.

Tempo and mood

At the end of the sixteenth century the whole range of medieval proportions was theoretically available to the composer, though in practice very few were used. From about 1475 the proportion signs ₵ and ₵ had been used as true time-signatures, implying duple and triple time respectively with the B as the beat (Morley P & E, 40, n.3). In fact, they seem commonly to indicate rather faster speeds than C and ○ (cf. the situation with ₵: Chapter 6, n.5). Probably there was a conflict of interests here between composers and theorists, with the latter maintaining a conservative position. However that may be, these two proportional signs normally appear as such after *c.* 1475 only if they were opposed to other signs in use simultaneously in another voice.

The old *quatre prolacions* had survived, especially C and ○, as signatures for duple and triple time. After the mid-sixteenth century, when the M finally became the beat, this caused much confusion, especially between C and ₵: for unless they were used in opposition (i.e. with proportional significance for ₵ or ₵) they could mean the same thing. Where a conservative composer, *c.* 1600, would use C and ○ to signify a M beat, a progressive, used to the C beat, would denote M beats by duple proportion—i.e. by ₵ and ₵.

This confusion apart, the signs available and in normal use *c.* 1600, with their meanings, were those shown in Figure 99 (Donington IE M, 406). A number of signs in which ₵ combined with numbers are discussed below. Whatever proportional significance some of these signs may have had *c.* 1600, they lost it in the course of the century. In duple measurement, then very simple notationally, the signs were not even much needed, which added to the existing confusion about C and ₵. While some writers continued to maintain that C, ₵ and ₵ indicated exact proportions of 4:2:1, an increasing number gave the more general interpretation relating to speed.

C   very slow
₵   moderate (marches and almains)
₵   brisk

(These all indicate four Cs to be counted in the bar.)
The figure 2 is used for some of these signs in French music: it is likely that 2 = ₵ (i.e. $\frac{2}{1}$ for dupla diminution) and $\frac{2}{2}$ = ₵, but this is not certain.

Figure 99. Time-Signatures

○ C ⊙ Ċ	as above, Figure 43, but not with the S beat
¢ or Ɔ	dupla diminution of C
Ɖ * (or ¢ = ⵦ)	dupla diminution of ¢
ɸ	dupla diminution of ○
$\frac{2}{1}$	dupla diminution
$\frac{1}{2}$	dupla augmentation
$\frac{3}{1}$ = 31 (or 3)	tripla diminution
$\frac{3}{2}$ (or 3) **	sesquialtera diminution

* Often called 'retorted time' because its commonest notation retorts (reverses) the C .

** This notation unfortunately confuses the issue of triple measurements (below).

Triple-mensuration signatures, of which there was a wider range, were used too loosely for their implied speeds to be listed with any certainty. For example, while corantos appear under a variety of time-signatures, those signatures were used also for sarabands, jigs and minuets, so that a study of their use in dance-music is less helpful than one would hope. Such clues as can be gleaned from the sources are incorporated into the summary that follows.

Throughout the seventeenth century the sign 3, the mark of triple diminution, was used also to denote three in the time of two—i.e. *sesquialtera* proportion. To add to the confusion it appears also as a general sign to denote triple measurement: indeed, some writers merely distinguished duple and triple time by ¢ and 3, irrespective of the actual mensurations. The sign Ɔ was also used generally, I think, but in a different way (see below). More specifically, at the beginning of the century Ɔ still retained its old *alla minima* meaning of twice 3 Ms, the stately triple time of the galliard. (In fact, at this early stage of barring the galliard was normally barred in three, not in six. Very rarely we find galliards notated in 3 Cs in the bar, for which ⅜Ɔ or a similar sign is used.) Playford confirmed the use of Ɔ for 'ayery songs and galliards' as late as 1654, but by then it was also used occasionally

189

for the English saraband, a much faster dance notated in Cs (Donington IEM, 401 f).

Playford gives the sign 31 (the tripla sign ⅔) as 'swifter' than ₵ in editions of the *Introduction to the Skill of Musick* from 1662 until 1687. This is lucky, for it allows us to fix other speeds relative to that indicated by 31 even after the disappearance of ₵ as an *alla minima* sign. The commonest triple-time signatures found from about the 1640s are, in tentative order of speed:

$\frac{3}{2}$ Three M beats take the time of two M beats in ₵. This is the slowest speed, and probably replaced the slow *alla minima* ₵.

C3 Probably = $\frac{3}{2}$: perhaps marginally faster.
(The rest are notated as six Cs in the bar unless stated to be in three and/or in Qs.)

31 'Swifter' than the old ₵: used for corantos, sarabands and jigs. (The 1694 edition of the *Introduction* allows this sign to be used for the faster tempo of six Qs in a bar.)

3 As 31, but faster (also allowed by the 1694 *Introduction* to be in Qs).

$\frac{3}{4}$ Quicker than 3, and notated as three Cs to the bar.

$\frac{3}{8}$ Like $\frac{3}{4}$ but much faster: three Qs in the bar.

$\frac{6}{4}$ Very brisk: used for jigs and passepieds. (Allowed by the 1694 *Introduction* to be in Qs.)

$\frac{6}{8}$ Like $\frac{6}{4}$ but faster: six Qs in the bar.

Here we see that notation in smaller values was generally accepted as implying faster tempo. We can probably assume that by the end of the century the increase was considerably less than the proportional increase (i.e. dupla) implied by the note-values, although still appreciable. The 1694 edition of Playford's *Introduction* (Donington IEM, 415), gives the following speeds:

Figure 100. Speeds Notated Metrically

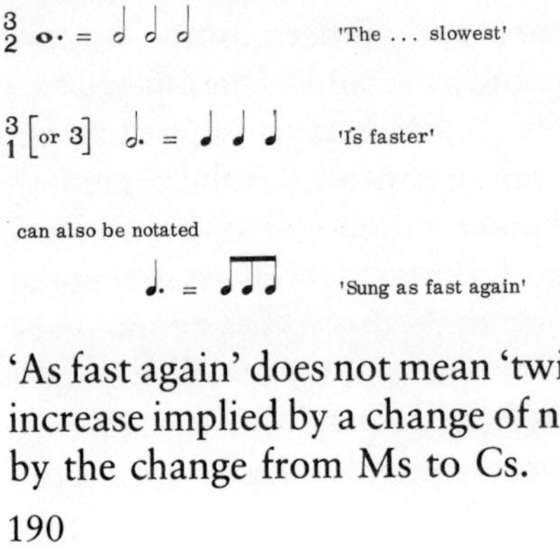

'As fast again' does not mean 'twice as fast': Playford is saying that the increase implied by a change of notation from Cs to Qs is that implied by the change from Ms to Cs.

190

As noted above, ⊙ most commonly appears in composite figures. Here it seems to have no numerical significance, only a general warning of triple measurement. The most common sign incorporating it is $\frac{\odot}{31}$, used for corantos, sarabands, jigs, etc.—too wide a range for a precise speed to be guessed at. $\frac{\odot}{3}$ appears to be the same, or perhaps a slightly faster, tempo: a rarer form, $\frac{\odot}{32}$, may indicate a slower speed. The retorted forms $\frac{\overline{\odot}}{31}$ and $\frac{\overline{\odot}}{3}$, for minuets and jigs, presumably indicate faster speeds than their forward-looking counterparts. These combined forms probably cover the range 31–$\frac{6}{4}$ in the list just given, but one cannot try to be more accurate.

In England the numerical forms retained the semblance of proportional signs to the end of the century: indeed, granted that we cannot be sure of the speed of 'common time' (C or ¢) from which proportions would be calculated, some proportional signatures are clearly used to notate tempo more precisely than was otherwise possible. Two examples from Purcell's contribution to the second part of *Musick's Hand-Maid* (1689) can easily be used as test-cases:

1. $\frac{3}{2}$ for 'Lilliburlero', notated in three Cs to the bar: the expected $\frac{3}{4}$ signature would give three fast beats in a bar. A proportion of two in the time of three makes the music more leisurely than this (though presumably not as slow as notation in $\frac{3}{2}$, since it it not thus notated).

2. $\frac{8}{6}$ for the 'Jigg' of the C major suite, notated in three Qs to the bar: the expected $\frac{3}{8}$ signature would provide a faster speed than $\frac{3}{4}$. A proportion of 8:6 is faster still.

Note that if these are correct interpretations the barring is itself an integral notational element.

Few practising musicians of the seventeenth century can have taken much pleasure in calculating speeds in this way. Fortunately there was a move towards a simpler form of time-signature, which we still use: the change started on the continent and began to affect England during the 1690s. Because the basis for all proportional calculations was the S in 'common' (i.e. duple) time, simple proportions usually took the form of fractions of a S. (In music that was barred regularly at this time, viz., keyboard music and most printed music with any didactic purpose, the S was the unit of barring in duple time.) Thus $\frac{3}{2}$ signified a bar of three half-Ss (Ms)—a view that was visually accurate although the Ms were not of the correct value. Similarly, $\frac{6}{4}$ signified six Cs (quarter-Ss) in the bar. This numerator/denominator system for time-signatures (as we can now call them with a completely clear conscience) replaced the last common vestige of divisive rhythmic organization.

191

The variety of speeds implied by the seventeenth-century 'time-signatures' was largely lost with the new system. From now on $\frac{3}{2}$ might be either faster or slower than $\frac{3}{4}$, depending on the type of movement involved. It is no coincidence that in the first half of the eighteenth century much interest was shown (though not for the first time) in defining the speeds of different types of movement— symphonies, dances, etc.—with reference to the human pulse, a pendulum, or the tick of a watch or clock. This was particularly necessary in duple time, for the old system had been simplified to a plain distinction between C (what the Italians called *tempo minore*) and ₵ (*temp maggiore* or—universally—*alla breve*).

Such mechanical means represented the attempt to define speeds absolutely. Earlier attempts to indicate tempo more precisely had used speed-words comparable to 'fast' and 'slow', relative terms that are always open to misinterpretation. While Purcell's 'brisk' and 'drag',[1] or the Italian Andante ('walking') and Allegro ('cheerful') may not be misunderstood in most contexts, they do require us to draw a line between what is fast and what is slow. Only then can we understand why Andantino ('a little Andante') generally implies a speed faster than Andante while Allegretto ('a little Allegro') is slower than Allegro.

Speed-words are not unambiguous, then, but their use in France, Italy and England in the last quarter of the seventeenth century shows that they were thought to be helpful. From the mid-eighteenth century, composers used them with increasing care: and although there was only a small range of tempo-words proper, even in Italian, this repertory has hardly increased since then, except for the addition of such qualifications as *poco* ('little'), *più* ('more'), *molto* ('much' or 'very'), *non troppo* ('not too much') and others. Gradual changes of tempo were also an eighteenth-century addition: *rall* [*entando*] and *rit* [*ardando*] ('slowing down'), *accel* [*erando*] ('getting faster'), with *a tempo* indicating a return to the original speed.

More important musically was the fact that many of these speed-words really indicated the mood of a piece and therefore showed speed only indirectly. Allegro (literally 'cheerful') need not necessarily be very fast; some other markings, such as the French *gaiement* ('gaily') and *tendrement* ('tenderly'), fix speeds even less accurately (see Donington IEM, 391, for Couperin's use of *vivement* in a piece which must be taken very steadily). Attempts to formulate a hierarchy of speeds run into difficulties if obvious mood-words are included. J.-B. Cartier, for instance (*L'Art du Violon*, 1798, cited by Donington IEM, 390), in a list of twenty-three terms, places Grazioso,

Affectuoso and Amoroso in ascending order of speed between Andantino and Moderato: how many of us would care to pigeon-hole Amoroso in this way? With the invention of the metronome and the consequent discovery that absolute speed-calculation is not such a Good Thing after all,[2] new indications have nearly always been descriptive modifications to a basic speed-word, indicating mood. These terms may imply an approximate tempo or a slight change of tempo: indeed, they may stand alone as if they *were* tempo-indications—terms like *pesante, con brio* and Elgar's *nobilmente*—but in fact they always presuppose an Allegro or other term which they qualify. In general such terms are useful, for they tell us what sort of effect the music should make: but they cannot be used as precise indicators of tempo. One wonders what speed Cartier would have chosen for Bliss's *Maestoso, con ardore—con somma passione* in the finale of his piano concerto.

Dynamics

As noted above, we may date the beginning of a general use of dynamic markings from Giovanni Gabrieli's *Sacrae Symphoniae* (1597), where *pian*[o] and *forte* distinguish the two contrasting dynamic levels required. Terraced dynamics—that is, contrasts of static volume-levels—were a feature of some early baroque music, and also of most of the concerto-style music of the seventeenth and early eighteenth centuries. For this reason such indications of medium as *solo/tutti* or *instrumentes/omnes* can be taken to imply general contrasts of dynamic levels as well as being practical indications for performance: and conversely, *piano* and *forte* may (in certain circumstances) imply *solo* and *tutti* sections rather than directions to the individual performer. In these circumstances there was no need for more subtle indications of dynamic. *Pianissimo* appeared early in the seventeenth century, but otherwise composers did not add much to *piano* and *forte*—often abbreviated to such forms as *pian, pia:, p°, p, for:* and *f*—until the eighteenth. Although other countries used comparable words in their own languages (*lowd* and *soft* in English, shortened to *lo:* and *so:; F*[*ort*] and *D*[*oux*] in Lully's music), Italian was the main language of verbal directions, as it has remained. Italian composers tended to be sparing in their use of dynamic markings. Handel rarely used more than the occasional *forte* and *piano*, though he added *pianissimo* to his palette for *Messiah*. (He was, however, often meticulous in his placing of such markings: see the beginning of 'Every valley' in the reproduction of the autograph score.)

It should not be thought, however, that terraced dynamics were the rule even in Italy during the seventeenth century. The *Nuove Musiche* (1602) of Giulio Caccini describes a number of vocal techniques involving the expressive increasing and diminishing of the voice (Strunk SR, 382–91)—in other words, crescendo and decrescendo. Indeed, such effects were normal throughout the century, in instrumental as well as vocal music (Donington IEM, 487 f). It remained largely a matter of style, and therefore conventional and unnotated: but there are isolated and mainly unstandardized examples. Monteverdi, in *Il Combattimento di Tancredi e Clorinda* (composed in 1624) required the last note to be played 'with a dying bow-stroke' ('questa ultima nota va in arcata morendo'); Locke used 'lowder by degrees' and 'soft and slow by degrees' in his music for *The Tempest* (1675); and a number of composers showed crescendo and diminuendo by a graded series of levels such as f – p – pp. This last method, used by Handel in *Messiah* (Winternitz MA i, 15), probably operated for much of the later eighteenth century, too, when alterations of *piano* and *forte* do not always imply a *subito* change.

By about the middle of the eighteenth century the terms *crescendo, decrescendo* and *diminuendo* were themselves in regular (if still fairly infrequent) use, often in abbreviated forms such as *cresc., decresc.* and *dim.* At about the same time some composers chose a graphic method for notating them, which may in fact ante-date the verbal forms. The signs used by Francesco Maria Veracini (*Sonate accademiche*, 1744) are wedge-shaped, the thin end signifying soft playing and the wide end loud: they thus use what was then a new dimensional convention of width for intensity (Figure 101(a)). Veracini's signs have to be read from bottom to top, whereas those of Geminiani (*Treatise of Good Taste*, 1749, R/1969, p. 2) take on a diagonal position (b). Neither of these is very accurate, for they are small and do not conform to the basic convention of duration on the horizontal axis: but then, it was not necessary for them to do so. Later void wedges employed by Gluck and Rossini (Winternitz MA, plates 102, 103) use the horizontal axis for time (and therefore the vertical or pitch-axis for intensity) but seem to be used for changes of only very short duration—almost phrasing rather than structural dynamics (c).[3] The familiar 'hairpins' (d), still in use, first appeared in Piani's violin sonatas of 1712, and thus ante-date all other types (though it is still occasionally suggested that they derive from the closed wedges). This type, at least from the later eighteenth century, has normally made full use of the duration convention on the horizontal axis, and has therefore been capable of considerable accuracy, especially in conjunction with specific volume-levels (e).

Figure 101. Dynamic Changes

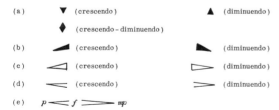

During the eighteenth and early nineteenth centuries composers used dynamic markings rather more. Four main developments can be seen, all indicating increased precision on the composer's part.

1. Throughout the period there was a general increase in finer dynamic distinctions, especially in the modifications of basic terms. J. S. Bach used *sotto voce* ('in an undertone') and also two modifications that were to become typical—*poco forte* and *più piano* ('more softly').[4] C. P. E. Bach used *m.f.* for *mezzo forte* ('half loud'), which has remained on our basic list of dynamic levels together with the later *mezzo piano* (*mp*). By Haydn's time the dynamic range went from *pp* to *ff* (*fortissimo*), though the outer extremes were still exceptional (and for a long time *pp* sometimes stood for the relative term *più piano* rather than the quasi-absolute *pianissimo*): both *ppp* and *fff* were used by Tromlitz (Warner, 'Tromlitz's Flute Treatise', 267). More important, Mozart used a range of subtle modifications such as *più crescendo, sempre crescendo* ('getting louder all the time'), etc., and a new term, *calando* ('lowering'), to imply a *diminuendo* and *rallentando* ('slowing down') together (Winternitz MA ii, plate 66). The nineteenth century used these markings much more lavishly, but added to them hardly at all. Even now the usual range is only from *ppp* to *fff*, a fourth degree in either direction being added 'rather for emphasis than exact measurement' (Donington in *Grove 5*, article 'Expression'). There are, of course, degrees of emphasis: but the addition by some later Romantics of a fifth or even a sixth degree is not often realistic (but see Chapter 16). The real advance in the nineteenth century was perhaps in the increased use of both verbal and graphic markings for *crescendo* and *diminuendo*.

2. The extension and refinement of the range of dynamic markings is partly indicative of a more dramatic style in the later eighteenth

195

century, shown particularly by a number of markings that apply to single musical events. The earliest is perhaps J. C. Bach's *sforzo* ('with force'), used to isolate a chord or note from its surroundings (Winternitz MA ii, plate 51). Haydn's use of *fz* (*forzando*) for the same purpose was followed by Mozart (*sf,* for *sforzando*) and ultimately by Beethoven and others. All the abbreviations so far mentioned could in theory be combined, and *mfp, fp, ffp, sfp* and *sfpp* are all found in Mozart's music. They imply sudden changes of dynamic on a single note or on two adjacent notes, so their effect is often to imply a method of attack or of large-scale articulation of a whole passage (see below).

3. The signs just discussed are all precise as to the note(s) to which they apply, and a similar precision had to be devised for the notation of *crescendo* and *diminuendo* (Figure 101(e) is a a nineteenth-century refinement). The verbal directions for *crescendo* and *decrescendo* were placed at the beginning of the gradation, the end being shown (if at all) by a final dynamic marking. In general the graphic forms are more immediately recognizable, and gradational precision was achieved first with them. Beethoven, for instance, often used wedges in preference to the verbal alternatives: they are much more striking in his autograph than in printed versions, and are sometimes used with considerable precision, his 'hairpins' extending over two bars or more, with the beginnings and endings very carefully placed.[5] The same accurate placing of wedges is seen in Chopin's autographs and—especially as regards the very short wedges to be discussed below—in those of many other composers. The precision of Beethoven's usage is seen in a version of his *crescendo* + *decrescendo* marking in which the wedges join at their open ends (that being the point of climax) to form a rhomboid, <> (Winternitz MA i, 16 and ii, plate 94: and see n.3, below). When his script is hurried the joins are not neat (ibid., plates 88 and 91), true also of Schubert's use of the sign (Hürlimann CA ii, plate 3), where it appears as two overlapped and not quite aligned wedges. Its use by Meyerbeer (ibid., plate 13) is much clearer, quite as good as Beethoven's best.

4. In the twelfth chapter of his *Versuch einer gründlichen Violinschule* Leopold Mozart makes some very interesting remarks about the use of loud and soft notes. For him, dynamics are often to be used somewhat analytically, highlighting certain points of rhythmic or melodic structure. In other words, the dynamics depend on the context. Hence certain chromatic notes should conventionally be played loud in contrast to surrounding notes, as should certain long notes sur-

rounded by groups of shorter-value notes. This use of dynamics (of which such signs as *fp*, *sfp*, *fz*, etc., are more precise notations) is therefore a means of showing points of phrasing and articulation (i.e. the articulation of several notes, not the attack and decay of a single note). One of the contexts in which Mozart requires a strong attack is the feminine cadence, then notated by *fp* (Figure 102(a)), which—according to his own warnings about exaggerated dynamics—Mozart probably played as a quick decrescendo (b). This latter version of the figure, notated with a short wedge (open or closed), is common from the early nineteenth century onwards.

Figure 102. Feminine Cadence (Leopold Mozart)

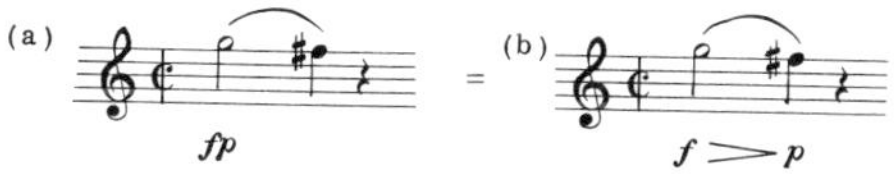

Accent and articulation

Baroque music depends for its idiomatic performance very largely on correct use of the 'silence of articulation'—that is, the shortening of a note so that part of its value is replaced by silence (Donington IEM, 473 ff). For most of the baroque period a *staccato* ('detached') note was indicated by a vertical stroke (ˈ) or a small wedge (▾ or ▴) above or below it. In the eighteenth century a dot took on the implication of *staccato*, too, and by the middle of the century these signs were interchangeable: indeed, their precise shapes depend partly on the pen and the speed of writing. C. P. E. Bach (*Versuch*, 1753) did not distinguish between them. Quantz (*Versuch*, 1752) and Leopold Mozart (*Versuch*, 1753), however, made a clear distinction between a strongly accented and separated note (ˈ or ▾: (Figure 104(b)) and a lighter, unaccented *staccato* (shown by a dot (a)).[6] Leopold Mozart, of course, was writing for violinists, and his use of the accent-sign implies a strong down-bow. Because of the lifting of the bow for down-strokes on consecutive notes, a strong articulation before the accent often results (shown by the arrows added to Mozart's examples, Figure 103). Although the accentual implication of the line or wedge gained general acceptance eventually, the various signs were not immediately used with complete conviction: as often happens, composers were a little uneasy about committing themselves to fine distinctions. W. A. Mozart used the distinction advocated by his father, but did not always make his intentions clear, and the same is true even of Beethoven.[7]

Figure 103. Bowing and Accentuation

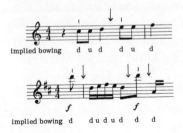

implied bowing   d   u   d   d   u   d

implied bowing   d   d u d u d   d   d

As might be expected, however, the distinction between the two types of *staccato* made other distinctions and refinements possible. The *tenuto* ('held') sign, occasionally used in the eighteenth century to show that a note should be held for its full length, acquired in the nineteenth century the implication of a slight accent when applied to several consecutive notes (Figure 104 (c)). A heavier accent, still *legato* ('smoothly'), was shown by a horizontal wedge very like a tiny *decrescendo* sign (d). (Indeed, they are often indistinguishable: see Ferguson KI, 160. However, the effect of a properly-phrased feminine cadence is much the same whether notated with a *decrescendo* (as in Figure 102(b)) or a *legato* accent.)

A later use of the *staccato* wedge (Figure 104(b)) is for bowing a stringed instrument with the heel of the bow, where most pressure and control are possible, to give an accent and *staccato* together (now notated ∧ or >). If the down-bow only is used, the *staccato* becomes pronounced (as in Figure 103, above).

Figure 104. Articulation

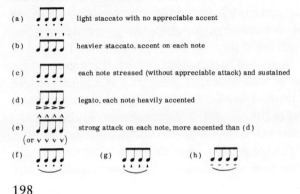

(a)   light staccato with no appreciable accent

(b)   heavier staccato, accent on each note

(c)   each note stressed (without appreciable attack) and sustained

(d)   legato, each note heavily accented

(e)   strong attack on each note, more accented than (d)
(or v v v v)

(f)   (g)   (h)

Like the foregoing signs, the slur was used increasingly during the baroque (Donington IEM, 473). As a tie, the sign had been in use since the early sixteenth century: as a mark of *legato* playing or unequal rhythm (see below), it dates from the first half of the seventeenth. Its placing is (or should be) from one note-head to the other when it is a tie, but more obviously above (or below) the two or more notes concerned when it is a slur. The distinction is fine but usually demonstrable (Read MN, 110 f), even with slurred notes at the same pitch.

The oldest use of the slur proper is probably to show an extreme *legato*. Normally this meant that the relevant notes were all to be played in one bow or breath (though wind players always articulate slightly by tonguing). In singing, the notes concerned took a single syllable: this notation was almost certainly not merely a convenient way to make the precise underlay clear, as it has sometimes been in later periods, for beaming or spacing were better ways of achieving that, and had been so used.

The *legato* slur could be modified to show degrees of articulation of the notes to be played with a single bow or breath. In particular, eighteenth-century composers often wrote a slur in conjunction with dots or wedges to indicate a light or accented *staccato*—a more specific form of Figure 104(a) and (b), in fact (shown at (f) and (g)). The wider range of modifications suggested by this, especially the *tenuto* (h), was commonly used in the nineteenth century. Composers have often used these signs as if they were universal or absolute, but they originally referred to specific instruments. Figure 104(a), for instance, would be interpreted by a keyboard player as a *mezzo-staccato*, while fast playing on a violin would produce *spiccato* ('springing' or 'jumping')—a very different effect (Donington, *Grove 5* article 'Staccato').

This ambiguity is a problem only in so far as composers prefer to use such signs universally (with a known musical implication) rather than specifically (with mechanical implications for particular instruments). The tendency towards notating the musical end rather than the instrumentally-conceived means to that end was fairly general in the nineteenth century, and gave rise to a very general notation for phrasing. Beethoven and many later composers used the slur to indicate large-scale *legato* phrasing, the internal articulation of bowing or breathing (not to be obvious to the listener) being left to the performer's musicality. The shorter of these slurs could be executed in a single bow or breath (although they are not necessarily better

199

performed that way), but the composer's intention is not often in doubt.

Verbal indications for these various styles of playing are found throughout the eighteenth century, in either full or abbreviated form: *leg[ato]*, *ten[uto]*, *sost[enuto]*, *stacc[ato]*, *spicc[ato]*and others, to which the nineteenth century, and the twentieth even more, have added. *Pizz[icato]* also became a standard term in the eighteenth century. However, the technique itself goes back at least as far as *Il Combattimento di Tancredi e Clorinda* (first performed in 1624), in which Monteverdi's 'notation' for it consists of the instruction to 'put the bow down and pluck the string with two fingers' ('Qui si lascia l'arco e si stappano le corde con duoi ditti'). Playford's use of the sign ʊ to indicate the 'thump' (i.e. left-hand *pizzicato*) seems a rare notation for what in any case was a short-lived and specifically English term (*Musick's Recreation on theViol*, 1682, R/1965, 33 f).

15. Notation and Convention

To a large extent, all musical notation is a matter of convention. Even graphic notations such as the 'pop' ukelele tablature (Figure 92(c)), or a notation which is pure visual analogue (see Chapter 18), rely on conventions of some sort. In the period up to about 1600 the conventions on which staff notation is based have been for the most part recognized and easily recognizable. There are of course many conventions of performance that we cannot fully appreciate and which for us take the form of more or less insoluble problems (e.g. the matters of *musica ficta* or the accompaniment of medieval song): but in general these are conventions which are not notated in any way. Conventions of which we have a notated record present us with a different sort of problem, and not always one which we have a better chance of solving. For example, the Renaissance notated certain transpositions by means of clefs (see below, especially n.7), and we cannot discover how the system worked with reference only to the notation, which is itself merely incidental to the convention.

In the period after 1600 the situation changed. The conventions of baroque and later music are normally notated, though the precise relationship between notation and the conventional practice is not always easy to see. In this chapter, therefore, we shall consider certain notated conventions found in music after about 1600, the chronological line being, as always, not sharply drawn.

Basso continuo and the notation of harmony

By 1600 it had long been customary for an organist to accompany the so-called 'a cappella' repertory by playing from the bass-line after first familiarizing himself with the composition as a whole. The harmonic vocabulary used was so limited that notational directions were unnecessary. From the end of the sixteenth century, however, the experiments of the Florentine *camerate* produced a type of solo monody which needed to be accompanied both more precisely and more flexibly, the singer and accompanist working closely together and allowing each other a greater rhythmic freedom. A system of harmonic notation became necessary, partly to lessen the memory-work required of the accompanist and partly to make clear those passages where the bass-line alone might be harmonically ambiguous. The result was figured bass, a system which first appeared in the year 1600, in the famous prints of music by Peri, Caccini and Cavalieri (see Bibliography).

The notation consists of numerals and accidental signs placed above the bass line. Jacopo Peri (*L'Euridice*, [vi]) explained it as follows:

> Sopra la parte del basso, il diesis congiunto col 6. dimostra sesta maggiore, e la minore senza 'l diesis; Il quale quando è solo, è contrassegno della terza, ò della decima maggiore: Et il b. molle, della terza, ò decima minore; . . .

> (Above the bass line a 6 together with a sharp shows the major sixth, and without a sharp the minor sixth; by itself [the sharp] is the sign of the major 3rd or 10th, and the b of the minor 3rd or 10th; . . .)

Although this treats the 3rd and 10th together, Peri, Caccini and Cavalieri all used higher numbers (9–14 or so) to show compound intervals. Cavalieri, in fact, figured as high as 18 to specify the octave of the note concerned, and his figuring sometimes leaves very little room for creativity on the part of the continuo-player. Cavalieri also used two numbers simultaneously, ranged one above the other, a principle that was later extended to three notes figured together. At this early stage the duration of the figures was shown in the notation of the bass: where necessary, the bass note was divided into smaller values which gave the rhythm of the harmony-changes. These notes would be tied to show that the bass-note itself was not to be articulated (Figure 105(a)).

During the seventeenth and early eighteenth centuries a number of changes took place in the details of the system. Very early on
1. compound intervals ceased to be shown (except in the 9–8 suspension), so that the figure 3, for example, was always understood to signify a 10th or 17th as well; and
2. composers stopped showing the rhythm of harmonic change in the bass line, relying instead on the horizontal spacing of the figures.

In the first few years of the eighteenth century
3. the figuring was placed below the bass line;
and soon afterwards
4. the alternative sharp (major) figures 3,4,5,6 and 7 came into being.

The system was not wholly concerned with the vertical aspect of the music, however, and there quickly grew up a notation—a horizontal line under the notes affected—that allowed the harmony of previous figuring to remain while the bass moved, either by step or through the notes of a chord (Figure 105(b)).

Figure 105. Figured Bass

(a)

(Peri, *L'Euridice*, (1600, R/1969), pp. 45 – 6 : text omitted)

(b)

(J. S. Bach, sonata in G minor, BWV 1020, for violin and harpsichord, 1st movement, bars 93 f)

Cavalieri's use of figured bass sometimes approached the precision of a shorthand version—a tablature, in fact—of a composed keyboard part. Otherwise, figured bass cannot be said to be a shorthand harmonic notation: it is merely a convenient way of showing intervals, conventional not in what it includes but in what it omits. The interval of a 3rd is assumed (so much so that a lone accidental is taken to refer to the 3rd) unless replaced by its dissonant alternatives the 2nd and 4th. The 5th is also assumed unless replaced by a 6th: its presence or absence in conjunction with a 7th depends on the context and the taste of the performer. Octaves, 5ths and 3rds (apart from chromatic inflexions) were normally figured only to show a dissonance and its resolution, which includes a 6th falling to a 5th.

A figured bass, then, really notates only deviations from a norm

203

consisting of root-position chords and the diatonic notes of the key involved. Of course, this 'norm' is not musically normal at all, but the result is that one can very quickly see from the figuring the chord to be constructed over any particular bass-note. As used by Italian and Italian-trained composers, it shows a remarkable economy of means. It is purely functional: the figuring does not dictate the part writing which it is the continuo-player's business to improvise, nor duplicate in the figuring information that can be seen in the solo part. Thus Handel, in the opening of the F major recorder sonata, figured only the keyboard part, although the chord at * is a passing $\frac{6}{4}$ (second-inversion dominant 7th) if we take the recorder into account (Figure 106(a)).

Figure 106. Styles of Figuring

(a)

(Handel, sonata for recorder and continuo, op. 1, no. 11, 1st movement)

(b)

(J. S. Bach, trio sonata from *The Musical Offering*, 2nd movement, bars 202 ff)

If anything, Handel erred on the side of under-figuring, as did most Italian-trained composers. With others the use of figuring may be very different. J. S. Bach tended to figure all the intricacies that could already be seen in the upper parts, perhaps so that the keyboard player should not double the upper parts or muddy the texture by resolving dissonances differently: but a keyboard player may sometimes feel that there is little left for him to do (Figure 106(b)). Indeed, Bach's figuring often seems prohibitive, for the more figuring there is the less the performer plays.

A harmonic abbreviation notation used for popular music in the twentieth century has something in common with *basso continuo,* though it is simpler in application and depends on modern harmonic nomenclature. Like figured bass, it is a way of notating chords: but it does not normally show the triadic inversions, and it cannot notate dissonance and resolution in melodic terms, only purely as an aspect of harmony. A major triad is shown simply as the letter-name of the chord's root, e.g. G = G major; a minor triad has the addition of 'mi', e.g. Gmi = G minor; upper powers, such as 7ths or 9ths, are shown in the same way but with a numeral (sometimes superscript), e.g. Gmi^7, G^9. Such a notation could no doubt indicate chord-inversions by some simple means such as subscript numbers: for example, the dominant 7th inversions in G major could be shown as D^7_1, D^7_2 and D^7_3, respectively. In general, however, this notation has been used for music where such a refinement is not necessary, since the player of a banjo, guitar or accordion using this instead of the staff notation would usually have a bass-player on the bass line of the music, so that the chord inversions would automatically be correct. As in figured bass, the precise result of the notation depends on the key, which is therefore given at the beginning: for instance, G^7 would be a major 7th in G major but a dominant 7th in C major (Figure 107(a)).

Figure 107. Guitar Tablatures

('When You Wish Upon a Star' from *Pinocchio*: music by Leigh Harline, words by Ned Washington. © 1940 Bourne Co.)

(Luis de Briçneo, *Metodo . . . para apprender a tañer la guitarra* (Paris, 1626): See Wolf HdN ii, 200)

(Lucas Ruiz de Ribayaz. *Luz y Norte Musical* (Madrid, 1677): see Wolf HdN ii, 201–2)

This last notation would not have been possible prior to Rameau's *Traité de l'harmonie* of 1722. Without modern harmonic theory and nomenclature the logical procedure would perhaps have been to list all the necessary chords in a key, to give them numbers or letters, and to use those numbers or letters as notational symbols: in other words, a harmonic tablature. Such is the basis of the notation for a large repertory of guitar music of the seventeenth and eighteenth centuries (Figure 107(b)). Its success depends (1) on a fairly simple chordal style; (2) on the chords not changing too frequently; and (3) on the harmonic vocabulary being limited enough for the player to memorize all the necessary chords and their symbols. It should be noted that whereas the first two notations described leave the spacing and texture of each chord to the player's discretion (that is, they are simply indications which act as a basis for creative improvisation), harmonic guitar tablatures dictate every note of each chord, since the 'strumming' technique of playing requires that all the strings be accounted for.

Purely as a phonetic system this tablature is fairly flexible: it can be used in conjunction with staff notation (e.g. for the accompaniment of a vocal part), with other forms of tablature, or—with the addition of notes to give the rhythm (as in lute tablature)—by itself. When used by a solo performer, the notation is suitable for chordal dance-music. Indications of *forte* and *piano* can be added without confusion. The strings of the guitar can be struck either from above or from below and the distinction is often made notationally. The usual way is to base the tablature on a horizontal line (or on several short lines, each one corresponding to a bar of the music): then symbols below the line represent downstrokes and those above it, upstrokes. The symbols concerned may be the letters themselves, or they may be short vertical strokes which also give the rhythm. Methods of rhythmic notation are too numerous to detail: in some the rhythm is shown by note-symbols, but the majority use the spacing of vertical strokes. (There are many variations on this notation, described in detail by Wolf, HdN ii, 171–203.)

Cues and aids to rehearsal

Prior to the seventeenth century performers had very few notational aids in rehearsal or performance. (I do not count verbal directives, such as the cues for plainsong verses in *alternatim* settings, as notational.) I suggested in Chapter 7 that the *signum congruentiae* was used, especially in *cantus lateralis*, to help a singer to keep (or even to find) his place. This does not solve all of the problems for a present-day singer attempting to perform from the original notation, however: and we must assume that in choral polyphony (1) the director rehearsed the boys separately and thoroughly, in the course of which certain starting-points became recognizable; (2) that the men were good sight-readers; and (3) that they were able to remember, and compensate for, those places where they could distinguish scribal errors.

For small-scale performance, both vocal and instrumental, the situation did not change until the nineteenth century, when cues were marked into parts as for orchestral players: in large-scale concerted music there is evidence of help being notated in the eighteenth century. Prior to the second half of that century the generally continuous style of baroque music made cues unnecessary for any player: even in a baroque concerto the soloist's music makes it fairly plain at what point the *ripieno* enters. The same is often true of a classical concerto, and for the completely unpredictable section—the cadenza—two infallible conventions were used: (1) the classical period took over the pause-sign, the usual baroque notation for the final chord before a cadenza, and in addition made sure that that chord was always a second inversion tonic chord; (2) the soloist gave warning to the orchestra of the end of his cadenza by playing a trill, under which he then placed the perfect cadence of which the cadenza was a decoration.[1]

In the seventeenth century, of course, the performance largely depended upon the continuo players. The keyboard player, in particular, must often have directed the performance, and he presumably knew the music well enough to bring the *ripieno* in without cues. With the classical style, it is a little different. In discussing the role of conductor, continuo-player and soloist in the classical concerto (*The Classical Style*, 191–6), Charles Rosen points out that because a keyboard soloist in the Baroque had played continuo in the *tutti* sections, the pianist in a classical concerto also took his cues from the cello part, even though he now played only in the solo sections. In consequence the printed solo part, even as late as Chopin's concertos, included the bass part, figured, between solo sections: and as an off-shoot of the same convention the organ part of Haydn's *Missa in Tempore Belli* includes figuring in the bass even in passages marked 'Senza org[ano]'. Rosen regards both of these as no more than a cueing system: but in the latter case the figuring would of course be useful in a rehearsal with voices and keyboard only, and I prefer to believe that that was its main purpose.[2] Another example of cueing cited by Rosen occurs in Mozart's Clarinet Concerto, the solo clarinet part of which originally included the first violin part throughout although there was no question of the clarinettist doubling the strings between solos.

The examples discussed by Rosen cause trouble in interpretation because we do not know the purpose of the passages in question and no longer have the conventions that brought the situation about. In the nineteenth century distance from the convention caused a notational change that we have retained ever since: the cues were printed in small type. Cues may come from the part of any other instrument or voice, and this sometimes causes confusion if the clef is different. Strictly, the clef at the beginning of the staff holds good until changed in large type, whereas a small clef refers to the cue only: but it is safer to repeat the clef in use (Read MN, 440).

In the present century full scores and orchestral parts (and chorus parts or vocal scores, where appropriate) have used a more consistent and helpful equivalent to the medieval *signum*—rehearsal letters. These date back to the nineteenth century, but were not regularly used until more recently. The principle is that at convenient starting-points in the music—often coinciding with major articulation-points in the structure of the music—a large letter is placed between sections of the score and over the bar-line in the parts. Conductor and players then have the same reference-points, starting at 'Letter A', throughout the work. In small-scale vocal music it is more usual to number the bars every five or so. The two systems have occasionally been amalgamated in modern scores, the bar-numbers every ten bars taking the place of rehearsal-letters: but this is an inconvenient system because (1) the numbers do not coincide with structural reference-points (e.g. the start of a new theme), and (2) it forces the players to count rests in groups of ten bars, which do not coincide with phrase-structures.

Rhythmic conventions

The rhythmic conventions to be discussed are all found in contexts where the rhythm of a piece of music is either known in advance or can safely be left to the discretion of the performer. They fall into three broad categories:

1. choral recitative and unrhythmed preludes;
2. *notes inégales*; and
3. certain types of rhythmic resolution, in which notated rhythms are modified in performance to be compatible with a prevailing rhythmic context, stated or implied.

Choral recitative must be as old as choral plainsong, for simple chanting is on a monotone with cadences. The monotone was normally written as a series of single notes (one for each syllable), and the Roman Church has retained this notation even in cases such as litanies, where several texts with different numbers of syllables are sung to the same music. Modern Anglican psalm-chanting, on the other hand, gives a single note (assumed to be of indeterminate length) to which all the syllables of the monotone are sung. It is assumed that a choir is capable of singing the recitation clearly, together and in speech rhythm, although this is very difficult to do if the choir is large. However, there are also a few examples in the Italian madrigal repertory, which show that with soloists or a very small choir choral recitative in speech rhythm is not only possible but very effective. Figure 108(a) shows the opening of Monteverdi's 'Sfogava con le Stelle'—perhaps the most famous example—in which the reciting-note is notated as a B.

Figure 108. Unmeasured Notation

(Monteverdi, *Quarto libro de Madrigali*, 1603)

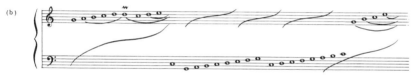

(Anonymous prelude, probably by Louis Couperin: see Louis Couperin, *Pièces de clavecin*, p 22)

Choral recitative is possible only because the rhythm of the music is known in advance. In the case of the unrhythmed instrumental preludes of the seventeenth century a general rhythmic style may be known, but the solo performer must decide on the precise rhythms of the piece. The keyboard preludes of Louis Couperin, d'Anglebert and others are written in non-committal note-values—usually Ss—which make the music appear slow: but in fact ornaments (e.g. written-out trills) and quite intricate decoration are notated. Davitt Moroney has argued that these preludes fall into two stylistic groups, of toccata and allemande-lament, whose musical characteristics were known ('The performance of unmeasured harpsichord preludes'): but he notes that the unmeasured notation was puzzling to non-professionals, and that printed sources (as opposed to the manuscripts in which most unmeasured notation is found) chose to notate such works in a rhythmically more explicit way. Moroney distinguishes three uses of the slur, the most important notational element after the notes themselves: (1) to show that a note is sustained, so that it forms part of a broken chord; (2) to show a purely melodic grouping, either a melodic phrase (on the large scale) or a written-out ornament (on the small scale); and (3) to show the synchronization of notes whose alignment disguises the harmonic structure of the music. The last of these is in fact only one possible interpretation (and a rare one) of a wide-ranging type of slur that may not obviously relate to any particular note. Figure 108(b) shows all three types of slur in a context which suggests no obvious interpretation for the third type.

Although this notation must be interpreted according to certain rhythmic conventions, the preludes for which it was used were certainly to be performed in a relatively free manner, even if not quite as freely as the notation now suggests to us. A seventeenth-century composer usually preferred this situation to writing in rhythmically precise notation that would inhibit the necessary element of improvisation. But, as Moroney points out, the historical trend was towards notational precision, and in this respect we should remind ourselves that even the preludes of J. S. Bach belong to the end of a long tradition of improvisation. For example, the first prelude of the '48' is written partly in plain chords (Winternitz MA ii, plate 26), the figuration being written in full for the first six bars. This was of course a practical expedient for Bach, since it saved space and the time and effort needed to write out a regular pattern of figuration, and in this respect we can see the chords as a shorthand version: but if we put it in its proper historical context, we can see these chords as the structural

210

basis for the figuration, itself a written-out realization such as would normally be improvised.

We saw in medieval mensuration (Chapters 3, 4 and 5) that it is often difficult to know the exact rhythms of figures composed of small-value notes. This is a matter of style, often depending on geographical location, and changing with time. In the baroque period there arose certain notational methods of indicating the ways of performing small-value groups, and especially of showing whether pairs of notes written as equal values were to be played equally or unequally. In all inequality the exact values are at the discretion of the performer and depend on many factors. It was normal to notate inequality in dotted rhythm or as triplets (Figure 109(a) and (b)): this is convenient, but rarely quite accurate.

Figure 109. Rhythmic Inequality

(Handel, sonata for oboe and continuo, op. 1, no. 8, last movement)

(François Couperin, 'Les Moissoneurs': *Pièces de clavecin* II, p. 2)

Robert Donington has stated concisely the conditions in which an *inégale* style may apply (IEM, 452 f). The most common form of inequality is the lengthening of the first of a pair and the corresponding shortening of the second, a rhythm that the French called 'lourer'. To give equal Qs or Sqs an unequal lilt in this way was so common that it is hardly ever notated. In fact, no recognized notation seems to exist for it: the use of a slur for this purpose—found in very rare

211

instances—occurs only if the rhythm is notated as a dotted rhythm elsewhere.[3]

More often the slurring of a pair of equal notes indicates the inequality known as 'couler', in which the first note is shortened and the second lengthened. This notation is entirely unambiguous when the notes slurred are thus distinguished from notes which could be expected to receive 'lourer' treatment (Figure 109(c)). More specifically, the 'couler' rhythm was notated in the eighteenth century by a slur with a dot over the second note (d), a meaning which is quite the reverse of the phrasing that is now implied. (François Couperin placed the dot above the slur, but it was more usually placed—as now—between the slur and the note-head.)

A composer who wished notes to be played equal when they might otherwise have been played *inégales* had to make his wishes known. In the seventeenth and early eighteenth centuries equality was shown by dots over (or under) the notes concerned: as we have seen, such dots did not imply staccato until well into the eighteenth century (Chapter 14). However, inequality was always precluded by any type of staccato, so the stroke or wedge, too, prevented *inégale* treatment. Similarly, since inequality could be applied only to pairs of notes, any phrasing applied to more than two notes precluded inequality. Another way of showing equality was to mark the music with some term such as *notes égales, détachées*, etc., which had the same effect.

Two terms often found in connection with inequality are *piquer* and *pointer*, both of which have the general sense of 'point the rhythm'. In a more specific sense they are used when equally-written notes are played with 'lourer' treatment and a notated dotted rhythm should be sharpened, i.e. exaggerated. The direction is needed, for a piece in 'lourer' style can be notated equally or in dotted rhythm, and many composers used either notation or a mixture of the two quite arbitrarily. This is partly for the composer's convenience, dotted rhythms being fussy and laborious to write: and composers of the seventeenth and eighteenth centuries often did not bother to write the necessary rests and short notes for up-beats (Figure 110).

Dotted rhythms are notoriously difficult to interpret in the baroque period. Traditionally, a dot of augmentation was valued at half of the note to which it was attached. Hence the first dotted rhythm of Figure 109(a) equals three-quarters + one quarter of a beat. In the seventeenth and eighteenth centuries, however, the dot was considered a variable quantity whenever the rhythm was not notated as it was to be played. (Otherwise, of course, it had its normal value.) Thus

212

Figure 110. Pointed Rhythms

(Froberger, Suite in G minor, Allemande)

in a dotted-rhythm piece played in 'lourer' style, with the note-values approximately two thirds + one third, the dot was worth much less than usual (Figure 111(a)): and in French overture style, where the rhythm was sharpened and a silence of articulation interposed, the values might be seven eights + one eighth, especially if a dotted rhythm had to synchronize with a group of smaller values (b). Notationally, these conventions showed hardly at all. Indeed, they can be recognized only when a composer has notated the short notes more accurately than the dotted note, so that the dot has to expand or contract in value before the group adds up to the right total duration (c).

Figure 111. The Variable Dot Principle

(a)

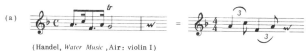

(Handel, *Water Music* , Air: violin I)

(b)

(Telemann, Suite in A minor for flute and strings, Ouverture: outer voices)

(c)

(François Couperin. Passacaille from 8th Ordre: *Pièces de clavecin* II, p. 54)

N.B. Rhythms to be performed in (a) and (b) are approximate only.

213

The 'variable dot' principle was immensely useful—so useful that its effects can be seen sometimes even in the nineteenth century. The notational conventions involved were not ambiguous, but the stylistic conventions sometimes were, so that it was not clear what the prevailing rhythm of a piece should be. Of course, much baroque music can legitimately be interpreted in two or more ways: but composers tend to prefer their own interpretations. It is perhaps for this reason that the double-dot notation gained acceptance around the middle of the eighteenth century as an indication of sharpened rhythms (*pointer*). We regard the second dot as valued at half of the first, and in theory we can continue to add dots in precise mathematical proportions (as in Figure 112(a)). The eighteenth century, however, regarded dots thus only if the context was right, and in other cases the second dot could be as variable as the first.

Figure 111(a) is symptomatic of a principle prevalent in the seventeenth and eighteenth centuries, which we have partly discussed in Chapter 7. The seventeenth century counted Cs, even when the beat was a M (as in ¢), and the C was in any case normally the beat. However the beat is broken down into smaller values, there is much to be said for the beat itself being instantly recognizable in notation. Hence Figure 112(b) is a better notation for the 'triplet' rhythm than (c), for in the latter case the C might be taken for the beat: compare (d) and (e) (the arrows show the position of the beats).

Figure 112.

(a) o···· = o ♩♩♪♪

(b) ♩.♪

(c) ♩ ♪

(d) 6/8 ♩ ♪♩ ♪|♩. |

(e) 3/4 ♩ ♪♩ ♪|♩. |

Our modern notation is not unambiguous, and it depends on an unequivocal time-signature. This simpler range of time-signatures was not in general use before the middle of the eighteenth century. Furthermore, that system had to be very well established before a dotted note would be accepted as the notation for a beat: and even so, it must be admitted that our 'compound-time' metres (⁶⁄₈, ⁹⁄₈ and ¹²⁄₈) are

214

difficult to read, awkward to notate accurately, and laborious to write. It is still not possible to write a bar of $\frac{9}{8}$ time as a single note, Figure 113(a) being the simplest form. Some musicologists have used (b) for this, but it is not yet universally recognized, and its notational parentage is not immaculate. The fact is that metres in which the beat has three parts are very easy to notate in divisive systems and very awkward in additive ones: and for a long time composers retained a divisive view where smaller note-values were concerned. Thus Arne—typical of his contemporaries—notated a $\frac{12}{8}$ piece in $\mathop{\mathbb{C}}$, writing triplet Qs against undotted Cs (c). This movement, as it happens, has Q-runs throughout: but in this metre, according to what has just been said, the long-short rhythm would be notated as dotted.[4] Another movement by Arne illustrates this (d).

Figure 113. Notation of Compound Metres

(Arne, *Sonatas*, 1756, p. 26)

(Ibid., p. 18, bars 8–12)

In fact, (d) is notationally transitional. Arne alternates inconsistently between the older and more modern notations, though for safety he uses a triplet sign for the C + Q grouping. This notation is not ambiguous, however, and it illustrates a general rule: the notated rhythms accommodate themselves to the basic metre required by the composer. In most cases, as here, this means that note-groups written in binary rhythm should be played or sung in ternary rhythm, the prevailing ternary metre being shown by triplets, etc. This notation rarely causes confusion once the performer has made the necessary mental adjustment. There are nevertheless a few contexts in which help is needed, and the precise interpretation must sometimes be decided not just with reference to the performer's experience and musicality, but taking the instrument and conditions of performance (e.g. acoustic) into account as well (Figure 114(a)).

Another general rule can be stated: in baroque music (i.e. *c.* 1600–*c.* 1750) a strict three-against-two was never performed, the duple notation being resolved to triple rhythm or—just possibly, and certainly rarely—triple notation being resolved to duple rhythm (Collins, 'The Performance of Triplets'). There are also examples of music notated wholly in one metre which seem to need interpretation in the other. For example, some seventeenth- and eighteenth-century gigues are rotated in duple time although we should expect them to be in triple rhythm (Figure 114(b)). Fortunately some of Froberger's gigues exist in two versions, one duple and one triple, which confirms what we should otherwise only suspect (Ferguson KI, 92). A similar consideration of style is responsible for my interpretation of the *Water Music* Air in triplets (Figure 111(a)). The Tempo di Gavotta in Bach's E minor Partita presents a more difficult problem (discussed by Collins, 'The Performance of Triplets', 310 f, and Donington IEM, 469): performance in triplets throughout seems much more probable than duple time, but the Sqs—especially the groups of four—do not fall into any recognizable pattern (Figure 114 (c)). Donington's solution is shown at (d) and my own suggestions at (e).

Figure 114. Rhythmic Assimilation to Prevailing Metre

(François Couperin, *Pièces de clavecin* II, p. 88: interpretation ibid., p. x.
A note between the staves reads, in translation, "Although the right-hand values seem not to agree with those of the lower part, it is usual to notate it thus".)

(Froberger, Suite in G minor, Gigue)

(J. S. Bach, harpsichord Partita 6, Tempo di Gavotta)

217

Donington's interpretation (d) relates to three specific points (IEM, 469):

1. that the Sq-Sq-Q group is 'a written-out slide, to be taken quite normally on the beat, unmeasured and a little quicker than notated';
2. that the groups of four Sqs 'are likewise to be taken ornamentally, unmeasured and a little quicker than they are notated'; and
3. that the metre is assimilated throughout to triplet rhythm.

It will be seen from this that Donington's points (1) and (2) do not admit of a precise notation, and (d) must be read with this in mind.

Point (3) need not be discussed here, for the evidence is overwhelmingly in favour of it, but points (1) and (2) are more difficult. The Sq-Sq-Q group appears during the piece nine times in all. Of these, five are in contexts where parallel 3rds or 6ths make a triplet interpretation harmonically the obvious solution (the examples in bars 6 and 7 are the first two of these five). None of the remaining four examples of this grouping (three of which can be seen in the first two bars of the piece) contradicts this interpretation. Before we can accept this solution, however, we must answer an important question: why should the Sq-Sq-Q group be used for triplet rhythm—even simultaneously with the triplet itself—when the triplet is available and used freely in the piece? Clearly, it is because of this problem that Donington favoured an interpretation beginning with short notes to correspond to the Sqs.

The answer to this question is, I believe, an important one not only for this piece. It concerns the consistency of Bach's notation. Bach used two metres at the notational level below the C, the C itself having a place in both metres. In one metre, binary division of the C gives 'dotted-rhythm' notation and Sqs; in the other, ternary division of the C gives Q triplets. His use of these metres is indicated in the diagram that follows, D showing the extent of duple notation and T that of triple. The vertical lines represent bar-lines, and the bars are numbered; an asterisk shows a single binary-notated beat in ternary division of the C, or *vice versa*. The music is strictly in two-part texture throughout.

Certain facts are immediately apparent in this diagram. To begin with, there are stretches of several bars where one voice consistently uses a particular metre. (I have ignored those half bars which the use of Cs or M makes notationally non-committal in this respect, but taking them into account would not affect this discussion.) Sometimes this consistency happens in both hands simultaneously, the two hands using different metres. A glance at the music will show that

218

this reflects the prevailing rhythms of each voice: that is, that certain characteristic rhythms require a particular metre; that these rhythms complement each other in the music; and that the hands therefore exchange metres when they exchange melodic/rhythmic material. Further, while the notational situation is very clear throughout the first half of the piece and the 'recapitulation' (which begins in the middle of bar 26), it is less so during the 'development section', in which all eight examples of irregular beats occur (asterisked). Indeed, in this section there are difficulties in deciding what is the prevailing metre of the left hand, which is not the case elsewhere.

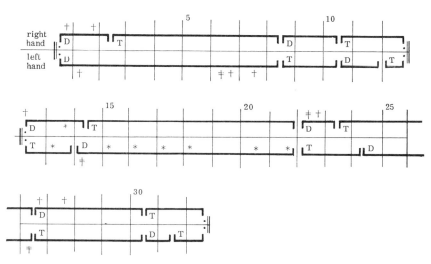

Without exception, the Sq-Sq-Q groups (marked+) fall outside the area of irregularity (bars 13–21), and occur in places where binary division of the C is being used consistently. It is important to recognize that the criterion for notational consistency is in respect of the melodic voice, not of the texture as a whole. That is, if the Sq-Sq-Q grouping is indeed rhythmically equivalent to Q triplets, the simultaneous use of the two notations should not be regarded as an inconsistency: for each notation is entirely consistent in its own melodic/rhythmic context.

What, then, of the irregularities of bars 13–21? These bars follow a long passage (in the repeat, too) in which triplet Qs are set against the dotted rhythm, and every one of the eight irregularities allows these two rhythms to be used almost exclusively: in fact, in all cases but one they allow triplet Qs in the left hand to be set against 'regular' triplet Qs in the right. The Sq-Sq-Q grouping would have been visually disturbing here, and I believe that in these few bars Bach felt that to

219

avoid such disturbance was more important than the intellectual satisfaction of complete consistency—if, indeed, it was a wholly conscious decision. This does not, of course, prove my interpretation of the Sq-Sq-Q group to be the correct one (at least one other solution has a strong claim and is hardly less satisfactory in performance): but it is potentially the best solution, and there is insufficient reason to discount it.

Finally, we must try to decide on the role of the group of four Sqs (marked ‡ in the diagram). It belongs unequivocally to the binary division of the C, as we should expect. Its melodic context gives little more help, however, and its harmonic context is such that almost any obvious interpretation assimilated to Q triplets would be acceptable. Harmonic considerations in bar 22 make Sq-Sq-Q-Q slightly the most probable there (as noted in square brackets above the left hand, Figure 114(e)), but it is not a strong argument. More important factors are
1. that in every case the first note of the four is tied to a C before it. By analogy with French overture style, this suggests the possibility of the first (tied) note of the group acting as a variable dot to the C in front (actually a variable *second* dot in modern terms, the beat by implication being that of a dotted C). In this case it is reasonable to see the remaining three Sqs as being the strictly-measured remnant of this beat. Thus my preferred solution looks like Donington's but, unlike his, is strictly measured.
2. The structural position of this group is always before a new phrase, if not a new section. The first is at the mid-point of the first half (bar 6); the second follows the two-bar phrase that begins the second half (bar 14); the third is at the start of a new phrase following a passage in B minor (bar 22); and the last introduces the 'recapitulation'. In each case, then, the last three notes of the four-Sq group are the anacrusis to a new phrase. This certainly strengthens the interpretation given at (1), above, and is no doubt also responsible for Donington's interpretation.

Bach's E minor Tempo di Gavotta is by no means unusual in its presentation of rhythmic problems. The foregoing discussion, unsuccessful as it has been in providing incontrovertible solutions, will serve to highlight some of the problems still to be solved. It may also suggest fruitful ways of approaching these problems. More importantly, for our present purpose, it can act as an object-lesson in a subject which has not generally been taken seriously enough by students of notation: the matter of a composer's or scribe's consistency. If we do not immediately see consistency where we expect to see it, we are usually ready to say that the scribe/composer was only human and that the most troublesome details of his work can safely be ignored. It may be that scribes and composers were sometimes more consistent than we realize, and that we throw away good evidence if we give up the search too easily. Certainly, on the subject of notational conventions we do now need to approach the available evidence in new ways.

Conventions of ornamentation

Prior to the seventeenth century ornaments were normally notated by special symbols only in instrumental tablatures (Chapters 10 and 11). The signs may be familiar to us from script or staff notation (e.g. ',♯, ✗), or the initial letter of a directive word may be used (e.g. t = trill). In staff notation, ornaments were to be added by the performer according to a long tradition: instrumental tutors say how this was to be done. Some music survives in two versions, one with written-out ornaments and one without.

Complexity of all types is usually seen at cadences more than elsewhere, and this is true of ornaments. Caccini's *trillo* and *gruppo* were intended for cadential places (SR 384), though they were unnotated. The *trillo* (a beating on a single note) had a short life, but the *gruppo*—which we should now call a measured trill (i.e. alternation of two notes) with a turn—can be applied to almost any cadence from the sixteenth century to the late eighteenth. Throughout the seventeenth century the note-groups of Figure 115(a) showed a trill and turn, with or without the slur (which, in string music, signifies a single bow-stroke): and this occurs not only at cadences. Similarly, the mainly eighteenth-century cadential figure of (b) needs a trill and sharpened rhythm, as shown.

These ways of writing cadences, which warn the performer of a required ornament, are really only more specific forms of the plain cadences shown at (c). More explicit indications for cadences were not needed until the nineteenth century, and the same is true of other contexts where ornaments were normal. This is why many early ornament signs were general in character. For instance, the English virginalists' ornaments (d) were used too loosely to be given specific interpretations except in specific contexts. From the mid-seventeenth century onwards many signs appeared (Donington IEM, 728–35 and *Grove 5*, article 'Ornaments'; Ferguson KI, 138 ff), often with very specific meanings explained by the composers who used them. Some of these signs are phonetic, like that for a double relish (e), but most are graphic—even diastematic—in origin, like the turn (f), the trill (g), and the forefall and backfall (h).

Figure 115. Ornaments

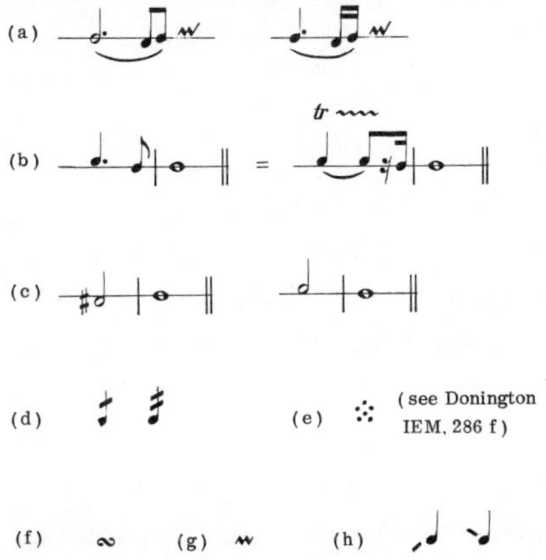

This notation for the forefall and backfall, the seventeenth-century English names, is only one method of writing an *appoggiatura*. Most of the earlier forms are obviously graphic, taking the shape of a stroke, comma (sometimes inverted) or curve. The close calligraphic affinity between these is obvious (Figure 116(a)): in particular, J. S. Bach's upward curve, distinguishing forefall and backfall by vertical position rather than direction, clearly derives from D'Anglebert's comma and not (as at first appears) directly from Purcell's notation. The signs used by Dieupart depend on the context for their interpretation: his vertical curve was used by D'Anglebert and others for a slide, and the two uses should not be confused.[5]

The signs used by Playford, Purcell and others in the second half of the seventeenth century imply a short appoggiatura with values of $\frac{1}{4}$ + $\frac{3}{4}$, but from the late seventeenth century the standard appoggiatura was longer. Robert Donington (IEM, 201) gives the following rules for its length:

(i) half of an undotted main note;
(ii) two-thirds of a dotted main note;
(iii) all of the first of two tied notes in compound metre;
(iv) all of a note before a rest.

Illustrations of these rules are in Figure 116(b). It can be seen that two notational pitfalls arise:

Figure 116. Interpretations of Ornaments

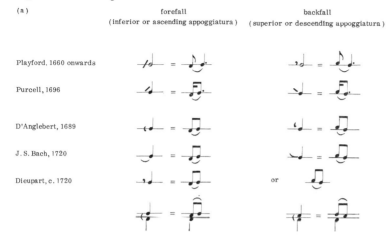

(a)

| | forefall
(inferior or ascending appoggiatura) | backfall
(superior or descending appoggiatura) |

Playford, 1660 onwards

Purcell, 1696

D'Anglebert, 1689

J. S. Bach, 1720

Dieupart, c. 1720

(b)

(i) See examples by D'Anglebert, Bach and Dieupart, above.

(ii)

(Bach, *Matthäus Passion*,'So ist mein Jesus nun')

(iii)

(Quantz, *On Playing the Flute*, 95 f)

(iv)

(Bach, E♭ prelude from Book I of the '48', interpreted by Dolmetsch in IM, 109)

(c)

1. in rule (iv), a rest is notated which necessarily disappears in performance. The resulting rhythm could easily have been notated differently, and it was sometimes suggested that this notation be discarded. Probably this figure had originally been interpreted with a short appoggiatura (the rest being observed) and had survived the growing predilection for a longer ornament;
2. from the early eighteenth century onwards, and almost invariably

223

from the middle of the century, an appoggiatura was shown as a small note—small because harmonically inessential. This can easily make one think of it as both unaccented and short, although it is neither.

There was no general consistency in the use of flags in this small-note notation. Quantz (1752) says that a single flag was normal, and he himself notated the appoggiatura as a small Q. However, he says that it does not matter how it is notated, except that the two-flagged (Sq) form always indicates a short appoggiatura: the reverse is not true, and short appoggiature can be notated in other forms. Similarly, there was no consistency in the use or omission of a slur between the notes.

Although the half-length appoggiatura remained standard, there was a tendency in the second half of the eighteenth century to play it longer. In addition, some appoggiature were played short: C. P. E. Bach (1753) recommends this before short main notes and when the ornaments are filling in a chain of 3rds ('falling' 3rds is understood, though this figuration is not unknown in its ascending form). His rule for the latter case is that the appoggiatura should take only a quarter of the main note, if not less; but that in Adagio it is better in triplet-rhythm (Figure 117(a)). Marpurg (1750) uses some very old-fashioned notation for this (b). The confusion resulting from this haphazard notation for a variety of appoggiature led to a rationalization by C. P. E. Bach, Marpurg and others in the middle of the century, in which appoggiature were notated as small notes of the value of the ornament.[6] Another innovation that partly resolved the problem is found in a few Italian sources (Donington IEM, 208), where a short appoggiatura is notated as in Figure 116(c). This shape became used, logically enough, for the *acciaccatura* in the nineteenth century: in the late baroque period it should not be confused with the full-sized note, which is a form of Sq.

The notation of Figure 117(a) was unfortunately also used for what is often called the 'passing appoggiatura', in which the small note is played before the beat (c). This is a misnomer, since a true appoggiatura occurs on the beat and takes the accent. Quantz says that the true appoggiatura is 'lively and bold' (he is not thinking of the Adagio interpretation, presumably), and that the passing appoggiatura is a more expressive device. Marpurg (1755) reversed the flags of the passing appoggiature, in order to distinguish them from appoggiature proper in this context (Neumann OBPM, 187), a useful and notationally neat device. The passing appoggiatura is in fact characteristic of French style: François Couperin had used the second of the notations shown in Figure 117(b) for it. This figure is really a special case of an ornament that was probably much used (even if not notated) by French composers, for J-J. Rousseau (1768) shows a notation for it that must have had a wide application (Figure 117(e), cited by Donington IEM, 227). Note that the slur covers all three notes.

The so-called double appoggiatura—that is, ornaments of two consecutive notes—are notated in a way analogous to other appoggiature. Whether disjunct or conjunct (the latter is a slide) they were written as two small notes before the main note (f). C. P. E. Bach requires a slur over all three notes of the disjunct form, but in practice this was not invariable: the conjunct (slide) form was often notated without the slur. The double appoggiatura starts on the beat but, unlike its single relative, it does not take the accent, which is reserved for the main note and is therefore delayed (Donington IEM, 216). Marpurg (*Principes du clavecin*, 1756) indicates a long first note by means of a dotted-rhythm ornament (g).

Figure 117. Interpretations of Ornaments

Conventions of transposition

Early conventions of transposition are very difficult to track down. For example, parts of Pierre de la Rue's *Missa L'Homme Armé* are notated so low that a transposition up a 4th or so seems to be intended, but no other indication is given; and Thomas Morley's remarks about 'high' and 'low' keys suggest a convention of transposition in which the clef disposition constitutes a 'code' for the performers' use.[7] To a large extent the problems of transposition in the seventeenth century must be related directly to the difference between organ pitch and choir pitch, or between church pitch and chamber pitch. In English sources the difference of a 5th made it possible for an organist to transpose by a mental substitution of a C-clef for an F-clef and a G-clef for a C-clef (Caldwell, *English Keyboard Music*, 53), which may well help to explain the increased use of the G-clef in England during that century.

This section, however, is not concerned with problems of transposition generally. Rather, I wish to discuss certain conventional transpositions relevant to specific instruments. These transpositions, used in the seventeenth and later centuries, fall into three main categories: octave transpositions for various instruments; *scordatura* notation for the violin; and the notation of transposing instruments generally.

The first of these is not really a type of notation at all, but mainly a warning to the player. In *concertante* passages a solo violin sometimes acted as the bass to two or more other instruments (e.g. in the slow movement of the Fourth Brandenburg Concerto). In such a case the *basso continuo* was suspended, so that the violin became the real, and only, bass to the texture. In the music of Hasse and his contemporaries the violin part is sometimes notated in the bass clef to remind the performer of his function (Drummond, 'The Concertos of . . . Hasse', 98). The part is thus notated one or two octaves too low, and must be transposed up by the player. This principle of transposing a passage comfortably notated in the bass clef is found also in parts for horn and for clarinet. Until about the beginning of the present century, a horn-part in the bass clef had to be read an octave above its notated pitch: thus a horn in F, sounding a 5th lower than written pitch in the treble clef (see below for transposing instruments) sounded a 4th above its written pitch in the bass clef. In the same way, the clarinet parts in Mozart's music, for example, must be thought of as an octave

226

higher when they use the bass clef. In the present century this practice has been discontinued, and the transposition is always in the same direction whatever clef is in use.

A similar principle, but with the opposite effect, is found in many cello parts of the nineteenth century. In its highest register the cello uses the treble clef, and this was often notated an octave higher than the intended sounding pitch.

The second type of transposition-convention is rather earlier in date, being found in the music of Biber and some of his contemporaries. It is basically a method of writing staff notation for a *scordatura* violin in such a way that the fingering, rather than the sound to be produced, is notated. Let us suppose that the top string of a violin is tuned to e″, as usual: then the violinist has certain fingerings with which he will normally produce the notes of Figure 118(a). Now suppose that he re-tunes the string to d″: with minor adjustments for intonation, that same fingering will produce the notes of (b). Hence, with this tuning the way to produce the sound of (b) is to ask the performer to finger the notes of (a) in the usual tuning.[8] Alternatively, the sound of (a) can be produced by fingering the notes of (c): in either case the fingering must be for the notes a tone higher than those required.

It follows that if the string is tuned a tone lower than usual, the notation must be in a key which is a tone higher than the key of the music (e.g. music in F major must be notated in G major): if a semitone higher, then in the key a semitone lower than the key of the music; and so on. Were all of the violin's strings re-tuned to the same interval higher or lower, the result would be a simple transposition of all the music. However, Biber used these tunings to facilitate the fingering of certain chords, so the *scordatura* usually affects only one or two strings, the others being tuned normally. Thus some of the music is notated in its own key, and some is notated in a higher or lower key according to the tuning of the strings. The disposition of keys is however decided by the tuning of the strings: for example, if only the top string is re-tuned, only the part of the staff from e″ upwards is given a different key-signature because only that music will be played in a different key (high positions were not much used then, so it was assumed that music from e″ upwards would always be played on the e-string). Figure 118(d) shows the notation for a scale of G major on an instrument with the top two strings tuned down a tone: from a′ upwards the music is notated in A major. An illustration of this notation is shown at (e).

227

Figure 118. Violin Scordatura

Scale of G major

in normal tuning
g d' a' e"

in *scordatura*
g d' g' d"

Accordo

Vln

Basso continuo

* In the original,
this bar is
notated as
follows:

etc.

(Biber, opening of Sonata IV from *Acht Violinsonaten*, 1681)

A similar use of *scordatura* is found in eighteenth-century fiddle-music in Scotland (Johnson, *Music and Society in Lowland Scotland*, 119 f). The three usual tunings are a d' a' e" for D major, a e' a' e" for A major, and a e' a' c♯", also for A major. The notation follows the principles outlined above in reference to Biber's music.[9]

228

The notation of transposing instruments generally is closely allied to that for *scordatura* violin. It concerns those instruments which, if played in their 'open' key, without chromatic notes, would produce a scale of some key other than C major. The notation was first used in the eighteenth century for horn parts, at a time when the horn had a very limited repertory of notes, based on the harmonic series of a particular key. The key could be changed by taking out the crook (a part of the instrument's tubing) and substituting a longer or shorter crook which would make a new harmonic series possible. The convention arose whereby the player's part would specify the crook to be used and then notate the music in C major. Thus a notated c″ would result in the note f′ if played on a horn with the F crook, g′ if the G crook were used, and so on. The same system applied to trumpets, and was later used also for clarinets, cor anglais, and other instruments.

All horns transpose downwards: that is, they produce a sound which is lower than that notated. Trumpets and clarinets in B flat and A transpose downwards; those in C play at pitch; and those in D and E flat transpose upwards. The cor anglais is in F, transposing downwards, and the same is true of the bass clarinet. Figure 119(a) shows the transpositions of the most common orchestral instruments (not all are used in modern scores).

Figure 119. Transposing Instruments

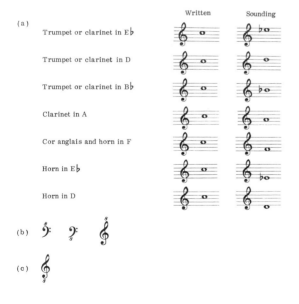

229

In addition there was a period in the late eighteenth and early nineteenth centuries when the timpani were also notated as transposing instruments. Like the horns, they had a limited series of notes which in any case had to be specified, although they were usually the tonic, dominant and subdominant of the key. It was therefore possible to notate the part entirely as if it were in C major.

In more recent scores the tendency has been not to treat instruments as transposing if it can be avoided. The timpani are always written at sounding pitch, following their musical liberation by Beethoven and later composers (helped eventually by the invention of pedal-timpani); composers usually write for trumpet in C now; and some even prefer to write horn-parts at sounding pitch, a procedure made possible by the common use of the 'double' horn in F and B flat. Transposed notation remains for clarinets (including bass clarinet) and cor anglais.

Some instruments are conventionally notated an octave away from their true sounding pitch. The reason for this notation is invariably to allow the use of normal treble or bass clef (G^2, F^4) without too many leger lines. The piccolo, written at the same pitch as the flute, sounds an octave higher: the same is true of all members of the recorder family, although their acoustic properties are such that this is not normally noticeable. The double bass and the double bassoon, often written with cellos and bassoons respectively, sound an octave lower. In recent decades there has been some attempt to introduce octave versions of the G and F clef (Figure 119(b)), analogous to the G clef used for the tenor voice (c) but specifically for instrumental use. These clefs are, however, quite unnecessary, and they are not in general use.

16. The Limits of the System

As this book may have indicated, musical notation is always in a state of change, constantly subjected to pressures which cause it to embrace innovations, to become more explicit, more flexible, or otherwise more suited to the prevailing musical style. That is why it is hard to generalize about notation. A statement about Mozart's staccato-markings may have to be modified for one of his contemporaries; and our inability to date a mid-thirteenth-century manuscript precisely may make it impossible to choose between two possible interpretations of its notation.

This is an historical view, however, and most musicians, working on the time-scale of their own lives, regard notation as static. That is why publishers sometimes impose a uniform house-style which 'corrects' notational innovations; and why so many of the theorists cited in this book were trying to correct errors in the usage of a system that they knew to be logical and practicable as long as everybody used it in the same way—their way.

In this story of constant change one period, the nineteenth and early twentieth centuries, stands out as unusual. The system as we know it was complete: it had all the signs and directives necessary to notate the great Romantic works, with enormous subtlety of nuance allied to considerable precision. Even the most imaginative Romantic composers were notationally conservative (after all, they wrote for posterity), while many of the rest—in their notation as in their music—were content with eighteenth-century ideals.

Yet the nineteenth century was not notationally moribund, for it was not easy to notate that subtlety of nuance with precision. (Verbal directives were much used: but they tend to become clumsier as their meaning is made more precise.) When we look at a Romantic score—often a fine example of penmanship and beautifully clear—we find that much ingenuity has been expended on the expressive subtleties of the music, however static the basic notational principles may be. In this chapter, therefore, we shall discuss first certain phenomena which might be termed mere idiosyncrasies of the individual composer.

Extensions of the system

Nineteenth-century extensions of the system were directed mainly towards the notation of expressive parameters such as phrasing, articulation and dynamics. These extensions often broke the 'rules' of notation in order to express the composer's intention in a clearer, more direct way—usually graphically, and often by an unconventional use of notational devices (cf. the tendency to a more visual notation in Dufay's time, discussed in Chapter 6). The very precise rhomboids used by Beethoven and others for dynamic markings (Chapter 14) is a good example, but a simple one because the function of the notation is not changed. More interesting in every way is the use of beams to show phrasing, articulation and melodic structure, a use which they did not originally have. Throughout the seventeenth and eighteenth centuries beaming showed metrical groups, at least in instrumental music (Chapter 13): in practice, this means that a beam does not cross a bar-line, that a new note or beam starts at the half-bar in duple time, and that separate beams are very often used to guide the eye to one-beat groups. The opening of Beethoven's piano sonata op. 14, no. 2 (Figure 120(a)) contravenes the second of these conventions in order to reinforce the slurs: the notation does not confuse the rhythm, and the visual effect is direct and clear. An example of slur-reinforcement at the beginning of Brahms's German Requiem, no. 5 (b), is more subtle. Indeed, in view of the different beamings in other parts it may even be subconscious. Here the rhythmic groups are not tampered with, since beaming as 5 + 3 would obscure the metrical structure of the music, but the separation of the fifth Q from the following group is just enough to guide the eye. Brahms did not isolate this note further by giving it an upward stem, as the 'rules' of stemming would require; his musical purpose transcended such rules. Printed versions, however, give an upward stem, and so do not reproduce the composer's notation accurately. Winternitz (MA i, 5 and ii, plate 46) cites the opening of C. P. E. Bach's B flat Fantasia (c) as another example in which the printed version fails to transmit the composer's notation: Bach's original retains the metrical divisions of the beaming, but stems the notes above or below the beams in such a way that the phrasing in threes is instantly recognizable.

232

Figure 120. Beams.

(a)

for

(b) 'correct' beaming

p dolce

(Vienna, Gesellschaft der Musikfreunde: see Hürlimann CA ii. 13)

(c)

printed
as

(Washington, D.C., Library of Congress:
see Winternitz MA ii, plate 46)

This ability of stems and beams to notate various parameters efficiently has been much used in the twentieth century (see Figure 125(b), for example). Indeed, a freer use of beams is perhaps the most obvious visual difference between the traditionally-notated music of the present century and that of the Romantic era. Cole (*Sounds and Signs*, 87 ff) shows how beaming has been used to indicate not only matters of articulation (rhythmic groups including rests, irregular additive rhythms, articulation-patterns divorced from metrical grouping, accentuation) but also to clarify motivic structure or to point out close imitative entries.

As the foregoing might suggest (especially Figure 120(a) and (b)), beaming often shows the phrasing that would otherwise be indicated only by slurs. This gives rise to a considerable freedom of usage, in which the beams define the individual voice-parts and show the extent of their phrases. Hence the beams themselves are able usefully not only to cross bar-lines but to move from one staff to another. Figure 121(a) shows this in the piano part of Berg's early song 'Die Nachtigall' (1907): a phrasing-slur is used in addition, which also moves freely between the staves (this helps to clarify the part-writing from bar 12 onwards, where there is crossing of parts). As far as I know, the crossing of beams between staves has been used only for the music of an individual performer, though such beaming could no doubt help a conductor when incomplete phrases are passed from one instrument to another. As it is, this latter situation can be notated by the crossing

233

of phrasing-slurs, often found in Berg's music. A good example is at the beginning of *Lulu*, where a phrasing-slur begins with the cellos and basses and ends two bars later when the second violins finish their phrase: the bold upward pen-stroke, impressive in the printed score, is even more so in the autograph (reproduced in Hürlimann CA ii, 22). This usage is of real help only to a conductor unless the orchestral parts have continuous cues showing the migration of the phrase. (As Cole points out (*Sounds and Signs*, 96) such a cue *is* used in the *Lyric Suite*, in order to show a crescendo affecting imitative entries at the beginning of no. IV. The crescendo wedge travels through the score from cello to first violin.) In the Violin Concerto Berg shows the performers exactly how the responsibility for a phrase is shared between them by means of Schoenberg's signs for *Hauptstimme* (principal part), ⌐ ⌐, and *Nebenstimme* (subsidiary part), N⌐ ⌐. Figure 121(b) shows the first bar of the work, in which the bass clarinet plays the first and last notes of the phrase (completed by the first clarinet), holding a less important pedal-note meanwhile. The dynamic markings help the player to achieve the effect.

Figure 121. Slurs

(Berg, 'Die Nachtigall' from *Seven Early Songs* (1907): voice part omitted)

(Berg, Violin Concerto, opening: harp and solo violin omitted)

These uses of beams and slurs are aids to the performer's comprehension of the music, though in general they make no difference to his interpretation. There are, however, notational devices of which this is certainly not intended to be true: that is, devices that

234

direct the performer's interpretation, not via the mechanical actions of his fingers, etc., but by an appeal to his appreciation of the musical effect required. The only certain criterion for this type of notation is that its execution is mechanically or otherwise impossible: but there is a large border-area between this and normal directive notation in which examples must be investigated separately. For want of a better term I shall refer to it as 'psychological' notation. One example of psychological notation—and it is surprisingly common, once one starts to look for it—is very easily overlooked altogether: the notated direction for a crescendo on a single chord played on the piano. A famous example in the postlude of Schumann's *Dichterliebe* (Figure 122(a)), which also includes a decrescendo, could be regarded as a Romantic composer's notation for an unattainable ideal, a musical event written as if for another medium. But further thought suggests that it is more than this, for even played at Andante Espressivo this Q is too short for the swell to be played on any instrument. We must conclude, therefore, that Schumann wished the pianist to linger over this chord—a breaking of the tempo that he achieves a few bars later by means of an arpeggiated chord and a leap.[1] Even so, there must be a purpose in the notation: and although it is physically impossible to play a single chord *crescendo* on the piano, that must surely be the effect required. How the pianist achieves this is another matter— through timing, certainly. (It is worth pointing out that the common notation of a *decrescendo* on a single chord presents a different problem. A chord played on the piano dies away in any case: but if the effect wanted were a more sudden decay, this could be achieved by half-pedalling, a device which is usually notated as a 'peak' in the pedal-line, ℗. ___∧___⌐ .)

This swell and decay on a single chord is common in Schumann's music, but it is no mere individual quirk: so hard-headed a composer as Schoenberg used precisely the same notation (*Three Piano Pieces* op. 11, no. 2—a string of them in bars 11–12, shown in Figure 122(b); *Six Little Piano Pieces* op. 19, no. 5, bar 5), as did Berg (c). In fact, a search through Berg's early songs and Sonata op. 1 and the opp. 11 and 19 of Schoenberg shows that both composers treated the piano as if it were capable of sustained and variable tone. Of course, this is often reasonable in the songs (both Berg's and Schumann's), where a crescendo in the voice may have to be matched by increased intensity in the accompaniment: but since the piano is incapable of a sustained crescendo we can only say that the notation of Figure 122(d), for instance, is

1. a direction to the pianist to *think* a crescendo and decrescendo through the bar, and

2. a neater notation than the realistic (e), which is what the pianist actually plays.

It should be noted, however, that (d) is much more precise than (e), although impossible to perform: and there are many examples where the accompaniment is independent.

Figure 122. Psychological Use of Dynamics

(Schumann, *Dichterliebe* , postlude)

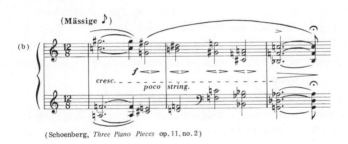

(Schoenberg, *Three Piano Pieces* op. 11, no. 2)

(Berg, 'Nacht', from *Seven Early Songs*)

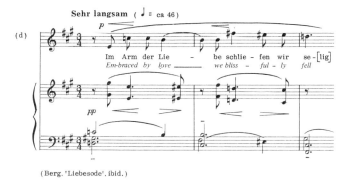

(Berg, 'Liebesode', ibid.)

Chromaticism and atonality

Pitch notation, based as it is on the writing of a diatonic scale in any key, was perhaps most suited to the music of the eighteenth century. In the Romantic period, with a more chromatic style growing, the tonal system was extended and the resources of the notation were further stretched. This can be seen in a great increase in the use of accidentals, including bb and ×, with a consequent use of double accidentals—i.e. the cancellation (by a ♮) of one accidental before another can be applied at the same pitch-level.

Tonal music and tonal notation go together. A composer who feels a passage of his music to be in a certain key will usually notate it according to that key, even if the music would be notated more simply (i.e. with fewer accidentals) using enharmonic alternatives. Even where the tonality is very fluid a composer will normally notate according to the harmonic structure. Thus Berg's Piano Sonata, clearly in B minor, goes momentarily into flat notation in the first bar because of a secondary seventh on C minor: and at the recapitulation (bars 111–12, shown in Figure 123(a)) a second harmonic twist to the flat side results in A sharp (the leading-note of the expected cadence) being notated simultaneously with a B flat.

Figure 123.

(Berg, Piano Sonata op. 1 (? 1907 - 08), bars 110 - 13)

Tonal notation is to a large extent preserved by sight-reading habits. A keyboard-player prefers a chord to be written tonally because he can assimilate it more easily, and his fingers have been trained to accommodate arpeggios and other chords in various keys. However, in the present century the habit of looking for triads and their inversions, diminished sevenths, etc., is partly broken in most of us. But in vocal music the difficulties are greater unless the singer has perfect pitch. For example, a doubly-augmented fourth or a diminished sixth are much harder to sing than their enharmonic equivalents, both perfect fifths (Figure 123(b)).

The way we notate music, then, has tonal, or at least harmonic, implications. If these implications are unwelcome (as they are in atonal music, at least from the composer's point of view), they must be eradicated, and this can be done successfully only by a random use of sharps and flats, which is difficult for the performer to grasp. In practice many composers allow themselves to use a majority of either sharps or flats in any given section, purely as a matter of notational convenience: but since notes have to be played which contradict these accidentals, there are also a large number of cautionary or other naturals. Thus the problem partly solves itself, most notes (some composers would now say *all* notes, for consistency and to avoid any possible ambiguity) being preceded by an accidental, so that no note is 'diatonic'. The result is less confusing to the eye than we might expect. In any case, bb and ✕ are redundant in atonal music, so that only 'first-degree' chromatic inflexion is involved. Nevertheless, there is an obvious advantage in a notation which has no accidentals, or one in which there is only one notation for any note (as in a tablature). It is

238

this advantage which leads to the kind of reform of pitch-notation discussed in the next chapter.

The limits of precision

In the Romantic period most composers specified as closely as possible the sound to be produced, and many searched for new sounds. This search resulted in the addition of new instruments to the orchestra (the cor anglais, for instance, and many percussion instruments) and in new ways for existing instruments to be played (e.g. Bartok's snap pizzicato and Elgar's use of side-drum sticks with timpani in the 'Enigma' Variations, no. XIII). We might expect this care on the composer's part to result in increased notational precision: and so it did.

In Chapter 14 I suggested that dynamic markings of a higher power than *fff* and *ppp* were merely for emphasis, but this must now be qualified to some extent. The highest-power marking known to me is Tchaikovsky's *pppppp* in the 'Pathétique' Symphony (first movement, 16 bars after letter G). Cole (*Sounds and Signs*, 76) regarded this as a matter of emphasis—almost of psychological notation—and not as a literal directive. But the direction comes at the end of a passage in which Tchaikovsky used *ppp, pppp* and *ppppp*, among other markings, with crescendos and diminuendos between; and it is clear that these different levels are intended to be aurally distinguishable. The distinctions may not be fully realizable in practice, but they are undoubtedly intended to be. (Cole also pointed out that a twelve-level dynamic scale, from *pppp* to *ffff*, is 'at least a practical possibility', and that player-pianos used to provide a fifteen-point scale of dynamics. A scale of *pppppp* to *ffffff*, with *mp* and *mf* at the centre, gives only fourteen levels, so perhaps Tchaikovsky's calculations were accurate.)

This example is a simple one, because only one dynamic scale is involved. Elgar's use of dynamics sometimes approaches the limits of precision because it is complex, working on two levels simultaneously. For example, four bars after fig. 41 in Part I of *The Dream of Gerontius* Elgar marked a *cresc.* which is to be taken as a general crescendo—it appears in all parts then playing or singing. Simultaneously with this there are other dynamic markings which are, however, to be understood as more detailed: in the first violins, for example, each bar in this passage is marked ⟨⟨ ⟩⟩, so that there are swells and decays within an overall crescendo. The distinction between 'phrasing' dynamics and longer-range 'structural' dynamics is important. The first clarinet has in this passage a one-bar figure with a 'phrasing' dynamic marking of ⟩⟩ : hence the bar in question carries an apparently contradictory marking of *cresc.* ⟩⟩ . This is by no means an isolated instance of dynamic marking on two levels in Elgar's music.

This use of dynamics is not self-evident to the performer, nor is it unambiguous. Later composers have been content to demand obedience to clearly-specified directives. Stockhausen has used note-head size to show dynamic values (see Karkoschka NNM, 153): the larger the note-head, the louder the note is to be played (an idea first proposed at the turn of the century: see Abdy Williams SN, 212). This is one substitution of graphic for phonetic notation that is perhaps not an improvement, for the traditional notaton of dynamics is more easily assimilated by the eye. Boulez is among those still using the traditional notation: but he, like Stockhausen, often gives a new dynamic level for each individual note. This makes severe demands on the performer, and adds to the extreme difficulty of playing the music as precisely as it is notated. The same applies to Cage's dynamics, where a wide range of dynamic levels is notated by numbers. (However, the short series from 1 to 8 used in *Imaginary Landscape No. 5*—for which see Karkoschka NNM, 97—is of course entirely realistic.)

The case of rhythmic notaton is different, for here the notational resources—based on the concept of a regular pulse—are quite inadequate for modern needs. In the present century composers have notated asymmetrical rhythms by showering accents over their music, by changing the metre (and therefore the time-signature) every bar, or by using the additive nature of notation to create unpredictable rhythmic periods. This last approach has been much favoured by Messiaen, especially in respect of two related devices:

1. the 'added dot' ('point ajouté'), a dot of addition causing asymmetry in what might otherwise be a normal metrical rhythmic group (Figure 124(a));
2. the 'unmetrical period' ('temps irrationel'), in which asymmetry is caused by an unmetrical additive grouping (b).

Figure 124. Additive Rhythms in Messiaen

(Messiaen. *Livre d'Orgue*, 1953, I)   (Ibid., VI)

Messiaen's usage is really only the distortion of regular pulses, and does not solve the problem of ametrical rhythmic notation: nor does Henry Cowell's division of the S into thirds, fifths, sevenths, etc., using note-head shapes to distinguish the different divisions (see Stone, 'Problems', 17). Interestingly, the problems of time-notation have been best solved in the simplest way, by making rigorous use of the time-axis principle, in which duration is proportionately shown by linear measurement on the page (see below, Figures 129, 131(d) and 132(a)).

A related problem—which is, however, a new one in the twentieth century—is that of the controlled ritardando or accelerando. Verbal directives have partly given way to a precise use of numbers (Figure 125(a)) or to graphic notations of various types (b). The difficulties arise rather over the very long-range structural changes of tempo, especially in music such as that of Elliott Carter, where two different changes take place simultaneously. The result is complex music written in a way that probably approaches the limits of acceptable notational complexity. (Examples of Carter's music are discussed by Stone, 'Problems', 18 ff: see also Perkins, 'Note Values'.)

Figure 125.

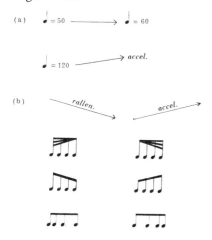

In pitch notation there has been for much of this century a need for a clear system of notating microtones. The most influential method until 1960 or so was that of Alois Hába (illustrated and discussed by Karkoschka, 2 f, n.5), still used in modified forms. Hába's notations for quarter-tones (Figure 126 (a)) and twelfth-tones (b), proposed in his *Neue Harmonielehre* (1927), use the ♯ and the ♭ as graphic bases

Figure 126. Hába's notations for microtones between 'white' notes a tone apart

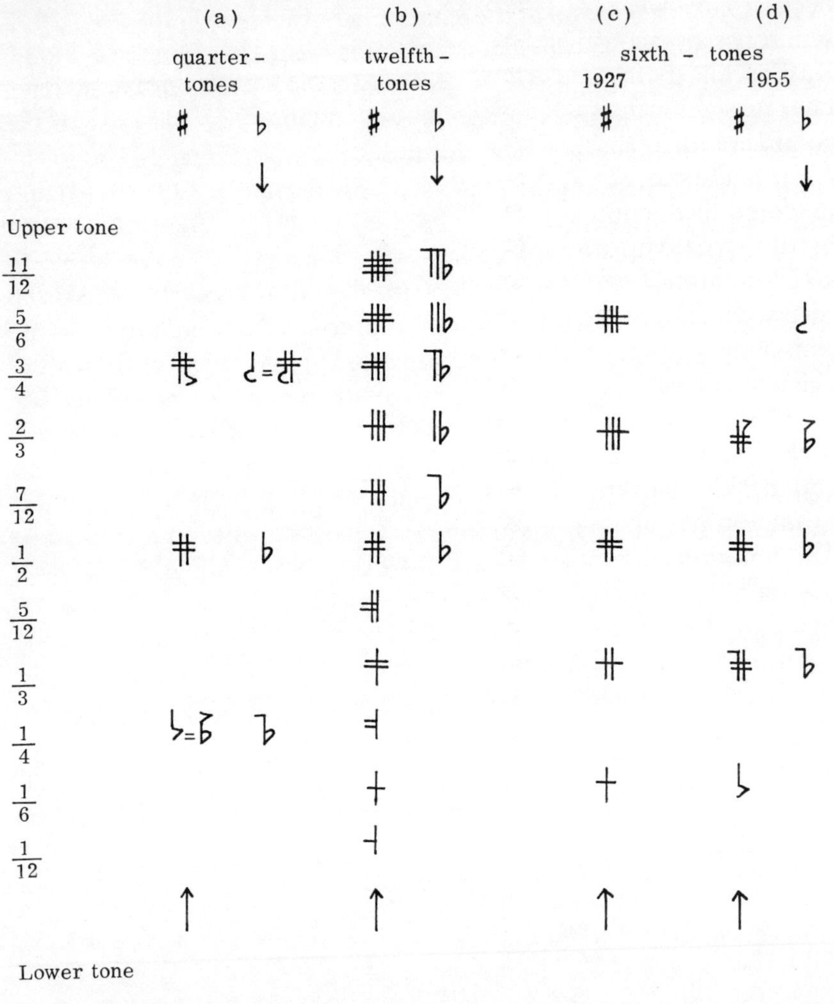

	(a) quarter-tones	(b) twelfth-tones	(c) sixth-tones 1927	(d) sixth-tones 1955

Upper tone

$\frac{11}{12}$

$\frac{5}{6}$

$\frac{3}{4}$

$\frac{2}{3}$

$\frac{7}{12}$

$\frac{1}{2}$

$\frac{5}{12}$

$\frac{1}{3}$

$\frac{1}{4}$

$\frac{1}{6}$

$\frac{1}{12}$

Lower tone

for the new signs. The signs for quarter-tones seem unnecessarily complicated. Those used for twelfth-tones should perhaps be regarded as two alternative series:

1. using sharp forms upwards through the interval of a tone;
2. using sharp forms upwards in the lower semitone, and flat forms downwards in the upper semitone.

Of these, (1) has the advantage of consistency and the disadvantage of an eleven-point series, while (2) is slightly more comprehensible, based as it is on the traditional concept of the accidental as a semitone sharper or flatter than the 'white' note. Purely theoretically, two other considerations are important: first, the concept of 'sharp' and 'flat' needs to be weakened in an age which largely treats the twelve semitones as acoustic equals (see below, Chapter 17); second, as Karkoschka pointed out (op. cit., 2, n.5), enharmonic equivalents have no significance in microtonal music, where temperament must be so precise as to forbid differences in tuning.

It is therefore particularly interesting to note that Hába himself made no distinction between the twelfth-note series (1) and (2), but used alternative forms as was convenient. Moreover, although his 1927 notation for sixth-tones (c) used only sharp modifications, he reverted to a dual system in the Suite for Violoncello Solo of 1955 (d). This suggests that there is a practical advantage in the availability of enharmonic equivalents, to the composer if not to the performer.

It will be obvious that to some extent these notations are mutually exclusive: for instance, the sign ♭ has different meanings in (a), (b) and (d). This weakness becomes more pronounced with a wider range of microtonal divisions (see Risatti, *New Music Vocabulary*, 17 f). The notation of microtones generally by means of additional signs based on the ♯ and b would be very cumbersome, even if a single set of signs could be devised to cover all useful microtonal divisions. Such a notation could hardly match the musical precision required (and obtainable). In such a case the solution is to discard the additional signs by devising a radically different system: some possible solutions will be described in Chapters 17 and 18.

17. Notational Reforms

The process of evolution by which staff notation came into being (described in Part I) resulted in limitations, illogicalities and apparently unnecessary difficulties in the notational system. Consequent innovations, apart from those which extended the system's possibilities, were usually for one of two reasons:
1. to circumvent difficulties of traditional notation for the musical learner;
2. to produce a simpler, more usable or more logical notation for general use.
The distinction is a fine one that cannot always be made with certainty. Moreover, history may change a notation's purpose: Rousseau's innovations were a deliberate attempt to supplant staff notation, but their survival is due entirely to their usefulness for teaching purposes. I have found it convenient for this and other reasons to include Rousseau's notation in Part II (Chapter 9, above), but it might have appeared here instead. In general, if I have been able to assign notational innovations to (1) or (2), above, the former are discussed in Part II and the latter are reserved for the present chapter.

Requirements and means

Some of the problems have changed since Rousseau's time. He, like other advocates of movable-do systems, sought to eliminate key-signatures, etc., by using the same notation in every key: we, who require equal status for all notes on the chromatic scale (not to mention different microtonal divisions), must necessarily reject this tonal concept and face the problems arising out of an 'octave' of twelve intervals. In order to understand in what ways staff notation needs reformation in the various parameters, it will be useful to tabulate the main notational needs and the means available.

244

Requirements	*Available Means*
PITCH	SPACE
tonality	vertical
accidentals	horizontal
octave-transposition	
DURATION	NOTE-HEADS
of notes (sounds)	size
of rests (silences)	shape
	colour
INTENSITY	STEMS
static	number
changing	length
	direction
PHRASING & ARTICULATION	+FLAG
	number
ATTACK/DECAY	direction
	shape (including extension
	as a beam)
	ADDITIONAL SIGNS
	shape
	number
	position
	VERBAL INSTRUCTIONS

In theory, any item on the left of this table could be notated by any of the means listed on the right.

This table is far from comprehensive, for I have omitted certain possibilities that seem unlikely to be used. For example, the colour of both stem and flag might be used notationally, although for purely practical reasons they are not—a red note-head takes a red stem and flag, and a black note-head a black stem and flag. (Nor is it possible conveniently to distinguish between full and void forms, so a full black note and a void black note have identical stems.)

The list of available means is in rough chronological order for diastematic notations, in which the vertical and horizontal axes were used from the beginning for pitch and time, and in which verbal directions appeared late. Additional signs, too, are mainly late (e.g. for staccato), but some of the earliest symbols—such as clefs—also belong to this category.

It is largely in relation to these additional signs that notational reform is most obviously needed. The more complex of them have been a source of confusion to eye and mind, even when their usage has been generally unambiguous (as is the case with clefs, for instance). The simplest signs, such as the slur, are by their nature prone to over-use, with consequent ambiguity. It would be possible to write a short book on the notational uses of the simplest of all symbols, the dot: but it will be enough here to refer the reader back to a notation already discussed (Chapter 12, especially Figure 89(a)–(c)) in which the dot has no fewer than three simultaneous purposes, none of which concerns either duration or articulation. Much notational reform has been concerned to substitute symbols for verbal directives, and then to eliminate additional signs by incorporating the signs for the relevant parameters into other categories of notational symbol.

If the multiple usage of certain notational means can be a difficulty, the variety of means used to notate some parameters is another. A moment's thought will show that in order to notate the duration of sounds we normally use five different means:
1. shape of note-head (we still use Bs in hymn-books);
2. colour of note-head (M distinguished from C);
3. stems;
4. flags;
5. an additional sign, the dot of augmentation.
Clearly, there are disadvantages in using so many means for a single purpose:

it uses up notational means that might be employed for other parameters;

it is inconsistent and therefore potentially confusing; and

it does not make full use of the means employed. For example, we use numbers of flags (in the order Q, Sq, Dsq, etc.) but do not alter their direction or shape, nor use them for values greater than a Q; we have both full and void note-heads, but do not use them consistently (the forms ⋈, •, ♪, etc., having fallen into disuse).

If we examine pitch notation we shall find that this, too, is illogical and wasteful of notational resources (see below). Pitch notation, however, raises a more general issue, which it is convenient to discuss here—the matter of series. We noted above (Chapters 10 and 11) the considerable demands made on the memory of a performer using Bermudo's first keyboard tablature or German lute tablature: the difficulty of these notations is the relatively large series (42 notes and at least 41 respectively) which form the basis of their pitch notation. Such a series is by no means outside the range of the average memory, but it invites mistakes because of its lack of 'land-marks'. The brain works much better with a shorter series repeated: hence the success of French and Italian lute tablatures, in which a series of eight or ten fret-positions is repeated for each of six visually-distinguished courses; hence also the move in Spanish keyboard tablatures, first to a shorter series (white notes only) and then to a seven-note series repeated, with easily-recognized differentiations for octave transpositions (Chapter 10). Even if we limit our range to that of a modern piano and include only the white notes, pitch-notation in the vertical axis on a staff may require a series of over 50 notes. In practice, however, this series is broken up in ways that help both eye and brain to choose the right note on the keyboard quickly:[1]

the notes are written on both lines and spaces, so that it is effectively a double series;

clefs impose certain visual limitations—the employment only of notes within a short distance of a fixed mark-point;

we use an *8va* sign for very high or very low notes in order to keep written notes on or near the staff, leger lines being difficult to read. This effectively means that much of the available range is notated as an octave-series, repeated with differentiations.

We are now in a position to state certain principles which an ideal notation could be expected to follow:

1. Each notational requirement should be met by a single means (left and right sides of my table, above).

2. Any means employed should meet only a single notational requirement.

3. The means chosen should offer a short series with differentiated repetitions, not a single long series.

4. The various symbols and their differentiations should be easily assimilable by the eye.

These principles cannot, of course, be applied in quite the simple terms in which I have stated them. Even so, it will be seen that our present staff notation is far from conforming to them. Reforms have tended to concentrate on four main areas: the staff; clefs; accidentals; and rhythm.

Areas of reform

Notational reforms have usually satisfied the first two of the principles just outlined, but not so often the third, and rarely the last. For example, the phonetic notation of Labatut in the early nineteenth century (Abdy Williams SN, 203), in which very simple signs take the place of letter-names, is made appallingly complex by the confusing graphical differentiations for accidentals, octave-displacement and durational values. The result is far from being the aid to sight-reading and quick learning which is the usual western requirement: rather, it must be studied and translated laboriously before any sound can be made. As Abdy Williams rightly remarked (SN, 199), such reforms appeal to the intellect rather than to the eye: and they illustrate the fact that it is much easier to see the faults of staff notation than to invent a more accessible system. The most successful reforms have been the clear phonetic systems, which are of course closest to a good tablature. It is outside the scope of this book to discuss all of the reforms attempted in the last four centuries (they are described by Abdy Williams SN, 196–212, and Wolf HdN ii, 335–86), but it will be useful to examine briefly the types of reform proposed for the four main notational areas mentioned above.

The staff is *per se* probably a very successful aid to pitch notation, especially with about five lines, which offer eleven positions without the use of leger lines. It is unfortunate that the staff has been so involved with the problem of notating chromatic notes, for many of the solutions to this latter problem actually make the staff much less usable (see below). The real drawback of our staff system is an intellectual rather than a practical one. We should like vertical displacement to be in direct ratio to the musical interval, which it is not: this can be seen in Figure 127, where the same written interval expresses two different musical intervals (a). This failure to define an acoustical interval precisely by its written interval does not normally matter for practical purposes, because we use additional signs (accidentals) to define the intervals unequivocally. However, accidentals are non-diastematic, and the result is—to state the most extreme position—that the written 3rd of Figure 127 can be made to stand for intervals containing as many as eight semitones (b), as few as none at all (c), or anything between (d).[2] (There are 25 possible combinations for any interval if we use $\times$, $\sharp$, $\flat$, $\flat\flat$ and $\natural$.)

248

Figure 127.

Clearly, this is logically unsatisfactory, and the simplest reform would be to use a staff in which adjacent line and space always represent the interval of a semitone. Seven lines are needed for a whole octave to be placed on this staff, but with octave differentiations a six-line staff is enough to make leger lines unnecessary, or five lines with a single leger line (Wolf HdN ii, 355 ff). The method of octave-differentiation proposed by Karl Laker for keyboard music in 1910 should be compared with that of Curwen (above, Figure 80(b)). He treated the nearest octave to c′ on each side as undifferentiated, these being on different staves: octaves below this in the left hand (i.e. from B downwards) have one or more short strokes to the left of the note-head; octaves above the first in the right hand (from c″ upwards) have one or more strokes to the right of the note-head.[3]

This system is neat, but it has two disadvantages:

1. Intervals are wide-spaced, and the eye does not take them in quickly without land-marks on the staff: since clefs are dispensed with (movable clefs would be confusing with such a spaced-out staff), no landmarks are available. This disadvantage was partly overcome by Mitcherd and others in the late nineteenth century by a grouping of the stave-lines into 2 + 3, as on the keyboard. Here, the larger gap in the staff represents the interval between e′ and f′, the lines representing the 'black' notes and the spaces the 'white'. (Mitcherd placed a dotted line in the centre of this space, which is visually disturbing: Wolf HdN ii, 359).

2. The octave transpositions do not necessarily coincide with melodic, rhythmic or fingering patterns, and cannot often be made to do so. For this to be possible it is necessary to have either a very much larger staff (resulting in a correspondingly larger series for the eye to take in) or a system of clefs.

Clefs have been the subject of attempts at reform since the sixteenth century. Early medieval usage, with a movable clef on a four-line staff, was flexible and visually clear, but the larger staff of six lines or more made a more static clef desirable. The use of particular clefs for specific voice-ranges also tended to immobilize clefs. During the nineteenth century the C-clef fell into disuse except for certain instruments (the C-clef being the last to appear in more than one position on the staff), and in the present century there is a move to abolish all but the clefs G^2 and F^4, octave-transposition signs being added as necessary (see above, Figure 119(b) and (c), for the octave-transposition clefs). Thus the present usage is quite different from the original one, and in the interim there has usually been some discrepancy between what the clef was best able to do and what was required of it.

The simplest solution would seem to be to abolish clefs altogether, either by devising a phonetic notation (such as tablatures, or the notations of Rousseau and Curwen) or by using a staff with some other means of pitch reference. The latter is no real alternative, however, for a clefless staff is merely a staff with a fixed clef implied. Thus, although the abolition of clefs has been regularly proposed ever since Sebald Heyden's *Musicae Stoicheiosis* (Nuremberg, 2/1532: see Abdy Williams SN, 199), the results are generally too limiting in application, unless in some situation (such as an instrument of limited range) in which a fixed clef might be sufficient in any case.

Attempts to reform the use of clefs have been aimed at standardization rather than at complete re-thinking of the problems. Standardization is, in effect, a limiting of resources which—as is suggested above—has in any case taken place. The best reforms are probably those that have used only one type of clef, but relating to different octaves: for these give a manageable series and—on a diatonic staff—a reasonably large range without too many leger lines. The problem is to find the right range. Thomas Salmon, in his *Essay to the advancement of musick*, 1672, chose g', g and G for the bottom line of his treble, mean and bass staves, respectively. This works well for bass and alto voices, but sopranos and tenors have to change clef too much for comfort (see Abdy Williams SN, 200 f). Salmon used the 'clefs' Tr (for treble), M (mean) and B (bass) for these staves. In the nineteenth century precisely the same idea was used again, but with C on the bottom line, the 'clefs' being numbers which defined the octave: and a series of C-clefs was also suggested (placed on the middle line in every case), in which the octave was shown by flags attached to a box surrounding the clef (Wolf HdN ii, 344).

The notation of accidentals is closely related to attempts to reform the staff. As we noted in relation to Spanish keyboard tablatures (Chapter 10), the 'black' notes of the chromatic scale can be treated in one of two ways:
1. As modifications of a diatonic series. A diatonic staff makes this inescapable: the modification may be by additional signs (♯, ♭, etc.;

dots above and below) or by modification of the note-shape (shape or colour of note-head; stem and/or flag).

2. As part of a chromatic series. This is the method adopted in lute tablatures, for instance, and it also follows automatically from the use of a chromatic staff. Because of the growing need for a tonally non-committal notation from the late nineteenth century onwards, many reforms in the last hundred years have favoured a chromatic series.

There are, however, two strong objections:

Such a series has no landmarks; and

keyboard instruments are built on the basis of a diatonic scale plus 'black' notes.

An alternative to the chromatic staff was a more refined use of the existing staff, notes being placed not only on lines and in spaces, but also in more precise positions between. This retained the 'white plus black' structure of the scale, and it also satisfied the intellectual demand for the graphical representation of intervals and eliminated the disadvantages of the chromatic staff. However, notes using the 'half-positions' are not easily distinguished by the eye (Wolf HdN ii, 354), and so other notational means, such as colour, shape of note-head, stem (and its direction), etc., were pressed into service. Two results follow from this: first, that the means employed cannot then be used for other parameters; and second, that the positional distinction between a 'white' note and its 'black' namesake is superfluous, since it is confirmed by some other and clearer means. In view of the latter result, a diatonic scale with chromatic differentiation is sufficient. Of all the possibilities for notating the differentiation (Wolf HdN ii, 349–70, passim) the best are those which add simple modifications to the note-head or use the shape of the note-head itself (not the colour, which is thus free to show duration). As always, the final test is that of legibility, and it must be admitted that none of these reforms really fulfils that requirement. (However, the continued use of Shape-notes (see Chapter 9) suggests that such means may be practicable if the series concerned is kept short.)

It was suggested above that our notation of duration is illogical and wasteful of resources. Strangely, little thought has been given to a radical reappraisal of rhythmic notation, most reformers having been content to extend systems of note-shapes or of stems and flags.[4] At its best this is hardly better than the traditional methods, except that it may release certain notational means for other purposes; it can be rather limiting, so that the range of values notated is too small; and at worst it descends to a naïve additive system of shapes or even the use of numerals (Wolf HdN ii, 422 ff, and Abdy Williams SN, 207). Perhaps the only really original system was that of Angel Menchaca in his *Nouveau système de notation musicale, c.* 1914 (Wolf HdN ii, 338 f). Here each note was represented by a pear-shaped void figure, the inclination of which above or below a horizontal line gave the twelve notes of the chromatic scale (Figure 128(a)); the duration was shown by the position of a dot on the figure's perimeter or, for rests, by a short horizontal line and a head corresponding to the dot (b); the octave was distinguished by a stem up or down, from the left or the right (c). In simple music this may work very well, but there are surely not enough easily-distinguishable dot-positions for rhythms of any complexity to be notated.[5]

Figure 128. Menchaca's Notation

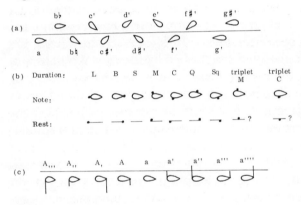

Three revisions of the staff

A considerable change of needs has led to further reforms in the recent past. As a result, a number of ideas in the types of reform just discussed have returned in the present century. There is room here for only the briefest discussion of each of three recent reforms, but they are all systems that merit study and serious consideration.

1. Klavarskribo (discussed by Karkoschka in NNM, 11 f) was invented by Cornelis Pot in 1931. As the name suggests, it is a keyboard notation, although successful use of it is claimed for other instruments and for the voice (*Klavarskribo,* 34–44). Klavar notation uses a chromatic staff with the lines in groups of 2 + 3, representing

the black notes of the keyboard. This staff is extensible, by repeating the octave pattern of lines as required. A 'clef', ₵ showing the position of middle C, was used in early Klavar prints. Later, the lines for c' sharp and d' sharp were shown as dotted: the clef was retained for some time after this (Figure 129(a)), but it was then strictly unnecessary and was eventually discarded.

The unique feature of Kavarskribo is that its staff runs vertically, so that the time axis is from top to bottom: this allows the lines of the staff to be seen in the same plane as the keys of the instrument. Regularly-spaced horizontal lines mark the beats and their divisions. The precise placing of the notes in time is shown by stems that extend horizontally from each note-head. The note-heads are placed on the staff to show the pitch by direct correlation with the piano keys, so that Klavar notation is close to being a tablature. Moreover, the note-heads for 'white' notes are void, while those for 'black' notes are filled in. This is strictly unnecessary, since black and white notes are clearly shown by the lines and spaces of the staff, respectively: but it adds a direct visual connection between notation and keyboard, of a type consistent with the best features of tablatures. A less happy feature (though it is the result of similar considerations) is that the black notes are turned above their stems and the void notes below them, in order to represent the different alignments of the black and white keys on the instrument. The problem here is that the positioning of the note-heads seems to relate to duration, which is the primary function of the vertical axis. If it were clearer to the eye that temporal placing is decided by the spacing of the stems and not of the note-heads, this would not matter: as it is, equal durations may seem unequally spaced (see, for instance, the first five notes of Figure 129(a)). This not only negates the fairly precise durational measurement on the vertical axis, but also makes it seem that the black notes in a chord should be played fractionally before the white notes.

Because temporal placing is shown by the horizontal stems, beaming in Klavarskribo can be used to clarify part-writing. No rests are necessary, but a stop, v, is needed to prevent a note being held too long (several can be seen in Figure 129(a)).

Karkoschka's complaint that Klavarskribo is diatonically based (NNM, 12) is surely misplaced, in view of the notation's specific purpose and near-tablature nature. His suggestion that Klavar notation should adopt certain features of Equitone (see (2), below) seems sensible at first sight but should be thoroughly assessed. The use of duration-lines, for instance, is not only probably unnecessary but could cause problems. Certainly a notation with so many stave-lines could hardly benefit from duration-lines drawn parallel to the staff, although angled duration-lines might be clear enough visually to be advantageous in certain types of music (cf. (3), below).

2. Equitone[6] (discussed by Karkoschka in NNM, 13 ff) was developed by R. Fawcett in 1958. Its staff consists of horizontal lines spaced an octave apart: the number of lines varies with the range of individual instruments. The number of the octave above or below c′ is shown by short vertical strokes joined to the beginning of the stave-line. Between the lines are another five note-positions, two of which are distinguished by a short line (like a leger line, but really an additional sign to the note-head). These give a whole-tone scale between one line and the next, notated by void stem-less circles: when these notes are black they represent the semitone above (Figure 129(b)). Microtones can be shown by means of other shapes, both black and void.

Durations are notated with regularly-spaced lines, as in Klavarscribo, but Equitone uses the horizontal axis for duration in the traditional manner. Moreover, Equitone has some features which Karkoschka argues (see above) should be incorporated into Klavarscribo: duration-lines, which not only show the precise duration of each note but can also indicate part-writing; and beams to clarify the rhythmic structure where necessary. In certain close relatives of Equitone the beams have the additional function of showing dynamics by their thickness, a feature that could be used in both Equitone proper and Klavarscribo (NNM, 88).

Klavarscribo and Equitone both offer some advance on traditional staff notation: the latter, especially, is visually clear and precise, and can notate complex music with a minimum of additional, phonetic, signs.

3. The last example was developed by András Szentkirályi for his own compositions: its basic principles are described in his article 'An attempt to modernize Notation' in *Music Review* 34/2 (1973). A chromatic staff was necessary, but Szentkirályi chose to use the normal five lines on the grounds that a composer must otherwise rule his own manuscript paper. The middle line of the staff is an A, the octave being shown by clefs from A to a² (i.e. the notes A, a, a′ and a″). Signs for the transposition of one, two or three octaves up or down (↑, ↓, ⇑, ⇓, ⇑ and ⇓) make the system flexible, and with four leger lines above and below, two octaves can be notated on a single staff. Quarter-tones can be shown by a + sign above or below the note-head, for raising or lowering the pitch, respectively.

Figure 129. Revisons of the Staff

(a)

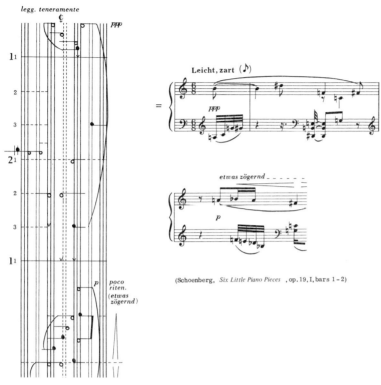

(Schoenberg, *Six Little Piano Pieces*, op. 19, I, bars 1-2)

(b)

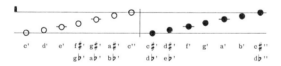

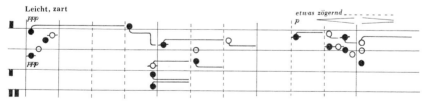

(Schoenberg, ibid. (c.f. (a), above))

(c)

Szentkirályi notates duration by a line following the note-head. Since the sound continues only to the end of the line, rests are superfluous, as are the various staccato and legato signs and the pause. (The duration-line is also used by other composers, in relation to a diatonic staff: see Figure 131(d), for example.) Szentkirályi's lines are rarely horizontal, but lead to the next note-head (or, if not legato, towards the next note, ending with a short cross-stroke). The time-unit of one second is taken as the most convenient 'bar'-length, giving a clear graphical spacing to the notes: but there is obviously a need to notate uniform time-intervals within these units, for which stems and beams are used (Figure 129(c)). These two types of measurement together allow quite complex relationships. However, the time-unit of a second need not be used when it is inappropriate (e.g. when consecutive events are spaced out over a much longer period), and the units can also be made to correspond with metronome speeds, being spaced at, say, 42 per minute (i.e. one 'bar' = MM 42).

Only five levels of intensity are used: *pp*, *p*, *mf*, *f* and *ff*. This supposes an inability of human performers to differentiate intensities more precisely, and it also discards any 'psychological' use of dynamics.

The three notations just discussed illustrate a phenomenon that is more noticeable now than at any time in the past—the inability of any one notation to cater for the needs of all composers. In the last chapter we saw how composers extended the 'rules' of their notation to suit their own purposes, and we have just discussed three notations developed for specific purposes, one by the composer who needed it for his own music. In the final chapter we shall consider certain types of notation which fulfil more general needs brought about by musical trends in the present century, and we shall also see the effect of a growing concern for standardization at a time of considerable notational creativity.

18. Innovation and Stability

In the Introduction I suggested rough categories of purposes to which notation has been put during the last thousand years or more (p. 3). In this final chapter we shall discuss the last three categories listed there, but first we must think again about categories (i)–(v). As I have tried to show, it would be possible to classify these categories rather differently, as

1. mnemonic notation, corresponding to (i) and usually (ii), in which the notation provides an analogue to the sound of music already learned by ear;

2. sight-reading notation, in which the object is to allow the performers to make at least a reasonably accurate attempt at the music at sight; and

3. notation which cannot be used except by a process of investigation and rehearsal.

This classification does not coincide precisely with the earlier categories, for (iii), (iv) and (v) could all belong to either (2) or (3) in the list just given. The obvious example of (1) is unheighted plainsong notation; of (2), all normal staff notation before the present century, and most instrumental tablatures; of (3), medieval canon and the more obscure uses of coloration. Clearly, (2) is by far the most common type of notation: that is, we have developed and used, as far as possible, notations which minimize the process of primary interpretation and the rehearsal-time spent on its problems.

Our discussion of the limits of staff notation in Chapter 16 was largely against the background of the sight-reading tradition. The reader will have noted that the limits of the system are less daunting if one assumes a different approach—not a sight-reading approach, but an assumption of careful and detailed preparation. Indeed, in the present century composers have tended to demand from the performer—and have received—a commitment to rehearsal-time that is largely unparalleled in other ages.

Precise notations

Once it can be assumed that a performer will spend a long time working out the main outlines and then the details of his performance, the composer is able to make demands that would be unthinkable in other circumstances. First, he can notate fine distinctions (e.g. of dynamic) that could not otherwise be obtained, secure in the knowledge that a performer will do his best to make them audible; second, the composer can notate patterns that are not easily assimilable by the eye—awkward additive metres, for example, or wide-spaced intervals. The recognition of this situation by composers has shown itself in two principal ways: the notation of fine distinctions has caused an increase in the precision of notation used and an extension of its vocabulary; and the exploitation of new performing techniques—especially in relation to particular instruments—has extended the range of necessary notational symbols.

The result, in both cases, is an enormous expansion of notational needs and means. For example, the notation of microtones—already confusing in the work of a single composer (Figure 126)—became much more confusing because of the range of distinctions required. While it is possible to perform and distinguish intervals as small as about a twelfth of a tone, most works use only a small selection of the intervals available. Thus, in the absence of a single series of interval-values as a means of notating the full range of microtones, composers have tended to use an individual notation for each work Risatti lists no fewer than five different signs based on a modified ♯ used to notate a sharp quarter-tone (*New Music Vocabulary*, 16: see Figure 130(a)): when we take into account the various other ways listed for notating this interval, it is clear that the notation of microtones generally is in a completely unstandardized state.

The notation of specialized effects for particular instruments is not new in the twentieth century—the 'thump' or left-hand pizzicato for viol is an earlier example—but the repertory of such effects has greatly increased in the last thirty years. Almost every instrument has acquired new playing-techniques, and the same is true of the voice: Bartók's snap pizzicato (against the fingerboard) and Schoenberg's *Sprechstimme* are only two early examples of what has become an extensive new range of technical resource. In this area, too, fine distinctions have caused proliferation in an already expanded notational system. For instance, when the piano was first played with the use of the forearm or the flat of the hand, the technique had to be explained verbally: but recent composers have tended to use symbols for this, and have in addition required the pianist to play with the closed fist, the closed palm of the hand, the edge of the hand, or the complete row of fingertips (Risatti, pp. 120 f). All these have their own symbols, so that a whole notational vocabulary has come into being for new ways of playing a keyboard.

As it happens, all of these signs in Risatti's list are pictorial, showing a stylized hand or fist in a position that is easily learnt as the notation for which it is designed. Most composers would probably agree with Schoenberg's opinion, offered in 1923 (*Style and Idea*, p. 351), that 'one should express as little as possible with letters, or even words, and make ever-increasing use of signs (if possible, pictures) . . .' The symbols that Schoenberg suggested in this essay are a little mixed in their success as self-explanatory notation (ibid., 352). The signs for *pizzicato, con sordino, arco* and *col legno* (bowed) are all more or less self-explanatory, and certainly would not need to be re-learned once a performer had used them (Figure 130(b)). On the other hand, there is no apparent reason why *col legno* (struck) and *spiccato* should substitute a wavy line ('used for arpeggios' and 'used for broken chords') instead of the hair in the representation of the bow (c). Very likely Schoenberg did not, on mature thought, find these signs very useful, for he appears never to have used them in any of his compositions.

The less successful of Schoenberg's signs may remind us that the difference between a picturegraph and an ideograph may be very small: indeed, we do not usually note the difference consciously (cf. the graphical and non-graphical road-signs shown by Cole, *Sounds and Signs*, 37). In the case of Figure 130(c) there is a mixture of the two, the bow itself being a picturegraph and the wavy line an ideograph. So, too, is there in his *senza sordino* sign (d), in which a mute (picturegraph) is cancelled (ideograph). Schoenberg has made use of the fact that an ideograph or phonetic sign may, because of its known associations or traditional use, be quite as capable of transmitting the composer's intention as a picturegraph, even without explanation. As with picturegraphs, use of non-pictorial symbols is a great space-saver, and such symbols are therefore a very efficient way of transmitting the composer's intention if the meaning is obvious. It is the last of these conditions, as we have already seen, that causes the problems. Pictorial means are not available for notating microtones,

259

for instance, so that we are again faced with the problem of finding a suitable set of symbols. Here, as in so many notational areas, the recent solution has been to fix on a series which the composer finds suitable for his immediate purpose—i.e., for that particular work—and to list the signs and their meanings at the beginning of the work. This is of course perfectly acceptable for individual works if the series is small. (One can imagine an orchestra giving a concert entirely composed of such works, and finding itself reading different symbols for the same meaning, and the same symbols with quite different meanings, in the various items. This will be extremely irritating to the players.)

It is perhaps because of this problem that verbal instructions on the score have taken so long to disappear. In the last resort, a clear verbal instruction is capable of considerable precision, and may well be the best way of achieving real precision in performance. One problem, that of the space needed, has already been mentioned. The other is also a serious one: the matter of language. As verbal instructions become less standardized, and as they carry increasingly precise meanings, ever heavier demands are made on the performer's vocabulary and his understanding of foreign languages. In the past there has usually been a *lingua franca* (though not French) capable of fulfilling the function of international communication—first Latin, then (from the seventeenth century onwards) Italian, and then to some extent German in the late nineteenth and early twentieth centuries. At the present time there is some move to treat English as the international musical language (see below), but there is no real evidence that any one language is likely to attain exclusive acceptance for the purpose. Although it is now reasonable to treat English, French, German and Italian as an international group, at least one of which is likely to be known by native speakers of other languages, there is still plenty of room for ignorance and misunderstanding within that group. Unless an internationally-recognized agreement can be made, therefore, verbal instructions will have to be very simple indeed if all misunderstanding is to be avoided, or else they must be given in parallel translation (as is, in fact, often the case). There is however a limit to the number of translations that can be accommodated in a score, especially in view of the space taken up by any verbal instruction. On the whole, one returns to acceptance of the fact that symbols are better: and one result of this is the symbols used to denote instruments—picturegraphs taking the place of written names (Figure 130(e)).

Figure 130.

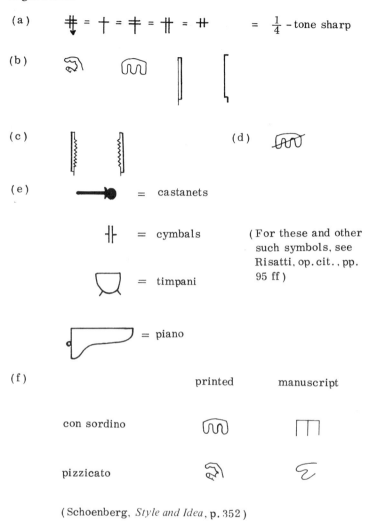

(a) ⧺ = ┼ = ╪ = ╫ = ╫   = $\frac{1}{4}$ – tone sharp

(e) = castanets

= cymbals

= timpani

(For these and other
such symbols, see
Risatti, op. cit., pp.
95 ff)

= piano

(f)   printed   manuscript

con sordino

pizzicato

(Schoenberg, *Style and Idea*, p. 352)

In general, it may be said that the distinction between picture-graphs and ideographs in music is not a sharp one. A symbol that started life as a picturegraph may well acquire a simplified or stylized form that is more easily classifiable among the ideographs, or the realism of the picture may for other reasons be insufficient to merit its classification as a picturegraph. Thus the classification into picturegraphs and ideographs requires the symbol to be well away from the borderline between them: only then can we be sure that the

261

picturegraph (unlike the ideograph) needs no explanation. The composer is in a dilemma here, as Schoenberg's essay of 1923 testifies. On the one hand, the symbol must be 'as realistic as possible' (*Style and Idea*, 352), so that explanation is unnecessary: on the other, the notation as hand-written by the composer must be simplified and stylized. Thus the symbols in Schoenberg's list that can be called picturegraphs in their intended printed form are virtually ideographs in their simpler, manuscript, form (Figure 130(f)).

Recognition of this fact forces on us two alternatives. The first is that of notational anarchy, in which each composer shall devise and introduce those symbols that seem most satisfactory for the work in hand, the symbols being explained verbally as necessary. The second is that a set of universally-understood symbols shall be used, for which no explanation is necessary. The two are not mutually exclusive, because the first becomes in time the second if it is used regularly enough by a majority of composers. This is of course what has happened to all our universally-recognized non-pictorial symbols, such as the clefs, accidentals, and dynamic 'hairpins'.

This is also true of certain basic concepts. For example, there is no need to explain any use of the vertical axis for pitch, at least in the West (there are, in fact, cultures in which the concept of 'high' and 'low' is reversed). Thus, even when several notational ideas are used simultaneously, each is individually comprehensible although the synthesis itself may be new. In certain works of Penderecki, for instance, the wedding of the notation for a note-cluster (Figure 131(a)) to that for a duration-line (b) causes no conceptual difficulties at all: what does have to be explained is the precise limits of the cluster (since quarter-tones are involved) and the distribution of the notes among the instruments concerned. These explanations are given in symbols below the principal staff (c).

In Figure 131(c) it will be seen that Penderecki has dispensed with musical time, together with its constituent concepts of tempo, metre, accelerando and ritardando, etc., in favour of an absolute method of

Figure 131.

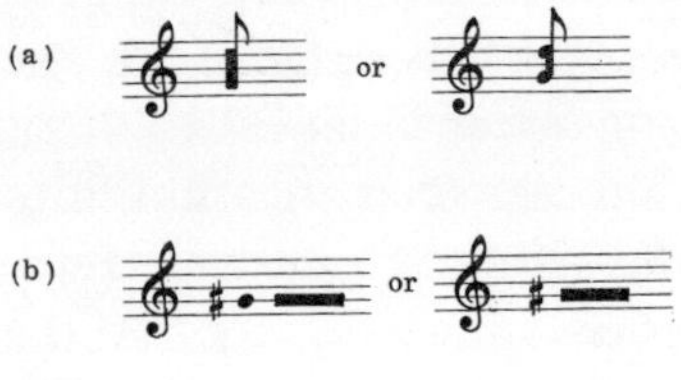

262

(c)

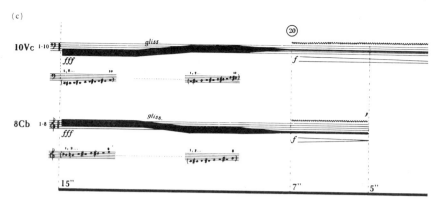

(d)

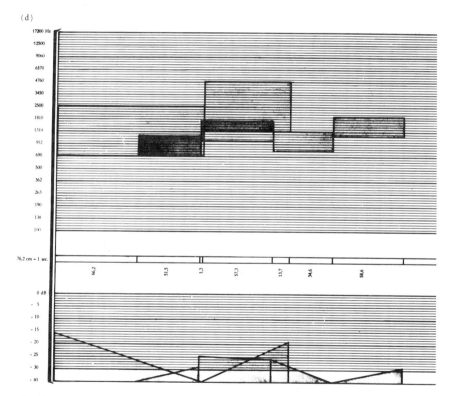

(Stockhausen, *Nr. 3 Elektronische Studien : Studie II* , p. 1)

timing each section in seconds. It is perhaps the more mathematical basis of electronic music, together with the general acceptance of mathematical ideas current in a culture where a pocket calculator is a common piece of personal equipment, that is responsible for such absolute methods of notating musical parameters. Indeed, it is in electronic music that the greatest precision is achieved, both in performance and in notation. In relatively simple electronic music the parameters can be notated in a very precise way by graphs. In Stockhausen's *Elektronische Studie II* two parallel graphs are used: the first, above the horizontal time-scale, plots pitch against time; the second, below the time-scale, plots intensity against time (Figure 131(d)). In each case the shapes delineated refer to particular types of sound, each type being a sound-mixture of five frequencies. There are only five sound-mixtures, all immutable for the duration of the piece. Since the two graphs share the time-axis, the shapes correspond: that is, the graphs represent the elevation and plan views of what would seem to be three-dimensional figures (although, since the different types of sound overlap in time, so do the shapes in space). Frequency (i.e. pitch), intensity (i.e. dynamics) and time are all plotted very precisely in appropriate units—respectively Hertz, decibels, and centimetres of tape (convertible to seconds). The values are given at the beginning of the score, as shown in Figure 131(d).

The main limitation of this method of notation is that only three parameters can be notated conveniently on a two-dimensional graph. In the case of *Elektronische Studie II* it would be more difficult to notate the piece thus if the types of sound were to change during their presentation—that is, if the constituent frequencies of any sound-mixture were to be altered. Pieces with a more complex use of frequencies have been notated as graphs (Karkoschka uses Ligeti's *Pièce electronique no. 3* as an example: NNM, 166 f), but in general other notational methods are used. The principal alternative (though by no means the only one) is to 'notate' the wiring diagram and the position of controls. Such a diagram is likely to make use of the normal vocabulary of symbols commonly available to electronic engineers, although they may have to be supplemented by other signs and/or by verbal instructions. The best way in which the composer can transmit instructions for building and using the generating circuitry for a particular piece will usually depend on his methods of sound generation and composition. With some of the most complex methods, there is no doubt that composers face the alternatives (1) that writing down their sound-generating processes is very laborious and results in an extremely complex set of mathematically-based instructions, or (2) that the composition, once committed to tape, need only be transferred to other tape copies, and need never be reconstructed afresh. In the latter case, clearly, no score is required, and therefore no notation is involved.

In computing terms, it may be said that the graphical method of notation concerns the 'software' of the piece—that is, its musical results in terms of accurately-measured pitch, loudness, timbre and time—whereas the circuit-diagram method concerns the 'hardware'— the tangible mechanism by which the results are generated. Thus it is the former, more limited, method that can be used in conjunction with traditional notation (e.g. for use with conventional instruments or the human voice), while the latter type cannot. In complex pieces in which electronically-generated sound is used in conjunction with conventional instruments, therefore, two requirements may be demanded in addition: first, someone (often the composer) may need to exercise control over the electronically-generated sound; second, the players of conventional instruments need a score notated in such a way that they can synchronize their playing with the electronically-generated sound as required by the composer. The first of these results in the use of a mixer to control the audible results of the electronic sound-generation. The second, with which we shall be concerned presently, results in a form of notation that I have called 'analogue notation'.

The expansion of notational resources, dating mainly from the middle of the present century onwards, continued unchecked for a long time, with composers using old devices or inventing new ones as their need dictated. The wealth of material threw up a certain amount of secondary work involved with the classification and, partly, the assessment of new notational devices. Karkoschka's book (NNM), first published in 1966 as *Das Schriftbild der Neuen Musik*, was by no means the first full-length study of new notations, for Chailley's *Les notations musicales nouvelles* had been published in 1950: but it was perhaps the first not only to present the main innovations in orderly manner (by then a very necessary task) but to assess them critically with a view to suggesting guide-lines on which future practice might sensibly be founded. By the end of the 1960s it was becoming increasingly difficult to keep up with notational practice as seen in the works of the many composers then using non-traditional symbols. At that stage it was clearly necessary to have 'dictionaries' of symbols with their meanings: Risatti's *New Music Vocabulary* (1975) provided such a dictionary for a selection of works dating mainly from the

265

1960s (the latest date is 1972, the earliest 1952 except for a small number of earlier major classics). Risatti's work is not avowedly critical (although the process of selection does presuppose some assessment), but the advertisement on the back cover stated the author's intention 'to standardize a body of symbols so that common usage will replace the present arbitrary and individual usage'. In that Risatti's work involved judicious selection and then the orderly presentation of notational procedures with the intent to show their logical relationships to each other, it is clear that the standardization did indeed involve a critical assessment, even if a covert one. The same view is evident in the Preface, where Risatti stated that it was 'evident that the sixties comprised a decade of musical discovery. The seventies promise to be a time of synthesis and development.'

Meanwhile, in 1970 Kurt Stone and others had started the Index of New Musical Notation. Taking its cue from Karkoschka's work, this project undertook the detailed scientific examination of the notation of a very large selection of works, the composers themselves, if still living, being invited to clarify ambiguities. By 1974 the work had progressed far enough for a conference to discuss various notational devices and to make recommendations as to their suitability: the conference took place at the State University, Ghent, in October that year. At the end of the discussions votes were taken on the various proposals. A two-thirds vote in favour was considered to endorse any proposal; a simple majority was a recommendation. In the introduction to the Report on the conference it is suggested that the endorsed proposals might be regarded as 'fulfilling all requirements for establishing them as notational *standards*', while any recommendation might be seen as 'an example, a tentative solution, a non-exclusive possibility' (Sabbe, *Report*, p. 15). (Only the endorsed and the recommended proposals are included in the Report, not the rejected ones.)

In this work it is obviously vital to have good criteria for making a proposal in the first place, and there is an eight-point list of criteria contained in the Report (ibid., p. 33). Some criteria refer to the notation's graphical recognizability or to its efficiency and economy of space: but more important is the element of previous usage— those criteria which refer to the extension of existing principles (no. 1) and to relatively common usage among composers (no. 5). It is perhaps this appeal to existing usage that sets this project apart from the kind of work that we have discussed under the heading of notational reforms: for, although the boundary is not a sharp one, reforming zeal

266

on the whole puts intellectual principles before traditional usage. In fact, a very noticeable feature of the list of endorsed and recommended proposals is its conservatism. This is not an adverse criticism, but rather the reverse, for it seems that the criteria for selection coincide often enough with current practice for a sensible choice to be made. In general, the Report probably offers an acceptable way forward. The unchecked growth of symbols seen in the 1960s has given way to a process of 'weeding out' by informed selection, leaving, one hopes, a stronger and more useful vocabulary of resources and principles for future expansion. Only in one area, perhaps, should one feel a little doubtful. Where words or initials have been used, the language is English. Will English really be the *lingua franca* of the foreseeable future?

Indeterminacy

Some music of the later part of this century, rather than prescribing precisely the role of the performer, has allowed him to take part in the creative process. Historically, there are precedents for music in which one or more parameters are entrusted to the performer: basso continuo does this, for example, and so do the unrhythmed keyboard preludes of Louis Couperin and his contemporaries (see Chapter 15). Twentieth-century indeterminacy does not, on the whole, make use of special notations. Often there is a verbal instruction that requires the performer to obey some symbol's instruction in a manner partly determined by his inclination or ability—for instance, to play the highest possible note on his instrument, or to repeat some action as quickly as possible for a prescribed time. The performer's choice may determine the order in which sections of the work are played. Usually in this case the original choice then leaves the performer no alternative in the subsequent order of sections, and the dynamics, tempo, etc., may also be pre-determined by this choice. In other words, the performer simply chooses which of several predetermined versions of the piece shall be performed.

When the performer is given real control over one or more parameters, however, the notation may reflect this. In some of Morton Feldman's works, for instance, the performer decides the durations, and the notes are written in an unrhythmed notation such as we sometimes use for plainsong or for analytical work (Figure 132). In these works other parameters are fairly precisely notated. (In *De*

267

Kooning, Feldman's performance notes require 'very low' dynamics and 'a minimum of attack', so that these parameters are not shown on ~he score itself.)

Figure 132.

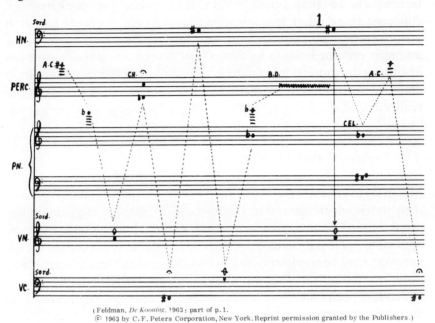

(Feldman, *De Kooning,* 1963: part of p.1.
ⓒ 1963 by C. F. Peters Corporation, New York. Reprint permission granted by the Publishers.)

Even further removed from precise notation are those notational devices that act as a catalyst to the performer's musical imagination, encouraging him to perform musical gestures which will then combine to make a piece. This notation may or may not include elements of traditional musical notation. Some does so, appealing to the performer's musical imagination through the associations of traditionally-learned symbols; but sometimes the 'notation' is purely graphical, without musical associations, and requires an even greater degree of partnership on the performer's part—indeed, the performer really becomes the composer, except at the fundamental formal level, where the composer's symbols determine the basic structure of the music.

Hugo Cole's discussion of indeterminacy (*Sounds and Signs,* 137–48) ends with a list of seven causes which, he thinks, have contributed to the use of experimental notations and indeterminacy in the last three decades or so. They are a realistic assessment of the

268

altered conditions in which composers have recently found themselves, and the effect that these conditions have had on them. Perhaps
the most important for our present purpose is his fifth point: that
notation is no longer necessary as a means of preserving music
permanently, because that function has been taken over by recording
techniques, so that notation can fulfil other functions instead.
Amongst these other functions we must include a purely graphical
purpose—i.e. a musical composition may now be a work of visual art,
and may even be hung in an art gallery as such—and the function of
liberating the musical imagination of the performer so that he is now a
creator, not merely a medium through whom musical sounds are
realized.

The needs of musicology

Musicologists have taken to using a number of notational symbols in
their work which are not a direct result of the need to notate in the
usual sense. The notation used may be regarded as auxiliary notation
applied to solve particular problems or to fulfil particular needs. Such
notation may be used for either of two basic purposes: as descriptive
notation, telling the reader about the original notation of a source
which has been edited; or as analytical notation, giving information
about the structure of the music under discussion.

Descriptive notation is needed because of the problems involved in
transcribing one type of notation into another. Since modern notation
does not use such devices as ligatures, coloration, *plicae* and
liquescents, and so on, some method must be used of marking the
position of these devices in the original if the scholar is to follow their
use when he reads the edition. Some of the commonly-used signs for
such devices have already been seen in earlier chapters of this book. In
general, such symbols are merely additional to those of traditional
notation: their function has no effect on the sound of the music. Only
in very few cases (such as the double-dotted note for compound
ternary metres, shown in Figure 113(b)) does musicological thinking
about notation add or modify a symbol in a way which affects the
main-stream use of notation.

Analytical notations of various types have been developed as an
aid to the analysis of music. To some extent it bears the same kind of
relation to traditional notation as descriptive notation does, in that it
may consist of additional signs which transmit information to the

scholar. Adding informatory symbols to a normal copy of the music, however, is only one way of 'notating' an analysis. Another is to make a modified copy of the music using notation of some sort to show the selected features of the music that form the basis of the analysis. Here, the symbols used must be recognizably derived from traditional notation, since it is primarily the parameters of pitch, phrase-structure, etc., that must be shown: but, on the other hand, the resulting symbols must be such that they are not mistaken for traditional notation. Most analytical notations of this type therefore make use of the staff and its incidental symbols (clefs, etc.), but notate pitch and rhythm in such a way that performing notation is clearly not being used. Heinrich Schenker's notation, for instance, uses stemless note-heads, together with beams that clearly show structure rather than rhythm. Part of Schenker's analysis of a chorale from Bach's *St Matthew Passion* will show this (Figure 133(a)), as well as the way in which Schenker uses slurs (e.g. to indicate the prolongation of a structurally important note) and beams.

Analogue notation

One more type of notation must be discussed, although it is less a notation than a number of notations used as an analogue. Such notations appear in scores designed solely for a listener, which are probably the only type of written music whose ultimate aim is not to enable a performance to be created or re-created. In this type of score, which might be called 'analogue notation', the precision of the notation is so much less than the precision of the composer's creation that one cannot adequately re-create the music from the score. This presupposes, among other things,

> that re-creation of the music is unnecesary, and
> that the 'score'—the visual analogue—came into being only after the music was created.

The notation of electronically-produced sounds in Henri Pousseur's *Electre* illustrates both of these premises: the piece can be performed only by playing a recording copied from the original tape made by Pousseur himself; and the 'score' was made after the tape, not even by Pousseur, but by Sylvano Bussotti.

The music consists of three distinct types:
1. Electronically-generated sounds.

Figure 133.

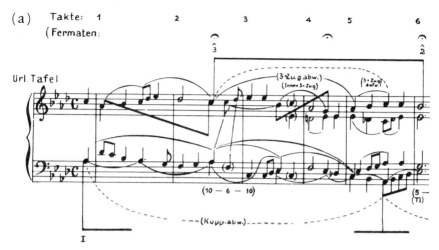

(Schenker, *Five Graphic Music Analyses*, p. 33)

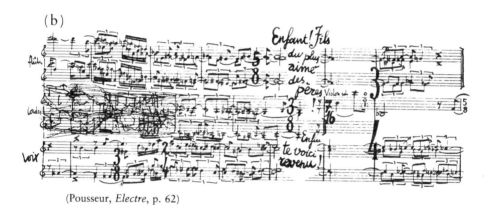

(Pousseur, *Electre*, p. 62)

2. Recorded voices, processed electronically and distorted to a greater or lesser degree.

3. Instrumental music, notated on staves in a conventional manner. The horizontal axis, as usual, represents time. The vertical axis represents the pitch-range used, but this is not precisely notated. The height of the score is only a few inches, while the total frequency-range used is very great: any attempt to represent frequency (pitch) precisely, therefore, would result in congested symbols and a lot of blank space, which would be illegible and wasteful. The notation of the electronic music, then, gives some idea of relative pitch, but certainly no more accurately than the staff-notation does.

271

The notation of the electronic music is an approximate analogue to the sound—almost a description in visual terms. A static note, for example, is represented by a straight line, a throbbing note by a wavy one; a sudden noise is shown by a dense patch of scribblings following a straight vertical edge; when the sound of instrumental music is obliterated by distortion or electronic noise, the staff-notation is gradually obliterated by ink-smudges. The use of the human voice introduces another, and in some ways less precise, element: duration and pitch are less accurately notated here, since the written word requires space on the score which may represent a greater duration and pitch-area than the spoken word takes up. This disadvantage apart, the volume, pitch, time-separation and distortion of the voices can be represented effectively enough (Figure 133(b)).

Although the score for *Electre* is purely for the benefit of the listener, it is worth pointing out that such a score could well have a more conventional purpose. When instrumental music and electronic sounds on tape come together in live performance, both the instrumentalists and the conductor must be able to synchronize the live instrumental sounds with the tape. A score of the *Electre* type, using analogue notation for the tape and conventional notation for the instruments, would then be a good solution: the performers would be able to see what was happening on the tape while reading their own part on a conventional staff. (In the case of *Electre*, of course, this is made impossible by the obliteration of parts of the conventional notation.)

At first it may seem that my book has now come full circle, for it began, as it ends, with a notation from which no performance could be reconstructed. The appearance is deceptive, however, for the two notations in fact fulfil completely different functions. Sangallian neumes were an aide mémoire for music transmitted aurally, through the singers' memories, while Bussotti's score for *Electre* transmits nothing from composer to performer in the electronic sections. We have not, then, returned in any sense to the position occupied by notation a thousand years ago. On the contrary, all our attitudes are now quite different, as are our requirements from musical notation.

If a parallel with a past age is to be made, it should perhaps be with the turn of the fourteenth century, although only in one respect. Then, a bewildering proliferation of notational means took place, with many varieties of semibreve variously notated for different purposes. Within a few decades the situation had simplified, giving a standardized set of symbols (or rather, two sets) which we now recognize as those of the Italian and French Ars Nova. The parallel has followed so far, in that a period of notational expansion seems now to be ending in favour of standardization. But we are certainly too close to events to be sure that the parallel is a close one, or to see in which directions notation will now develop. Of one thing we may be sure: if musical notation survives, it will certainly change with the changing needs of composers, performers and listeners, and with the changing relationships between them.

Notes

Preface

1   In the University of California at Berkeley: the event was reported in *Time* and *Newsweek* (both on 18 March 1974), and in various newspapers. Wulstan described the piece in 'The Earliest Notation'.

Introduction: The Nature of Musical Notation

The best general and comprehensive introduction to western notations (and with fascinating asides on oriental notations) was Thurston Dart's article 'Notation' in *Grove 5*. This is now superseded by the article in *The New Grove*, contributed by several distinguished scholars, which was published too late to be consulted during the writing of this book. Cole's *Sounds and Signs*, a mainly non-historical enquiry, is both readable and thought-provoking: it raises many pertinent questions for the general reader. Wolf's *Handbuch der Notationskunde* is a much more technical and comprehensive book, invaluable for its descriptions of a very large number of notations.

The arrangement of music on the page is discussed by Krummel, *English Music Printing*, 79 ff, where a variety of layouts are shown; also in the *Grove 5* articles 'Partbooks' and 'Score'.

PART I

Chapter 1: The Notation of the St Gall Manuscripts

The development of Sangallian notation is discussed by Abdy Williams (SN), Apel (GC), Parrish (NMM), Reese (MMA) and Stanbrook (GM). The most detailed work, however, is Dom Cardine's 'Sémiologie grégorienne', which I have used almost exclusively in writing this chapter: it represents a radically new approach that makes all previous work based on the Solesmes methods more or less obsolete. It is unnecessary to give many precise references to 'Sémiologie grégorienne' because it is so clearly ordered, according to neumes, that the reader can easily find the section needed.

Much is to be learned from a study of the *Graduale Triplex* and *Graduel neumé*, in both of which neumatic and square-notation versions of the music are presented in parallel: such comparative study of these versions is a useful tool in gaining an understanding of a neumatic notation and its transcription. The facsimiles listed in the notes to Chapter 2 are relevant also to Sangallian notation.

274

1 The reader should test all such graphological considerations for himself. On the mechanics of writing music, see Winternitz, *Musical Autographs* i.
2 See More, 'The Performance of Plainsong'.

Chapter 2: Later Neumatic Notations and the Development of the Staff

The works listed in the notes to Chapter 1 are also relevant here. Parrish gives a clear exposition of the various rhythmic theories (NMM, 31–9), and he discusses also the rhythm of secular monody (ibid., Chapter 2, passim). Further on plainsong rhythm, see More's writings and Murray GC.

For facsimiles, the various volumes of *Paléographie Musicale* are indispensable: Parrish NMM is very useful, and so is a handy collection published by the monks of Solesmes, *La Notation Musicale*. Bannister's *Monumenti Vaticani* uses photographs to classify the neumes of a number of neume-schools.

1 Hence also the German use of *moll* and *dur* for minor and major keys. From the note G the third is either minor (to B *mollus*) or major (to B *durus*). Compare also the English terminology, p. 181, above.
2 Smits van Waesberghe, 'Notation of Guido', considers that Guido d'Arezzo invented not only the use of coloured staff-lines but the staff itself as we know it, with lines a third apart and clefs at the beginning.

Chapter 3: Modal Notation

The authoritative study of modal notation is still Waite's *The Rhythm of Twelfth-Century Polyphony*, which includes a transcription of the *Magnus Liber Organi* of Leonin. The subject-matter of this chapter is well dealt with by Hoppin MM and Caldwell MM (both of which have excellent bibliographies), as well as by Apel NPM and Parrish NMM. Hoppin AMM and Marrocco and Sandon MM include recent transcriptions of St Martial and Compostella polyphony, as well as examples from the modal repertory.

All the main sources of modal polyphony are available in photographic reproduction, including Baxter, *St Andrews*, and items in the *Publications of Medieval Music Manuscripts* (see the Select Bibliography, and also the bibliographies in Hoppin MM and Caldwell MM). I have cited the St Victor MS exclusively here because it is easily available and because the reproduction (Thurston, *St Victor*) is the most legible.

1 See Anderson, 'Magister Lambert and Nine Rhythmic Modes'.
2 There has been much argument about this, but Waite (in his first chapter) is surely right.
3 In this chapter, note-names are written in full to remind the reader that note-values do not have corresponding *nota simplex* (single note) shapes in modal notation. (See the note on p. xiv.)
4 Occasionally, also, it is better to treat the rest as unmeasured, a breathing-space. The rests are used to divide up the music into phrases, or *ordines* (singular, *ordo*). The ordines are not vital to a basic study of the

notation, but they are very important indeed to a full understanding of the nature of the music and the compositional principles involved: see Waite, Chapter 1, and especially pp. 40 ff.

5   Waite, 70 and n.20, quotes the theorists.

6   There is a general rule that the penultimate note of a ligature shall be a brevis and the final note a longa. Here the single notes are regarded as metrically a part of the ligature. Note that the punctum and virga are used more or less indiscriminately, and cannot safely be identified with short and long values (Waite, p. 82).

7   According to Magister Lambertus, writing *c*. 1270: CS I, 273a, translated in Apel NPM, 226. I have accepted the dating of *c*. 1270 and *c*. 1280 for the works of Lambert and Franco, respectively, and have used them for such chronological discussion as I have entered into here and in Chapter 4: but there is no universal agreement on them—on the contrary, they are still subject to much debate—and it is possible that the notational changes concerned actually took place as much as twenty years earlier.

8   There is no certainty of this, but it seems very likely that the semibrevis was at this time a true half-brevis, the speed of the brevis beat being such that it did not lend itself to subdivision into more than two parts.

Chapter 4: The Later Thirteenth Century

On the dating of Lambert's and Franco's work, see Chapter 3, n.7: the same problem arises over Dietricus and other theorists.

The treatises of Lambert and Franco, along with other important treatises of the later thirteenth and early fourteenth centuries, are printed in Coussemaker, *Scriptorum* I. Franco's work is translated in Strunk, *Source Readings*, 139-59, but some of the musical examples are omitted. Extracts from the work of James of Liège are also translated by Strunk (SR, 180–90). Part 6 of Odington's *De Speculatione Musicae* is translated in MSD 31. Both Apel NPM and Parrish NMM have sections on this period, and much of my chapter is based on their work.

Coussemaker's edition of Adam de la Halle has good examples of simple mid-century notation: his transliterations are clear, though not always accurate. Facsimiles of late thirteenth-century music are less accessible: Aubry's *Cent Motets* presents the Bamberg MS, and this has been reprinted. A number of chansonniers are available, of which the *Chansonnier d'Arras*, with an introduction by Jeanroy, has been reprinted. Anglés's *Cantigas de Santa María* has many plates (though relatively few of the cantigas are notated mensurally); and there are plates in Wooldridge's *Early English Harmony* and Stainer's *Early Bodleian Music*.

1   The old term 'divisio modi' refers to its use as a rest showing the end of an ordo in modal notation: 'signum perfectionis' is a newer term depending on the concept of perfection.

2   'With opposite propriety', the usual translation, seems quite meaningless. I choose 'shared' because John of Garland says (CS I, 100) that the two Ss

stand in place of the B of a ligature 'with propriety': that is, the Ss share the quality of propriety (not necessarily equally) between them.

3   Explained by Master Lambert (CS I, 273: translated in Apel NPM, 227).

4   Tail to the Left is a bReve plica:
Tail to the Right is a Long plica.
(See Thurston Dart's mnemonics for ligatures, Chapter 5, n.3 and relevant text.)

5   The example of Fig. 33(c) is from the motet *Dame bele/Fi mari/Nus niert ja joli* (Montpellier MS, f. 300v). See Coussemaker, *Adam de la Halle*, 421, end of the second voice.

6   However, Lambert's *signum perfectionis* spans a space, like a S-rest (CS I, 271). Some sources of the period use Lambert's rests rather than Franco's, so it is important to know which series is in use.

7   Strunk translates this passage (SR, 186) in the same way as Apel. We should also ask why, if three or more Ss were equal, Petrus retained the old triple division for two Ss (minor S + major S: see CS I, 388, rule VII).

Chapter 5: Ars Nova

Apel NPM deals well with Ars Nova notations (chapters V.C, VI and VII): the best short descriptions are in NOHM III, 2–6 and 48–52.

The fullest account of Italian Ars Nova notation is in Gallo, *La teoria della notazione*: see also Gallo's article 'Marchetto da Padova' in *The New Grove*. The second book of the *Pomerium* (1318) of Marchettus is translated in Strunk SR, 160–71, with illustrations from the *Brevis Compilatio*: the originals are in GS IiI, 121–88 and CS III, 1–12. The *Tractatus . . . ad modum Ytalicorum* of Prosdocimus is in CS III, 228–58. I have not discussed the secondary interpretation of imperfect time in Italian notation, but Marchettus describes the French (unequal) and Italian (equal) rhythms (translated in Strunk SR, 166–71).

Part of the *Ars Novae Musicae* of Jean de Muris is translated in Strunk SR, 172–79: on the original texts of the treatise (GS III and CS III, passim), see Strunk's n.1 (SR, 172). The *Ars Nova* of Philippe de Vitry is in CS III, 13–22. The *Speculum Musicae* is in CS II, 193–433 (where it is attributed to Muris): that part which attacks the New Art is in Strunk SR, 180–90.

On Ars Nova in England, see Bukofzer *Studies*, Chapter III ('The Fountains Fragment'), especially pp. 86–98; Andrews and Dart, 'Fountains'; and Stevens (D.), 'Second Fountains Fragment'. On the English note-shapes, see n.4, below. Two important publications appeared too late for their findings to be incorporated in this chapter: Margaret Bent's section of *The New Grove* article 'Notation' dealing with the Ars Nova in England (section III, 3 (vi)), and Harrison and Wibberley, *Manuscripts*. Bent pin-points English characteristics, which can be seen in the facsimiles presented by Harrison and Wibberley; and the latter work sets out (among other things), for the first time in print, the results of Wibberley's study of the extraordinary way in which the values of notes in ligature were determined by the graphical slanting of the notes (Harrison and Wibberley, *Manuscripts*, pp. xxiv–xxv).

Facsimiles and transliterations of much Ars Nova music will be found in Wolf GdM and HdN i; Parrish NMM and Apel NPM both have facsimiles. An Italian source is published as MSD 13; the Escorial MS V.III.24 is in facsimile; the work by Harrison and Wibberley mentioned above presents much English material; and the various 'Fountains Fragments' are in preparation for BMS, with an introduction by Margaret Bent. See also Hughes (Anselm), *Worcester Mediaeval Harmony*, 128 f.

1 See especially the remarks of James of Liège: CS II, 427–32, and the translation in Strunk SR, 183 f.
2 However in the fifteenth century this patterning is often used without strict measurement, simply to indicate that the voice concerned rests for a whole section (e.g. of a mass or motet). In this case the patterning itself seems to be largely decorative: usually a text cue is provided to tell the singers where to enter after the rests.
3 The mnemonic rules marked with an asterisk are among those printed in Thurston Dart's *Grove 5* article 'Notation', and were used by him in his teaching.
4 Discussion of these shapes is confused by Coussemaker's transcription (CS I, 244) and subsequent corrections of his text: see NOHM III, 369, and MSD 31 (Odington's *De Speculatione Musicae*, part vi, ed. Huff), 23 f.
5 For the Fountains music, see above. See also NOHM II, 88, on the notation of the New College motets.
6 The swallowtail was later used to correct the pitch of a note that had been misplaced by the scribe, being attached to any note-value, and either above or below the note-head according to the correction needed. See Wolf HdN i, 431.

Chapter 6: Mannerism and the Fifteenth Century

Apel treats mixed and mannered notation exhaustively (NPM, chapters VIII and IX), as does Wolf (HdN i, 381–427; GdM i, passim). Wolf also supplies many transliterations (GdM ii) and their transcriptions (GdM iii).

Proportions are dealt with by Sachs, *Rhythm and Tempo*, 205–17; Apel NPM, 145–79, who lists the main relevant medieval theorists (on p. 145); Morley, *Plain and Easy Introduction*, ed. Harman, 42–99 and 126–37; Gafurius, *Practica Musicae*, ed. Young, 165–267; and Tinctoris, *Proportionale Musices*. The Gafurius is also available as a reprint.

Canon is discussed by Apel (NPM, 179–88).

The main facsimile publications are those of the Cambridge song book (BMS 1), the Escorial MS V.III.24 (ed. Rehm), the Trent Codices, the Locheimer Liederbuch and the Mellon Chansonnier. There are important collections in Stainer's *Dufay and his Contemporaries* and *Early Bodleian Music*.

1 Baude Cordier's 'Belle bonne' in the Chantilly MS, *c.* 1400 (Apel NPM, 427); the 'Cordiforme', or Jean de Montchenu chansonnier (Paris, BN, MS

Rothschild 2973), late fifteenth century; Baude Cordier's 'Tout par compas' in the Chantilly MS (Parrish NMM, 187–93 and plate LXII).

2 The early mannerist sources are hard to date: Apel dates all the main continental sources at *c.* 1400 (NPM, chapter IX). Margaret Bent dates the Old Hall MS at *c.* 1410–20 ('Sources of the Old Hall Music').

3 A partly illegible reproduction, with a transcription, is in Wolf HdN i, facing 364 and 365 f. My use of ⦂ ⦂ to show red void notes follows Hughes and Bent, *The Old Hall Manuscript.*

4 On this last point, Margaret Bent records a change of mind in Old Hall no. 73 (*The Old Hall Manuscript: a Paleographical Study,* 211). The scribe started by using a red void Sm, distinguished from a full red colored M: then he changed it to black void on finding that he needed red void for the F. Presumably he did not wish to use a tailed note.

5 However, Margaret Bent believes (ibid., 209) that *tactus alla minima* implied a slightly slower beat.

6 *Rota* = canon at the unison: *Rondellus* = a round (Harrison, 'Rota and Rondellus'). For the summer canon, see Parrish NMM, 127 f and plate XLIII, and Harrison MMB, 142 ff.

7 See MB 18, no. 53, where the canonic part is explained entirely without musical notation (this is a sixteenth-century example).

8 See the four-part example by Pierre de la Rue, reproduced and partly transcribed by Apel (NPM, 181 and Appendix, no. 27): also Ockeghem, *Omnia Opera* ii, for the Missa Prolationum.

9 Harrison MMB, 143 f; Stevens, 'Fountains', 148; Oxford, Bodleian Library, MS Arch. Selden B.26 (in Stainer EBM).

10 For instance, in London, BL, Add. MSS 29996 and 30513. For the latter, see MB 1, p. xiv.

Chapter 7: The Age of Transition

The standard background book on rhythm generally is still Curt Sachs's *Rhythm and Tempo.* Margaret Bent's account of stroke and strene notations ('New and Little-known Fragments', pp. 149–53), though very brief, is an excellent summary: Andrew Hughes discusses the usage of stroke-notation in 'The Choir in Fifteenth-Century English Music'. Krummel describes the making of music-type (*English Music Printing*, p. 6), giving the background to my discussion concerning Figure 70.

With respect to ternary metres and the features of staff notation there is little by way of previous discussion, though Donington's *Interpretation of Early Music* is of course invaluable for its informative presentation of source-material. Otherwise, the reader should refer to the musical sources themselves, for which such collections as Hürlimann's *Composers' Autographs* and Winternitz's *Musical Autographs* are excellent.

1 Both Caldwell (*English Keyboard Music,* p. 75) and the editors of MB 14 (no. 28) are inconsistent in their use of time-signatures for this piece. Bull's proportional increase of his mensuration is exact, so that the metre of the last

section is not $\frac{33}{8}$ (i.e. $\frac{12}{8} + \frac{12}{8} + \frac{9}{8}$) but $\frac{6}{4} + \frac{6}{4} + \frac{9}{8}$. The occasional use of hemiola in the $\frac{6}{8}$ part of the metre is merely Bull's additional commentary on his metrical manipulation.

2 Stephen Williamson is currently making a study of these notations, together with an inventory of sources, at the University of Leeds.

3 The stroke-notation principle, if used in the Robertsbridge pieces, could of course have been forgotten and then re-invented in the fifteenth century. Leaving aside such historical considerations, I do not think that the internal evidence for a stroke-notation interpretation of the Robertsbridge Bs is particularly convincing.

4 To the sources listed by Bent, 'New and Little-known Fragments', pp. 149 f, nn.20 and 21, we should add Grafton's two versions of *An Exhortacion unto Praier* (1544), illustrated by Steele, *The Earliest English Music Printing*, Figs. 9 and 10.

5 Figure 13 is, of course, from a nineteenth-century source: but its notation is that of earlier chant sources, as a glance through Steele's facsimiles will show.

6 This section avoids specifying the beat in the original notation as far as possible: the S-beat gave way to the M-beat early in the sixteenth century, which in turn gave way to the C-beat *c*. 1600. The principle is of course the same, whatever the beat may be.

7 The extra lines can often be regarded as extended leger-lines: see, for instance, the Escorial chansonnier and Fig. 66(a), lower staff.

8 See MSD 10.

9 See, for instance, Arne's *Sonatas*, 1756, especially pp. 16–19.

10 See Scholderer, *Gutenberg*; King, *Four Hundred Years of Music Printing*; Toledo, *The Printed Note*.

11 Rankin, 'Shrewsbury', argues convincingly that the Shrewsbury Fragment is a part-book. If this is so, it is the earliest (*c*. 1430), though an isolated example chronologically and of a type (a processional) that is otherwise unknown.

PART II

Chapter 8: Early Didactic Notations

Apel (NPM, 204–8) and Parrish (NMM, chapters 1 and 3, *passim*) treat these notations comprehensively: my chapter is largely based on their work. Wolf examines them against the background of Greek and Byzantine notations at various points in the first three chapters of HdN i.

Apel (NPM, 21) lists the theorists of Fig. 71 as found in Gerbert, *Scriptores* I, 96 f (Notker), 118 ff (Hucbald), 152–72 (*Musica Enchiriadis*, not in Apel's list), 173–212 (*Scholia Enchiriadis*), 213–29 (*Commemoratio Brevis*), 253 and 265 (Odo of Cluny), 326 ff (Bernelinus) and 342 (Anonymous II).

Chapter 9: Later Didactic Notations

Different versions of 'Ut queant laxis' are discussed in Harbinson, 'Ut queant laxis'. Solmization is discussed in Morley's *Plain and Easy Introduction*, part 1, and a slightly different approach is in Ornithoparchus and Dowland,

Compendium. There is a good brief summary in Rainbow, *Land Without Music*, pp. 169–71: see also Dobbs, *Three Pioneers*.

A number of dictionary articles cover the development of Tonic Sol-fa extremely well. In Scholes's *Concise Oxford Dictionary* the articles 'Buckwheat notation', 'Lancashire Sol-fa' and 'Sight-singing' give good brief accounts. In *Grove 5* the articles on 'Character notation', 'Chevé', 'Solfège', 'Solfeggio', 'Solmization' and 'Tonic Sol-fa' are well worth reading.

Wolf discusses cipher-notations in HdN ii, 387 ff: Rousseau's *Projet* is reprinted, with a translation by Rainbow.

1   The Golden Legend account of the Nativity of St John (24 June) includes the story of the composition of 'Ut queant laxis' (Jacobus de Voragine, *Golden Legend*, p. 326). This stanza was clearly very appropriate for Guido's purpose. This version of the tune comes from GS II, 45: it is very close to the Roman (Solesmes edition) version.
2   See Aldrich, 'The Analysis of Renaissance Music', especially pp. 3–5. There is room for much argument over the rules of solmization: those offered here will give sensible results for most medieval and renaissance music.
3   The first use of this dual system was probably in Loys Bourgeois's *Le droict chemin de musique* (1550).
4   Exponents of Tonic Sol-fa have always insisted that the phonetic notation used is only a part of the total teaching method, and that the final aim of the method is to teach staff notation. Nevertheless, Tonic Sol-fa notation is a quite independent notational system, used as such by many people.
5   These are, of course, English phonetic spellings. Curiously enough, Glover used the spelling 'Sol-fa' for the system, though not for the individual notes. In this chapter I use the simpler spellings in discussion.

PART III

Chapter 10: Keyboard Tablatures
Keyboard tablatures are well covered by Apel NPM, Chapter III, including numerous facsimiles: see also Thurston Dart's article 'Tablature' in *Grove 5*, and Wolf HdN ii, Chapter 1.

Paumann's *Fundamentum Organisandi* is included in the facsimile of the Locheimer song-book (Ameln) and in Arnold, *Locheimer Liederbuch*; the Buxheim book is in Wallner, *Buxheimer Orgelbuch* (both facsimile and edition); and Bermudo's *Declaración* is reprinted, as is Schlick's *Tabulaturen*.

1   London, British Library, Add. MS 28550. See RISM B IV², p. 237: also Parrish NMM, plate LXI.
2   Berlin, Staastbibliothek der Stiftung Preussische Kulturbesitz, theol. lat. quart. 290 private collection.
3   With the Locheimer Liederbuch: Berlin, Staatsbibliothek der Stiftung Preussische Kulturbesitz, mus. MS 40613. Edition in Arnold, *Locheimer*, and Apel, *Keyboard Music.*

4 Munich, Bayerische Staatsbibliothek, Cim. 352b. See Wallner.
5 Schlick, *Tabulaturen etlicher Lobgesang und Lidlein* (Maintz, 1512: R/1977).
   On descending M-tails, see p. 116, above.
6 Zurich, Zentralbibliothek, Cod. 284; and Basle, Universitätsbibliothek, MS
   F.I.8.
7 Basle, Universitätsbibliothek, MS F.IX.22.
8 Vienna, Österreichische Nationalbibliothek, MS 18491.
9 St Gall, Stiftsbibliothek, MS 530.
10 Berlin, Deutsche Staatsbibliothek, MS P283 (1717–23). See Apel NPM, 39.
11 Antonio de Cabezon, *Obras de musica para tecla, harpa y vihuela ...
   recopiladas y puestas en cifra por Hernando de Cabezon su hijo* (Madrid
   1578).

Chapter 11: Lute Tablatures

Wolf (HdN ii, 35–114) and Apel (NPM, 54–81) deal comprehensively with
lute tablatures. The *Grove 5* articles 'Lute' and 'Tablature' give a good
introduction to the subject. On ornamentation in lute music, see Wolf HdN
ii, 147–57, and Robert Spencer's introductions to BMS 9 (The Board Lute
Book) and BMS 11 (The Robarts Lute Book).

Many reproductions of the lute sources are now available, including Robert
Dowland's *Varietie*, various English manuscripts in the Musical Sources
series (Boethius Press), the English Lute Songs series (Scolar Press, now
published by Early Music Centre Publications), and several continental
sources (which include the works of Denis and Ennemond Gaultier)
published by Minkoff. Virdung's *Musica Getutscht* has been reprinted, as
have Schlick's *Tabulaturen* and Milan's *El Maestro*. Gombosi, *Capirola*,
includes some colour facsimiles.

1 Some sources require the instrument to be tuned in A (the most usual after G)
   or F: see Fuenllana, *Orphenica Lyra*, ed. Jacobs, pp. xxxi ff.
2 For example, the strings of the lowest course would be tuned to G and g. This
   is ignored for notational purposes, and we regard this course as a whole as
   being tuned to G.
3 For the main seventeenth-century lute-tunings, see the *Grove 5* article 'Lute'.
   The tunings shown in Figure 86 can be found in BMS 3 (The Burwell Lute
   Tutor) and BMS 9 (The Board Lute Book).

Chapter 12: Miscellaneous Tablatures

In this chapter, too, Wolf's descriptions of tablatures (HdN ii) are the fullest
work on the subject. He discusses many tablatures which, because of the
relative rarity of their notation, I have not mentioned here.

Ganassi's *Regola Rubertina* is available in facsimile. Two lyra-viol
sources are available, and are suitable for performance: Playford's *Musick's
Recreation on the Viol, Lyra-Way* of 1682, and the Marsh lyra viol
manuscript (BMS 10). Further information on the lyra viol is in the *Grove 5*
article 'Lyra-viol'.

Cittern sources in facsimile are so far rare. There is a cittern part in Allison's *Psalmes* of 1599 (R/1968), and nos 39–46 of the Willoughby lute book (BMS 13) are for cittern. A list of cittern sources by James Tyler is in *Early Music* 2/1 (1974), 25–9. New thoughts on many aspects of the cittern, including its pitch and tuning, are in Abbott and Segerman, 'The Cittern in England'.

1 Kärgel: *Renovata Cythara* (Strasburg 1578); Sammenhammer: Thorn (Trouń, Poland), Gymnasialbibliothek, manuscript dated 1590.
2 Music intabulated by Fray Benito: Sotheby sale catalogue of 25–26 June 1973, and Maggs Bros. catalogue 956 (1974), no. 592 and plate 8.
3 Berlin, Deutsche Staatsbibliothek, Mus. MS 40145 (1765), discussed by Wolf, HdN ii, 143.
4 *Pleasant Companion or new lessons and instructions for the flageolet* (London 1672 or earlier). See also Lindley, 'A 17th-Century Flageolet Tablature'.

PART IV

Chapter 13: The Perfection of the System

Robert Donington's *Interpretation of Early Music* is a comprehensive survey as regards the baroque period, and it supersedes all earlier work on the subject. However, Winternitz MA is extremely useful.

Donington discusses accidentals at length in IEM, pp. 123–51 and 610–19. My section on accidentals is indebted in several places to Michael Talbot: some of his work on accidentals—much more detailed than my treatment here could be—is incorporated into the Appendix of the Editorial Guidelines for the New Vivaldi Edition (forthcoming).

Suitable reproductions are not easy to find for this period. Apart from those cited in the text of this chapter, the following should be consulted: Monteverdi's *Poppea*; Purcell's *Sonnata's of III Parts*; and several keyboard publications, including d'Anglebert's *Pièces de Clavecin, The Harpsicord Master* and *The Harpsicord Master* II and III (BMS 15).

1 Most singers will recognize this problem if they have performed from a nineteenth-century score. Operatic recitative probably presents the most difficulty in this respect.
2 This is of course a radically new way of thinking: it makes each of the twelve notes of the octave an independent entity, rather than regarding the 'black' notes as dependent on the 'white' ones (using the keyboard to define the notes in question). It is true that tablatures treated the chromatic scale as a series of equal members (Bermudo's first keyboard notation, for instance): but there the player is not concerned with the nomenclature of the note he plays, only with its position on the keyboard.
3 See above, Figure 76(b) and relevant text.

Chapter 14: The Notation of Expression
This chapter is largely concerned with problems of secondary interpretation. Donington's *Interpretation of Early Music* is vital for this, since he cites and comments on all the main authorities: I have also used Winternitz's discussion of expression-marks in *Musical Autographs* (i, 14 ff), Ferguson's *Keyboard Interpretation*, Newman's *Performance Practices in Beethoven's Piano Sonatas*, and the excellent short history of expression-words in David Fallows's *New Grove* article 'Tempo and Expression-Marks'. For full listings of words and signs in current use, see Read, *Music Notation*.

The three famous treatises by Quantz, C. P. E. Bach and Leopold Mozart are all available in modern translation (see Bibliography), and Strunk translates sections of them in *Source Readings*.

Part 2 of *Musick's Hand-Maid* is edited by Thurston Dart (Stainer and Bell 1958).

1   Earlier examples are in fact known, in the works of Gibbons and Marini: see Donington IEM, 387.
2   For comments on this matter, see Donington IEM, 382; Ferguson KI, 49 ff; Newman BPS, 51 ff; and Fallows, article 'Tempo and Expression Marks' in *The New Grove*.
3   Rossini used types (c) and (d) together, which suggests a distinction. Type (c) was used by Tromlitz (1791) in conjunction with the closed double wedge (see p. 196), so it seems that the closed types belong together: $\lhd + \rhd = \diamond$. See Warner, 'Tromlitz's Flute Treatise', 272.
4   *Poco forte* is almost untranslatable, though it has the implication of 'not very loud', which depends on context. On the difference between *poco* and *un poco*, see Eric Blom's *Grove 5* article 'Poco'.
5   Beethoven also refined his use of verbal directives, as has been demonstrated by Fritz Rothschild: Newman (BPS, 82 f) lists the terms used by Beethoven before 1812 for *crescendo* and for expressive playing, and contrasts them with the much longer list of more precise terms used after that date.
6   The dot could hardly indicate *staccato* playing until it was less commonly used for *notes inégales* (see p. 212). However, while the older notation does not necessarily imply *staccato*, the use of a dot for *staccato* does preclude inequality, since notes must be phrased in pairs (impossible with *staccato*) to be eligible for *inégale* treatment (Donington IEM, 453).
7   See Eric Simon's introduction to Mozart, *Eine kleine Nachtmusik*, x; and Newman BPS, 68–71.

Chapter 15: Notation and Convention
The three operas by Cavalieri, Caccini and Peri are all available in facsimile reprints (see the Bibliography). The most comprehensive authority on the figured bass is Arnold's *The Art of Accompaniment from a Thorough-Bass* (1931, R/1961 and 1965): but C. P. E. Bach also treats the subject at some length (*Essay*, pp. 172–445), and Donington gives an excellent shorter account (IEM, pp. 288–372).

On rhythmic problems, Donington IEM and Collins, 'The Performance of Triplets' should be read. It should be said here, however, that many of the accepted views have been questioned by Frederick Neumann, and that any detailed assessment of the problems should take into account the debate which Neumann's work started, and in which both Collins and David Fuller have joined. A convenient place to begin studying this interchange would be Neumann's article in *Early Music* 7/1 (1979), pp. 39–45 (where he surveys the debate itself and its bibliography), together with a bipartite article on 'The French style and the overtures of Bach' by John O'Donnell (*Early Music* 7 (1979), pp. 190–6 and 336–45) and Fuller's letter (ibid., p. 279).

Ornamentation is comprehensively covered by Donington IEM and Neumann's *Ornamentation in Baroque and Post-Baroque Music*. To these can be added Ferguson KI for a wider historical perspective (a masterly survey in its scholarship, readability and sheer common sense), and Brown, *Embellishing 16th-Century Music*, which discusses the subject in the light of the early instrumental tutors.

1 A similar convention must govern the improvised slow movement of the Third Brandenburg Concerto, at the end of which the keyboard player (or does the 1st violin play it?) presumably brings in the strings for the notated phrygian cadence. The effect is that of the parallel place in the Fourth Brandenburg Concerto.

2 Rosen also cites the *Missa Solemnis*, where the same arguments apply.

3 Donington IEM, 461, quotes the opening of Handel's sonata op. 1 no. 1, in which equal notes slurred return later in the prevailing dotted rhythm.

4 This notation can be seen as late as Schubert, whose 'Wasserfluth' from *Die Winterreise* (1827, published in 1828) should be played in triplets throughout: other songs by Schubert also raise the question of rhythmic assimilation.

5 The re-use of a limited number of signs for different purposes by different composers makes it impossible to discuss the notation of ornaments in general terms.

6 Bach's examples are very interesting, and repay study: see the *Essay*, pp. 87 ff.

7 David Wulstan, 'Vocal colour', 33–8, and Morley, *Plain and Easy Introduction*, 274 f.

8 This has some of the features of *Griffschrift*, for which reason Wolf included it among the tablatures (HdN ii, 237 f).

9 Information on these tunings and notation was given by Dr Johnson during the Conference for Music Research Students at Edinburgh University, December 1979.

Chapter 16: The Limits of the System

For a survey of the ways in which composers have used notation as a positive part of the creative process, a selection of autographs is obviously essential: Winternitz MA and Hürlimann CA are excellent anthologies, with informative introductions. The number of nineteenth-century autographs available in facsimile is now increasing rapidly, with such series as that published by Scolar Press and that recently started by the British Library.

Some of the matters discussed in this chapter overlap with the subject of Chapter 18, and the reader is referred to the notes to that chapter, and especially to the works by Karkoschka, Sabbe and Stone.

1 An earlier example, in Beethoven's Sonata op.81a ('Les Adieux'), bar 11, should be treated cautiously, perhaps. A six-note chord would in any case sound louder than a four-note chord played with the same force, and the Adagio marking would allow this to be heard. It may be worth noting that this relates to two possible methods of obtaining a crescendo on a harpsichord: (i) by increasing the number of notes in successive chords, and (ii) by arpeggiating a sustained chord so that the volume grows with each added note.

Chapter 17: Notational Reforms

Some earlier notational reforms are described by Abdy Williams (SN, 196–212) and Wolf (HdN ii, 335–86). For more recent reforms see Karkoschka NNM: in addition, Klavarskribo is described in *Klavarskribo*; Equitone is lucidly discussed in Stone, 'Problems', pp. 10–12; and Szentkirályi's article gives details of his own notation. A somewhat undigested proposal by Schoenberg for a chromatic staff is in *Style and Idea*, pp. 354–62: those interested in the problems will find it instructive to assess the main features of this notation (which Schoenberg apparently never used).

1 I choose a keyboard for its large range; but even for a singer (with a range of two octaves or so) the series would be too long for easy note-finding.
2 I assume equal temperament here, so that all semitones are the same size.
3 This system was used for keyboard music on two staves, but it could easily be modified for voices or other instruments. Laker's notation is described by Wolf HdN ii, 356 f.
4 For a good example of the extension of the tail-series, see the notation of Démotz de la Salle, 1726 (Wolf HdN ii, 421–3). Seven stem-directions show the chromatic scale without the need for a staff; the note-heads show the octave by their shape (round, square or rhombic) and colour (black or void). The flag at the end of the stem notates anything between a S and a Hdsq (sixty-fourth note), and this series could certainly be extended.
5 Wolf's description does not explain how dotted rhythms are notated: nor is it clear what effect the various inclinations of the figure have on the position of the duration-dot and the stems. I have not been able to consult Menchaca's work.
6 The original German spelling, Equiton, is often used in English: but for an English-speaking reader the form 'Equitone'—used by Karkoschka's translator, Ruth Koenig—is more accurate as regards both meaning and pronunciation.

Chapter 18: Innovation and Stability
On the subjects of this chapter, Cole's *Sounds and Signs* contains much useful material and relevant comment. Apart from the cited books by Karkoschka, Risatti, and Sabbe *et al.*, an enlightening work on the general aspects of modern notation is Kurt Stone's 'Problems and Methods of Notation': Stone has further developed his work in the recent *Music Notation in the Twentieth Century*, an authoritative work unfortunately published too late to be consulted in the writing of this chapter.

Further on indeterminacy, see Behrman, 'What Indeterminate Notation Determines'. I have already cited other articles from Boretz and Cone's *Perspectives on Notation and Performance*, but it may be said here that the whole book should be read by those interested in the subject of this chapter.

Select Bibliography

A full bibliography on notation would be larger than could reasonably be encompassed in this book, and my list of sources is necessarily very selective. More detailed bibliographies will be found in *Grove 5*, The New Grove and the periodical RILM Abstracts (*Répertoire International de Littérature Musicale*) under 'Notation' and related headings. In the present list, I have generally cited only those works that are still easily accessible: with few exceptions, therefore, works published before the present century are not included unless they have been reprinted. Where more than one edition or version of a work is listed, the last-mentioned is that cited in this book. I have not listed the editions of works by major composers.

Abbott, Djilda, and Segerman, Ephraim. 'The Cittern in England before 1700', *Lute Society Journal* 17 (1975), 24–48.

Agricola, Martin. *Musica instrumentalis deudsch*. Georg Rhaw, Wittemberg, 1529: R/Georg Olms, Hildesheim, 1969.

Abdy Williams, C. F. *The Story of Notation*. Walter Scott, London, and Charles Scribner's Sons, New York, 1903.

Adam de la Halle: s.v. Coussemaker.

Aldrich, Putnam. 'An Approach to the Analysis of Renaissance Music', *Music Review* 30 (1969), 1–21.

Allaire, Gaston G.: s.v. MSD.

Allison, Richard. *The Psalmes of David in Meter*. William Barley, London, 1599: R/Scolar Press, Menston, 1968.

Ameln, Konrad, ed. *Lochamer-Liederbuch und das Fundamentum organisandi* (facsimile edn). Bärenreiter, Cassel, 1972.

Anderson, Gordon A. 'Magister Lambertus and Nine Rhythmic Modes', *Acta Musicologica* 45 (1973), 57–73.

Andrews, H. K., and Dart, Thurston. 'Fourteenth-Century Polyphony in a Fountains Abbey MS Book', *Music & Letters* 39/1 (Jan. 1958), 1–12.

Anglés, Higinio. *La Música de las Cantigas de Santa María del Rey Alfonso el Sabio*. Barcelona Central Library, Barcelona, 1943–64.

Apel, Willi. *Gregorian Chant*. Burns and Oates, London, [1958].

—— *Keyboard Music of the Fourteenth and Fifteenth Centuries*. Corpus of Early Keyboard Music 1: American Institute of Musicology, Rome, 1963.

—— *The Notation of Polyphonic Music 900–1600*. The Mediaeval Academy of America, Cambridge (Mass.), 1942: 5/1953.

Arne, Thomas A. *VIII Sonatas or Lessons for the Harpsichord*. John Walsh, London, [1756]: R/Stainer & Bell, London, 1969, with an introductory note by Gwilym Beechey and Thurston Dart, as *Eight Keyboard Sonatas*.

Arnold, F. T. *The Art of Accompaniment from a Thorough-Bass*. Oxford University Press, London, 1931: R/Dover Publications, New York, 1965.

Arnold, F. W., ed. *Das Locheimer Liederbuch*. Breitkopf & Härtel, Leipzig, 1926.

Aubry, Pierre. *Cent Motets du XIIIe Siècle*. Paris, 1908: R/Broude Brothers, New York, 1964.

Bach, C. P. E. *Versuch über die wahre Art das Clavier zu spielen*. Berlin, 1759 and 1762. Translated by W. J. Mitchell as *Essay on the True Art of Playing Keyboard Instruments*. Eulenburg, London, 1974.

Bank, J. A. *Tactus, Tempo and Notation in Mensural Music from the 13th to the 17th Century*. Bank, Amsterdam, 1972.

Bannister, H. M. *Monumenti Vaticani di Paleografia Musicale Latina*. Leipzig, 1913: R/Gregg, Farnborough, 1969.

Baxter, J. H. *An Old St Andrews Music Book*. Oxford University Press, London, and Champion, Paris, 1931: R/American Musicological Society, New York, 1973.

Behrman, David. 'What Indeterminate Notation Determines'. In Boretz and Cone, *Perspectives*, pp. 74–89.

Benham, Hugh. '"Salve Regina" (Power or Dunstable): a Simplified Version', *Music & Letters* 59/1 (Jan. 1978), 28–32.

Bent, Margaret. 'New and Little-Known Fragments of English Medieval Polyphony', *Journal of the American Musicological Society* 21/2 (1968), 137–56.

—— *The Old Hall Manuscript: a Paleographical Study*. Unpublished PhD dissertation, Cambridge University, 1969.

—— 'Sources of the Old Hall Music', *Proceedings of the Royal Musical Association* 94 (1968), 19–35.

—— 'The Transmission of English Music 1300–1500: Some Aspects of Repertory and Presentation'. In H. H. Eggebrecht and M. Lütolf, eds., *Studien zur Tradition in der Musik: Kurt von Fischer zum 60 Geburtstag*. Katzbichler, Munich, 1973, pp. 65–83.

Bergsagel, John D. 'An English Liquescent Neume'. In Jack Westrup, ed., *Essays Presented to Egon Wellesz*. Clarendon Press, Oxford, 1966, pp. 94–9.

Bermudo, Juan. *Declaración de instrumentos musicales*. 1555: R/Bärenreiter, Cassel and Basle, 1957, with notes by M. S. Kastner.

Berry, Mary: s.v. More, Mother Thomas.

Biber, Heinrich. *Acht Violinsonaten* (1681), ed. G. Adler. Denkmäler der Tonkunst in Österreich, 11: Graz, 1898.

Blezzard, Judith. 'The Wells Musical Slates', *Musical Times* 1631 (Jan. 1979), 26–30.

BMS   Boethius Press, *Musical Sources.*
    1 *A Fifteenth-Century Song Book.* Leeds, 1973.
    2 *The Turpyn Book of Lute Songs.* Leeds, 1973.
    3 *The Burwell Lute Tutor.* Leeds, 1974.
    5 John Dowland. *Lachrimae* [1604]. Leeds, 1974.
    9 *The Board Lute Book.* Leeds, 1977.
    10 *Narcissus Marsh's Lyra Viol Book.* Kilkenny, 1978.
    11 *The Robarts Lute Book.* Kilkenny, 1978.
    13 *The Willoughby Lute Book.* Kilkenny, 1979.
    15 *The Harpsicord Master* II and III. Kilkenny, 1980.

Boretz, Benjamin, and Cone, Edward T., eds. *Perspectives on Notation and Performance.* Norton, New York, 1976.

Brown, Howard M. *Embellishing 16th-Century Music.* Oxford University Press, London, 1976.

Bukofzer, Manfred F. *Studies in Medieval and Renaissance Music.* Dent, London, 1951.

Buxheim Organ Book: s.v. Wallner.

Caccini, Giulio. *L'Euridice.* Marescotti, Florence, 1600: R/Forni, Bologna, 1968, with a note by Rodolfo Paoli.

Caldwell, John. *English Keyboard Music Before the Nineteenth Century.* Praeger, New York, 1973.

—— *Medieval Music.* Hutchinson, London, 1978.

Campion, Thomas. *The Third and Fourth Booke of Ayres.* Thomas Snodham, London, [1618]: R/Scolar Press, Menston, 1973.

Cardine, Eugène. 'Sémiologie Grégorienne', *Études Grégoriennes* 11 (Solesmes, 1970), 1–158.

Cavalieri, Emilio del. *Rappresentatione di Anima e di Corpo.* Muti, Rome, 1600: R/Gregg, Farnborough, 1967.

Chailley, Jacques. *Les notations musicales nouvelles.* Paris, 1950.

Chansonnier d'Arras: s.v. Jeanroy.

Cole, Hugo. *Sounds and Signs: Aspects of Musical Notation.* Oxford University Press, London, 1974.

Collins, Michael. 'The Performance of Triplets in the 17th and 18th Centuries', *Journal of the American Musicological Society* 19 (1966), 281–328.

Couperin, François. *Pièces de Clavecin* 2, ed. Kenneth Gilbert. Heugel, Paris, 1969.

Couperin, Louis. *Pièces de Clavecin*, ed. Alan Curtis. Heugel, Paris, 1970.

CS   Coussemaker, Edmond de, ed. *Scriptorum de Musica Medii Aevi.* Paris, 1864–76: R/Georg Olms, Hildesheim, 1963.

—— ed. *Adam de la Halle: Oeuvres Complètes.* Paris, 1872: R/Gregg Press, Ridgewood (N.J.), 1965.

Crocker, Richard L. *The Early Medieval Sequence.* University of California Press, Berkeley, Los Angeles and London, 1977.

Curwen, John. *The Standard Course . . . in the Tonic Sol-fa Method of Teaching Music*. Tonic Sol-fa Agency, London, 2/1872.

D'Anglebert, J. H. *Pièces de Clavecin*. Paris, 1689: R/Broude Brothers, New York, 1965.

Dittmer, Luther A. 'Binary Rhythm, Musical Theory and the Worcester Fragments', *Musica Disciplina* 7 (1953), 39–57.

Dobbs, J. P. B. *Three Pioneers of Sight-Singing in the Nineteenth Century*. The Institute of Education of Durham and Newcastle Universities, Newcastle upon Tyne, 1964.

Dolmetsch, Arnold. *The Interpretation of the Music of the Seventeenth and Eighteenth Centuries*. Novello, London, 1915: 2/1946, R/University of Washington Press, Seattle and London, 1969, with an introduction by R. Alec Harman.

Donington, Robert. *The Interpretation of Early Music*. Faber and Faber, London, 1963: revised version, with corrections, 1975.

Dowland, Robert. *Varietie of Lute Lessons*. Thomas Adams, London, 1610: R/Schott, London, 1958, with an introduction by Edgar Hunt.

Drummond, Pippa. 'The Concertos of Johann Adolf Hasse', *Proceedings of the Royal Musical Association* 99 (1973), 91–103.

Eppelsheim, Jürgen. 'Buchstaben-Notation, Tabulatur und Klaviatur', *Archiv für Musikwissenschaft* 31 (1974), 57–72.

Escorial Palace, Madrid, MS V.III.24. Facsimile edition, with an introduction by Wolfgang Rehm, Bärenreiter, Cassel and Basle, 1958.

Expert, Henry, ed. Jacques Mauduit, *Chansonnettes mesurées*. Les Maîtres Musiciens de la Renaissance Française, 10. Paris, [?1899, 1900]: R/Broude Brothers, New York, n.d.

Fallows, David. '15th-Century Tablatures for Plucked Instruments: a Summary, a Revision and a Suggestion', *Lute Society Journal* 19 (1977), 7–33.

—— 'Tempo and Expression Marks'. In *The New Grove*. Macmillan, London, 1981.

Ferguson, Howard. *Keyboard Interpretation*. Oxford University Press, London, 1975.

Fitzwilliam Virginal Book, The, ed. J. A. Fuller Maitland and W. Barclay Squire. Breitkopf & Härtel, [Leipzig], 1899: R/Dover Publications, New York, 1963.

Frescobaldi, Girolamo. *Recercari et Canzoni Franzese*. Bartolomeo Zannetti, Rome, 1615: R/Gregg, Farnborough, 1967.

Fuenllana, Miguel de. *Libro de musica para vihuela, intitulado Orphenica Lyra*. Seville, 1554. Edited by Charles Jacobs as *Orphénica Lyra*: Oxford University Press, Oxford, 1978.

Fuller, David. Correspondence, *Early Music* 7/2 (April 1979), 279.

Gabrieli, Giovanni. *Sonata pian' e forte*. In A. T. Davison and Willi Apel, eds, *Historical Anthology of Music*. Harvard University Press, Cambridge (Mass.), 1946, i, no. 173.

Gafurius, Franchinus. *Practica Musicae*. Milan, 1496: R/Gregg, Farnborough, 1967. Translated and edited by Irwin Young as *The Practica Musicae of Franchinus Gafurius*. University of Wisconsin Press, Madison, 1969.

Gallo, F. Alberto. *La teoria della notazione in Italia dalla fine del XIII all'inizio del XV secolo*. Bologna, 1966.

Ganassi, Sylvestro di. *Opera intitulata Fontegara*. Venice, 1535. Edited by Hildemarie Peter, translated by Dorothy Swainson. Lienau, Berlin, 1956.

—— *Regola Rubertina*. Venice, 1542–43: R/Leipzig, 1924, with an introduction by Max Schneider.

Geminiani, Francesco. *A Treatise of Good Taste in the Art of Musick*. London, 1749: R/Da Capo Press, New York, 1969.

GS Gerbert, Martin. *Scriptores Ecclesiastici de Musica Sacra Potissimum*. St Blaise, 1784: R/Georg Olms, Hildesheim, 1963.

Glover, Sarah. *Scheme to Render Psalmody Congregational*. Hamilton and Jarrold, Norwich, 1835.

—— *The Sol-fa Tune Book*. Hamilton and Jarrold, Norwich, 1839.

Gombosi, Otto, ed. *Compositione de Meser Vincenzo Capirola*. Société de Musique D'Autrefois, Neuilly-sur-Seine, 1955.

Graduale Romanum. Abbaye Saint-Pierre de Solesmes, Sablé-sur-Sarthe, 1974.

Graduale Triplex. Abbaye Saint-Pierre de Solesmes, Sablé-sur-Sarthe, 1979.

Graduel Neumé. Abbaye Saint-Pierre de Solesmes, Sablé-sur-Sarthe, [1972].

Grove 5 *Grove's Dictionary of Music and Musicians*. 5th edition, ed. Eric Blom. Macmillan, London, 1954. Articles include 'Expression' (Donington), 'Notation' (Dart), 'Proportions' (Dart), 'Staccato' (Donington) and 'Tonic Sol-Fa' (Shaw).

[Grove 6] *The New Grove* (*Grove's Dictionary*, 6th edn), ed. Stanley Sadie. Macmillan, London, 1981.

Hába, Alois. *Neue Harmonielehre*. Leipzig, 1927.

Händel, G. F. *Das Autograph des Oratoriums 'Messias'*, ed. F. Chrysander. Deutsche Händel-Gesellschaft, Hamburg, 1892.

Harbinson, Denis. 'The Hymn "Ut queant laxis"', *Music & Letters* 52/1 (Jan. 1971), 55–8.

Harpsicord Master, The. John Walsh, London 1697: R/Price Milburn, Wellington, and Faber, London, 1980. [See also BMS 15.]

Harrison, Frank Ll. *Music in Medieval Britain*. Routledge and Kegan Paul, London, 1958: 2/1963.

—— 'Rota and Rondellus in English Medieval Music', *Proceedings of the Royal Musical Association* 86 (1960), 98–107.

—— and Wibberley, R. *Manuscripts of Fourteenth Century English Polyphony*. Early English Church Music 26: Stainer & Bell for the British Academy, London, 1981.

Henning, Rudolf. 'German Lute Tablature and Conrad Paumann', *Lute Society Journal* 15 (1973), 7–10.

Hoppin, Richard H. *Medieval Music*. Norton, New York, 1978.

—— *Anthology of Medieval Music.* Norton, New York, 1978.

Huff, J. A.: s.v. MSD.

Hughes, Andrew. 'The Choir in Fifteenth-Century English Music'. In Gustave Reese and Robert J. Snow, eds, *Essays in Musicology in Honor of Dragan Plamenac.* University of Pittsburgh Press, Pittsburgh (Pa.), 1969: R/Da Capo Press, New York, 1977, pp. 127–45.

—— 'Mensuration and Proportion in Early Fifteenth Century English Music', *Acta Musicologica* 37 (1965), 48–61.

—— and Bent, Margaret, eds. *The Old Hall Manuscript.* Corpus Mensurabilis Musicae 46. American Institute of Musicology, Rome, 1969–73.

Hughes, Anselm. *Worcester Mediaeval Harmony.* Plainsong and Mediaeval Music Society, London, 1928.

Huizinga, Johan. *The Waning of the Middle Ages.* 1924: DoubledayAnchor Books, New York, 1954.

Hürlimann, Martin, ed. *Composers' Autographs,* translated by Ernst Roth. Cassell, London, 1968.

Jacobs, Charles. *Tempo Notation in Renaissance Spain.* Institute of Medieval Music, New York, 1964.

Jeanroy, Alfred. *Le Chansonnier d'Arras.* Société des Anciens Textes Français, Paris, 1925: R/Johnson, New York, 1965.

Johnson, David. *Music and Society in Lowland Scotland in the Eighteenth Century.* Oxford University Press, London, 1972.

Karkoschka, Erhard. *Das Schriftbild der Neuen Musik.* Celle, 1966. English translation by Ruth Koenig published as *Notation in New Music.* Universal Edition, London, 1972.

King, Alexander Hyatt. *Four Hundred Years of Music Printing.* British Museum, London, 1964.

Kinkeldey, Otto. *Orgel und Klavier im 16 Jahrhundert.* Breitkopf & Härtel, Leipzig, 1910.

Klavarskribo. *What is Klavarskribo?* 1934: 2/[Klavar Music Foundation, 1948].

Krummel, D. W. *English Music Printing 1553–1700.* The Bibliographical Society, London, 1975.

LU *Liber Usualis.* Desclée, Tournai, 1896 and several subsequent editions.

Lindley, David. 'A 17th-Century Flageolet Tablature at Guildford', *Galpin Society Journal* 31 (1978), 94–9.

Lochamer/Locheimer Liederbuch, Das: s.v. Ameln; Arnold, F. W.

Lowens, Irving. 'Andrew Law and the Pirates', *Journal of the American Musicological Society* 13 (1960), 206–23.

Marrocco, W. Thomas, and Sandon, Nicholas, eds. *Medieval Music.* Oxford University Press, London, 1977.

Martino, Donald. 'Notation in General—Articulation in Particular'. In Boretz and Cone, *Perspectives*, pp. 102–13.

Mellon Chansonnier, The, ed. Leeman L. Perkins and Howard Garey. Yale University Press, New Haven (Conn.) and London, 1979.

Merbecke, John. *The booke of Common praier noted.* London, 1550: R/Nottingham Court Press, London, 1979.

Milan, Luis de. *Libro de musica de vihuela de mano intitulado El Maestro.* Facsimile and edition by L. Schrade. Breitkopf & Härtel, Leipzig, 1927: R/George Olms, Hildesheim, and Breitkopf & Härtel, Wiesbaden, 1967.

Monteverdi, Claudio. *L'incoronazione di Poppea.* Facsimile, with an introduction by G. Benvenuti. Bocca, Milan, 1938.

—— *L'Orfeo: Favola in Musica.* Amadino, Venice, 1615: R/Gregg, Farnborough, 1972.

More, Mother Thomas. *The performance of plainsong in the later Middle Ages and the 16th century.* Unpublished PhD dissertation, Cambridge University, 1970.

—— 'The Performance of Plainsong in the Later Middle Ages and the Sixteenth Century', *Proceedings of the Royal Musical Association 92* (1966), 121–34.

Morley, Thomas. *A Plaine and Easie Introduction to Practicall Musicke.* Peter Short, London, 1597: edited by R. Alec Harman, 2/Dent, London, and Norton, New York, [1962].

Moroney, Davitt. 'The performance of unmeasured harpsichord preludes', *Early Music* 4/2 (April 1976), 143–51.

Mozart, Leopold. *Versuch einer gründlichen Violinschule.* Augsburg, 1756: translated by Editha Knocker as *A Treatise on . . . Violin Playing.* Oxford University Press, London, 1948, 2/1951.

Mozart, W. A. *Eine kleine Nachtmusik.* Facsimile and edition, with an introduction by Eric Simon. Dover Publications, New York, 1968.

Murray, Gregory. *Gregorian Chant According to the Manuscripts.* Cary, London, 1963.

MB Musica Britannica. Stainer & Bell for the Royal Musical Association, London.

   1 *The Mulliner Book*, ed. Denis Stevens (1951).

   14 John Bull, *Keyboard Music* I, ed. John Steele and Francis Cameron (1960).

   18 *Music at the Court of Henry VIII*, ed. John Stevens (1962).

MSD Musicological Studies and Documents. American Institute of Musicology, Rome.

   10 *The Faenza Codex: An Early Fifteenth-Century Italian Source of Keyboard Music* (1961).

   13 *The Manuscript London, British Museum, Additional 29987*, with an introduction by Gilbert Reaney (1965).

   24 Gaston G. Allaire. *The Theory of Hexachords, Solmization and the Modal System* (1972).

   31 *Walter Odington: De Speculatione Musicae, part vi*, translated by Jay A. Huff (1973).

Neumann, Frederick. 'Once more: the "French overture style"', *Early Music* 7/1 (January 1979), 39–45.

—— *Ornamentation in Baroque and Post-Baroque Music*. Princeton University Press, Princeton (N.J.), 1978.

New Grove, The: s.v. Grove.

Newman, William S. *Performance Practices in Beethoven's Piano Sonatas*. Norton, New York, 1971, and Dent, London, 1972.

NOHM *The New Oxford History of Music*. Oxford University Press, London, 1954– .

Ockeghem, Johannes. *Collected Works* ii, ed. Dragan Plamenac. American Musicological Society, New York, 1947.

Odington, Walter: s.v. MSD.

O'Donnell, John. 'The French style and the overtures of Bach', *Early Music* 7 (1979), 190–96 and 336–45.

Ornithoparchus, Andreas, and Dowland, John. *A Compendium of Musical Practice*. Comprising Ornithoparchus's *Musice Active Micrologus* (2/1517) and Dowland's *Andreas Ornithoparchus His Micrologus* (1609). Both R/Dover Publications, New York, 1973, with an introduction by Gustave Reese and Steven Ledbetter.

Page, Christopher. 'The 15th-century lute: new and neglected sources', *Early Music* 9/1 (January 1981), 11–21.

PM *Paléographie Musicale*. Editions de L'Abbaye Saint-Pierre de Solesmes, Sablé sur Sarthe, 1889– .

Parrish, Carl. *The Notation of Medieval Music*. Norton, New York, 1957, and Faber, London, 1958: 2R/Pendragon, New York, 1978.

Peri, Jacopo. *Le Musiche sopra L'Euridice*. Marescotti, Florence, 1600: R/Forni, Bologna, 1969, with a note by Rossana Delmonte.

Perkins, John MacIvor. 'Note Values'. In Boretz and Cone, *Perspectives*, pp. 63–73.

Piae Cantiones. Greifswald, 1582: R/Fazer, Helsinki, 1967.

Pike, Lionel. 'The Performance of Triple Rhythms in Peter Phillips' Vocal Music', *The Consort* 28 (1972), 88–105.

Playford, John. *An Introduction to the Skill of Musick*. Playford, London, 1674: R/Gregg Press, Farnborough, 1966.

—— *Musick's Recreation on the Viol, Lyra-Way*. Playford, London, 1682: R/Hinrichsen, London, 1965.

Pothier, J. *Les Mélodies Grégoriennes*. Desclée, Lefebvre et Cie., Tournai, 1881.

Praetorius, Michael. *Syntagma Musicum*. Wittemburg and Wolfenbüttel, 1614–19: R/Bärenreiter, Cassel and Basle, 1958–59.

Publications of Medieval Music Manuscripts. Institute of Medieval Music, New York, 1957– . Introductions, etc., by L. Dittmer and others.
1 Madrid MS 20486.
2 Wolfenbüttel MS 1099 (1206).
3 *A Central Source of Notre-Dame Polyphony*.
4 Paris, BN MSS nouv. acq. fr. 13521 (La Clayette) and lat. 11411.
5 Worcester Add. MS 68, Westminster Abbey MS 33327, and Madrid, Bibl. Nac. MS 192.

6 Oxford, Lat. lit. D 20, London, BL Add. MS 25031, and Chicago, MS 654 App.

7 *Opera omnia Fauges.*

8 Seville, MS 5–1–53, and Paris, BN MS nouv. acq. fr. 4379.

9 *Carmina Burana.*

10 Florence, Biblioteca mediceo-laurenziana, pluteo 29.1.

Purcell, Henry. *Sonnata's of III Parts.* London, 1683: R/Nottingham Court Press, London, 1975.

Quantz, J. J. *Versuch einer Anweisung die Flöte traversiere zu spielen.* Berlin, 1752: 3/Breslau, 1789, R/Bärenreiter, Cassel and Basle, 1953. Translated by E. R. Reilly as *On Playing the Flute.* Faber and Faber, London, 1966.

Rainbow, Bernarr. *The Land Without Music.* Novello, London 1967.

Rankin, Susan. 'Shrewsbury School, Manuscript VI: A Medieval Part Book?', *Proceedings of the Royal Musical Association* 102 (1976), 129–44.

Rastall, Richard, and Seaman, Ann-Marie, eds. *Four 15th-Century Religious Songs in English.* Antico Edition, Newton Abbot, 1979.

Read, Gardner. *Music Notation: a Manual of Modern Practice.* Gollancz, London, 1974.

Reese, Gustave. *Music in the Middle Ages.* Dent, London, 1941.

—— *Music in the Renaissance.* Norton, New York, 1954: 2/1959.

RISM *Répertoire International des Sources Musicales* Bärenreiter, Cassel, 1971– (Series A), and Henle, Munich and Duisburg, 1960– (Series B).

Ringmann, Heribert, ed. *Das Glogauer Liederbuch.* Bärenreiter, Cassel and Basle, 1954.

Risatti, Howard. *New Music Vocabulary.* University of Illinois Press, Urbana, 1975.

Robertson, Alec, and Stevens, Denis, eds. *The Pelican History of Music.* Penguin Books, Harmondsworth, 1960–68.

Rosen, Charles. *The Classical Style.* Faber and Faber, London, 1971: 2/1972.

Rousseau, Jean-Jacques. *Projet concernant de nouveaux signes pour la musique.* Paris, 1742. Translated by Bernarr Rainbow, with an introduction, as *Project Concerning New Symbols for Music.* Boethius Press, Kilkenny, 1982.

Sabbe, Hermann, Stone, Kurt, and Warfield, Gerald, eds. *International Conference on New Musical Notation: Report.* Swets & Zeitlinger, Amsterdam, 1975 (*Interface* 4/1, November 1975).

Sachs, Curt. *Rhythm and Tempo.* Dent, London, 1953.

St Victor Manuscript: s.v. Thurston, Ethel.

Schenker, Heinrich. *Five Graphic Music Analyses,* with a new introduction by Felix Salzer. Dover Publications, New York, 1969.

Schlick, Arnolt. *Tabulaturen etlicher Lobgesang und Lidlein uff die Orgeln und Lauten.* Maintz, 1512: R/Bärenreiter, Cassel, 1977.

Schoenberg, Arnold. *Style and Idea.* New edition, ed. Leonard Stein, Faber and Faber, London, 1975.

Scholderer, Victor. *Johann Gutenberg.* British Museum, London, 1963.

Scholes, Percy. *The Concise Oxford Dictionary of Music.* Oxford University Press, London, 1952: 2/1964.

Smits van Waesberghe, J. *Expositiones in Micrologium Guidonis Aretini.* Amsterdam, 1957.

—— 'The musical notation of Guido of Arezzo', *Musica Disciplina* 5 (1951), 15–53.

Solesmes, The Monks of. *La Notation Musicale des Chants Liturgiques Latins.* Solesmes, 1960.

—— s.v. *Graduale Romanum; Liber Usualis; Paléographie Musicale.*

Spiess, Lincoln B. 'An Introduction to the pre-St Martial Practical Sources of Early Polyphony', *Speculum* 22 (1947), 16–17.

EBM Stainer, J., J.F.R. and C. *Early Bodleian Music.* Novello, London and New York, 1901: R/Gregg, Farnborough, 1967.

Stainer, J. F. R. *Dufay and his Contemporaries.* Novello, London, 1898: R/Knuf, Hilversum, 1966.

Stanbrook, Benedictines of. *Gregorian Music.* Art & Book Co., London and Leamington, 1897.

Steele, Robert. *The Earliest English Music Printing.* The Bibliographical Society, London, 1903: R/1965.

Stevens, Denis. 'The Second Fountains Fragment: a Postscript', *Music & Letters* 39/2 (April 1958), 148–53.

Stone, Kurt. *Music Notation in the Twentieth Century.* Norton, New York, 1980.

—— 'Problems and Methods of Notation'. In Boretz and Cone, *Perspectives,* pp. 9–31.

SR Strunk, Oliver. *Source Readings in Music History.* Norton, New York, 1950, and Faber and Faber, London, 1952.

Szentkirályi, András. 'An Attempt to modernize Notation', *Music Review* 34 (1973), 100–23.

Thurston, Ethel. *The Music in the St Victor Manuscript.* Pontifical Institute of Mediaeval Studies, Toronto, 1959.

Tinctoris, Johannes. *Proportionale Musices.* c. 1475: R/Gregg Press, Farnborough, 1967. Translated by Albert Seay as *Proportions in Music.* Colorado College Music Press, Colorado Springs (Colorado), 1979.

Tischler, Hans. 'A Propos the Notation of the Parisian Organa', *Journal of the American Musicological Society* 14/1 (1961), 1–8.

—— 'The Earliest Lute Tablature?', *Journal of the American Musicological Society* 27/1 (1974), 100–3.

Toledo Museum of Art. *The Printed Note.* Toledo (Ohio), 1957.

Tomkins, Thomas. *Songs of 3, 4, 5 and 6 Partes,* ed. E. H. Fellowes. Stainer & Bell, London, 1922.

Trent Codices. [MSS 87–93 in the Castello del Buon Consiglio, Trento, in facsimile.] Bibliopola, Rome, 1969–70.

Tyler, James. 'A checklist for the cittern', *Early Music* 2/1 (January 1974), 25–9.

Virdung, Sebastian. *Musica getutscht*. Basle, 1511: R/Bärenreiter, Cassel, 1970.

Voragine, Jacobus de. *Legenda Aurea*. Translated by Granger Ryan and Helmut Ripperger as *The Golden Legend*. London, 1941: R/Arno Press, New York, 1969.

Waite, William G. *The Rhythm of Twelfth-Century Polyphony*. Yale University Press, New Haven (Conn.), 1954: R/Greenwood Press, Westport (Conn.) 1973.

Wallner, Bertha, ed. *Das Buxheimer Orgelbuch*. Bärenreiter, Cassel and Basle, 1958–9.

—— *Das Buxheimer Orgelbuch* (facsimile). Bärenreiter, Cassel and Basle, 1955.

Warner, Thomas E. 'Tromlitz's Flute Treatise: A Neglected Source of Eighteenth-Century Performance Practice'. In Edward H. Clinkscale and Claire Brook, eds, *A Musical Offering: Essays in Honor of Martin Bernstein*. Pendragon Press, New York, 1977, pp. 261–73.

Winternitz, Emanuel. *Musical Autographs from Monteverdi to Hindemith*. Princeton University Press, Princeton (N. J.) 1955: 2/Dover Publications, New York, 1965.

Wolf, Johannes. *Geschichte der Mensuralnotation von 1250 bis 1460*. Leipzig, 1904: R/Georg Olms, Hildesheim, 1965.

—— *Handbuch der Notationskunde*. Leipzig, 1913–19: R/Georg Olms, Hildesheim, 1963.

Wooldridge, H. E., ed. *Early English Harmony*. Plainsong and Mediaeval Music Society, London, 1897.

—— *The Oxford History of Music* I. Oxford University Press, Oxford, 1901.

Wulstan, David. 'The Earliest Musical Notation', *Music & Letters* 52/4 (October 1971), 365–82.

—— 'Vocal colour in English sixteenth-century polyphony', *Journal of the Plainsong and Mediaeval Music Society* 2 (1979), 19–60.

INDEX